FRASERBURGH ACADEMY LIBRARY

D1092656

GenD

THOMAS HARDY

In this series

THOMAS HARDY

LANCE ST JOHN BUTLER

Lecturer in English Studies, University of Stirling

CAMBRIDGE UNIVERSITY PRESS

CAMBRIDGE

LONDON · NEW YORK · MELBOURNE

Published by the Syndics of the Cambridge University Press
The Pitt Building, Trumpington Street, Cambridge CB2 1RP
Bentley House, 200 Euston Road, London NW1 2DB
32 East 57th Street, New York, NY 10022, USA
296 Beaconsfield Parade, Middle Park, Melbourne 3206, Australia

© Cambridge University Press 1978

First published 1978

Printed in Great Britain by
Cox & Wyman Ltd, Fakenham

Library of Congress Cataloguing in Publication Data

Butler, Lance St John.
Thomas Hardy.
(British authors, introductory critical studies)
Bibliography: p.
1. Hardy, Thomas, 1840–1928 – Criticism and
interpretation.
PR4754.B8   823'.8   77–23532
ISBN 0 521 21743 1 hard covers
ISBN 0 521 29271 9 paperback

823 HAR

m005081   6347

General Preface

This study of Thomas Hardy is the tenth in a series of short introductory critical studies of the more important British authors. The aim of the series is to go straight to the authors' works; to discuss them directly with a maximum of attention to concrete detail; to say what they are and what they do, and to indicate a valuation. The general critical attitude implied in the series is set out at some length in my *Understanding Literature*. Great literature is taken to be a large extent self-explanatory to the reader who will attend carefully enough to what it says. 'Background' study, whether biographical or historical, is not the concern of the series.

It is hoped that this approach will suit a number of kinds of reader, in particular the general reader who would like an introduction which talks about the works themselves; and the student who would like a general critical study as a starting point, intending to go on to read more specialized works later. Since 'background' is not erected as an insuperable obstacle, readers in other English-speaking countries, countries where English is a second language, or even those for whom English is a foreign language, should find the books helpful. In Britain and the Commonwealth, students and teachers in universities and in the higher forms of secondary schools will find that the authors chosen for treatment are those most often prescribed for study in public and university examinations.

The series could be described as an attempt to make available to a wide public the results of the literary criticism of the last thirty years, and especially the methods associated with Cambridge. If the result is an increase in the reading, with enjoyment and understanding, of the great works of English literature, the books will have fulfilled their wider purpose.

ROBIN MAYHEAD

For Debbie

Contents

Introduction

Thomas Hardy was born in 1840 and died in 1928. During the eighty-eight years of his life he published fourteen novels, four volumes of short stories, eight volumes of verse and an 'epic-drama', *The Dynasts*.

During his lifetime the most fervent criticism of Hardy concerned itself with his morality: up to and including T. S. Eliot's *After Strange Gods* critics were largely concerned with Hardy's 'pessimism' and his view of God, the universe and marriage. After 1928 there was a swing towards a biographical approach to Hardy occasioned by the almost immediate posthumous publication of *The Life of Thomas Hardy*,[1] ostensibly written by his widow but largely written or dictated by the writer himself.

In more recent years these moral and biographical emphases have given some ground to what we have come to regard as 'normal' criticism; that is to say, to an effort to see Hardy as a novelist and poet and not as a philosopher or a Dorsetshire Victorian. Recent critics have not ignored 'Hardy the man' or 'Hardy's view of life', of course, but a balance has usually been struck along the lines of J. I. M. Stewart's *Thomas Hardy* (1971) in which the first three chapters are 'Hardy's Autobiography', 'Private Life' and 'Intellectual Background'; the ensuing chapters deal with the novels and poems in an objective analytical manner.

In this book I attempt to achieve something of the same balance, with an emphasis on the overall meaning of Hardy's major works. I offer no résumé of his biography, nor do I present a systematic exposition of his views (something he maintained to be impossible), although I believe that his world picture is coherent and that this should be recognized. In chapter 1 I try to elucidate the universe of the Wessex novels and the poems 'from within' and not from a standpoint influenced too greatly by Hardy's own comments (in the *Life* and elsewhere). Naturally, certain main themes emerge from this process, but I do not think that there is any formula or straitjacket into which Hardy can be bundled. As a result, each of the works dealt with here, especially each of the major novels, is

[1] Referred to hereafter as the *Life*. For full details, see Reading List.

given a different and, I hope, an appropriate sort of analysis. Thus in writing about *Far from the Madding Crowd* I try to work progressively through the novel in order to expose its procession of emotional and seasonal developments, whereas in the chapter on *The Return of the Native* I consider Egdon Heath rather more statically, as I hope befits that novel. In writing about *The Woodlanders* I spend some time analysing Hardy's vocabulary and his language in detail; when we come to *Tess of the d'Urbervilles* I am more concerned with the integrated cosmic vision presented in that book, and so on.

There certainly seems to be agreement about which works of Hardy's are most important; it is a consensus with which this book largely concurs, as a glance at the chapter headings will show. I think there is a clear gain to be made by relegating Hardy's less successful performances to their minor rôle and concentrating on the acknowledged masterpieces. It would be wrong, however, to ignore the minor work entirely and I recommend the less-well-known novels to the student of Hardy for the light they throw on his methods and concerns. Even his least-successful productions have an idiosyncratic flavour or a remarkable episode that saves them from ordinariness.

Hardy's own listing of his novels and stories (done for the Wessex Edition of 1912 and given below) makes it clear that his judgement of his work coincided with our own. Not only do the Novels of Character and Environment come first on his list but their very title proclaims them to be serious literature in a way that the words 'Romance', 'Fantasy' and 'Ingenuity' clearly do not. However, although his judgement may have been impeccable his inclination seems to have been pleasantly wayward. For instance, *The Well-Beloved*, a novel of almost no interest whatever except as an imaginative scheme of one of the ways of love, was written after *Tess of the d'Urbervilles*, after *The Woodlanders* and only very shortly before *Jude the Obscure*. Indeed, Hardy revised this oddest of his novels for publication in book form after the publication of *Jude*. The result of this uneven production is that critics are given an unfair stick to beat Hardy with. The vices they find in the minor novels can be unearthed, somehow or other, in the major novels. If the plot of *Desperate Remedies* creaks rather loudly then we can be forgiven for shaking our heads over the plot of *The Mayor of Casterbridge*; if the style of *A Laodicean* is sometimes forced and precious, surely we can find these same faults in *The Return of the Native*. The unfairness of this reasoning is evident.

Although we cannot dismiss the minor novels, then, we should pay greatest attention to the novels listed first by Hardy. Chapters 2 to 7 are each centred on one of the major Novels of Character and Environment and present them in chronological order. In each case some reference is made, where appropriate, to the other novels and to the poems. In chapter 8 I discuss the two most important of the Romances and Fantasies and the other minor fiction, and in chapter 9 the poetry, including *The Dynasts*.

The importance of Hardy's poetry has recently been recognized in various ways; among these I would point out a study of the poems and their influence by Donald Davie[2] and the twenty-seven Hardy poems that open Philip Larkin's new edition (1973) of the *Oxford Book of Twentieth Century English Verse*. It must also be significant that in Helen Gardner's edition (1972) of the *New Oxford Book of English Verse* Hardy is given more space than any other poet save Shakespeare and Wordsworth. As with the novels, Hardy seemed able to write poems in both more and less successful styles throughout his life; but there is no doubt that, whether we take the bulky *Complete Poems* as a unified work or whether we confine ourselves to the 'anthology' pieces, Hardy is an important poet as well as an important novelist.

In the following table the numbers 1 to 4 give Hardy's own categories for his prose as it appears in the Wessex Edition of 1912. I have added the volumes of poetry to the list (item 5) and the date of publication of all the works mentioned (often different from the date of writing). In the right-hand column I give the abbreviations used to refer to the works in this book.

HARDY'S WORKS

1 Novels of Character and Environment

1	*Tess of the d'Urbervilles*	1891	TD
2	*Far from the Madding Crowd*	1874	FFMC
3	*Jude the Obscure*	1895	JO
4	*The Return of the Native*	1878	RN
5	*The Mayor of Casterbridge*	1886	MC
6	*The Woodlanders*	1887	WL
7	*Under the Greenwood Tree*	1872	UGT
8	*Life's Little Ironies* (stories)	1894	LLI
9	*Wessex Tales* (stories)	1888	WT

[2] *Thomas Hardy and British Poetry.* London: Routledge and Kegan Paul, 1973.

(Poetry nos. 2–9 above are all referred to as 'CP', i.e. *The Complete Poems*, ed. James Gibson, Macmillan, New Wessex Edition, 1975. This edition also contains Hardy's uncollected poems.)

All references to the fiction cite the *chapter* in question. This is designed to avoid confusion. Most of Hardy's chapters are short, and reference to page numbers is rendered impracticable by the large number of editions of his work, all of which have different pagination. The Wessex Edition is the 'authorized version' and it forms the basis of all good subsequent editions. Currently the standard edition is the New Wessex series published by Macmillan; the pagination of the New Wessex hardbacks differs from that of the paperbacks.[3]

Most details of the confusing publishing history of Hardy's fiction and poetry are to be found in R. L. Purdy, *Thomas Hardy: A*

---

[3] Hardy's early novella *An Indiscretion in the Life of an Heiress* (1878), not included by Hardy in the Wessex Edition, is now available in an edition published by Hutchison (1976); see note 1, chapter 2 below.

Bibliographical Study (O.U.P. revised edition, 1968). It is worth remembering that most of Hardy's fiction appeared first in serial form in periodical publications whose editors were even more cautious about offending their readers than were the publishers of novels in book form. Consequently we have various versions of some novels, representing not only Hardy's second thoughts as he corrected proofs but also the definitive book versions that superseded the serial version. We can be sure, however, that the standard editions we now use largely reflect Hardy's final preference.[4]

[4] However, cf. R. C. Schweik, 'Thomas Hardy: Fifty Years of Textural Scholarship', in *Thomas Hardy after Fifty Years*, ed. L. St J. Butler. London: Macmillan, 1977.

I

'Life offers – to deny!'

The only honest answer to the question 'What are Hardy's novels and poems about?' is that they are about love. There is a temptation to think that Hardy's main concern is agricultural, provincial, sociological; that his work is about Wessex and the traditional ways of Wessex life. Raymond Williams, for instance, argues a sophisticated version of this case,[1] pointing out that although Hardy is not a peasant chronicler of peasant tales (there were no real *peasants* in nineteenth-century Dorset) we should see him 'in his real identity: both the educated observer and the passionate participant in a period of general and radical change'. Now it is true that there is a tension in Hardy between the 'educated' voice and the Wessex dialect, and a tension between old ways and new methods, and a tension between the social classes; but these are images or examples of the fundamental tension – which is that between the possible and the actual. And this basic issue appeared to Hardy most forcibly not in social or economic life but in the realm of love.

Among all creatures man alone has a view of the possible; so only man observes how far short of the possible the actual falls; this is the curse of consciousness. All other beings live by one law – the law of nature, evolution, what Hardy calls the Immanent Will. Man lives by two laws – the law of nature and the law of his own desires and aspirations. But the law of nature does not stop short at the boundaries of something called the 'natural world': it runs for man and society as much as for ants and anthills, so the conflict between the two dispensations lies as much within man as between him and hostile external forces.

The causes of any event are unimaginably complex. When Gabriel Oak is ruined in the early stages of *Far from the Madding Crowd* because his sheep run over the cliff to their deaths, we have a perfect example of the natural law in operation. Gabriel's desire is that the sheep should grow fat and healthy and improve his income. Nature decrees otherwise. But 'decrees' is the wrong word, because nature is quite impersonal, unconscious, unmalign. There is no malicious design against Gabriel, there are just the natural

[1] In *The English Novel from Dickens to Lawrence.* London: Chatto and Windus, 1970.

6

facts: the excitable dog, the weak fence, the proximity and height of the cliff. The Immanent Will is the energy that sustains the universe and is as much responsible for Gabriel's desire to succeed as a farmer as it is for the death of the sheep. But the Will is not God 'out there' controlling all things, aware of man's desires. It is definable only as the sum total of the energy involved in all events. Hardy's early sonnet 'Hap' (CP p. 9) helps to make clear how he saw the workings of the Will.

> If but some vengeful god would call to me
> From up the sky, and laugh: 'Thou suffering thing,
> Know that thy sorrow is my ecstasy,
> That thy love's loss is my hate's profiting!'
>
> Then would I bear it, clench myself, and die,
> Steeled by the sense of ire unmerited;
> Half-eased in that a Powerfuller than I
> Had willed and meted me the tears I shed.
>
> But not so. How arrives it joy lies slain,
> And why unblooms the best hope ever sown?
> – Crass Casualty obstructs the sun and rain,
> And dicing Time for gladness casts a moan . . . .
> These purblind Doomsters had as readily strown
> Blisses about my pilgrimage as pain.

This poem illustrates G. K. Chesterton's remark that Hardy combined a disbelief in God with a hatred of him for not existing.

It will be clear that on some occasions man's will coincides with the Immanent Will while on other occasions man may propose what he wants but the Will disposes that quite different things should come about. 'The all-enacting Might', we are told (in 'Let Me Enjoy'), 'That fashioned forth its loveliness/Had other aims than my delight' (CP p. 238). Surely man's strongest desires are good examples of the working of the Will; yet what thwarts them if not the Will itself? In 'Yell'ham Wood's Story' (CP p. 298) the final words of the mournful trees are 'Life offers – to deny!' The point is that the Will is quite unaware of man's aspirations, and in the face of that fact man's best choice is withdrawal, resignation, learning not to desire.

The importance of this disparity between the possible (the desired) and the actual (what the Will wills) varies according to the strength of the will or desire thwarted. 'I wanted brown bread but the baker had only white' is a trivial example. 'I had an aptitude as a scholar but society would not admit a stonemason to

Oxford' is a considerably more important example. What is the highest and most important example we can give? Perhaps it should be my desire for salvation, for union with God. But God does not exist and I am already as united to the Immanent Will as it is possible to be; indeed, I *am* the Will in one of its aspects. What is man's highest, strongest desire, then? What is his greatest thwarting? Surely his experience of love, described in the Preface to *Jude the Obscure* as 'the strongest passion known to humanity'. Love, for Hardy, has an almost religious power. It is like Jove's thunderbolts; it can kill (Sue Bridehead's first Oxford boyfriend, for example; also see 'Her Dilemma' (CP p. 13)). It can also destroy (Boldwood), torture (Fanny Robin, Giles Winterborne) and elevate its objects to the highest level (Grace Melbury for Giles Winterborne, Clym Yeobright for Eustacia until she has married him, Angel Clare for Tess). It can even do a little marginal good to the lover himself; Gabriel Oak, Marty South and Diggory Venn are better for their loving.

Love, in Hardy, is essentially passionate love, but not always. As we shall see in *Far from the Madding Crowd*, Hardy also countenances the possibility of a love based on affection and on mutual involvement in a joint enterprise. Gabriel Oak is certainly passionately attached to Bathsheba, but his final union with her promises permanence and satisfaction precisely because it has more to it than passion or infatuation. We have only to think of the situation just before the storm, in chapter 36, to see this point. Troy is drunk, satisfied, careless; Boldwood is infatuated, suicidal, careless; Oak is working on the ricks beside Bathsheba, working because he cares. And he cares not merely about the woman (Boldwood does *that*) but about the corn too.

Being thwarted, particularly in love, is the stuff of all Hardy's work. In *The Dynasts* it is Napoleon's ambitions that the Will happens to work against. In *The Mayor of Casterbridge* Henchard suffers disappointment in love and also in business, in friendship and in the affection of his daughter. This novel is a fair example of how these thwartings and disappointments are brought about. The causes of action, I have said, are unimaginably complex, and among them must be numbered the protagonist's own doings. This operates at the fundamental level at which all action is an offering of hostages to Fortune: Oak only fails as a sheep farmer because he *tries to be* a sheep farmer. It also operates at the level familiar to us from the traditions of tragedy: Henchard has flaws in his character, he is impetuous, headstrong, overfond. We sow the seeds of our own disasters. But then we are as we are because of a long and many-stranded web of cause and effect constantly wrought by the Immanent Will. This largely determinist view of human action led Hardy to describe man's freedom as being like the freedom of the pianist's fingers to move. Analysis of this image will make it clear that it leaves nothing at all of human freedom; elsewhere Hardy suggested that we have freedom to change the course of events only when everything else is momentarily 'equal' or in balance.

The main area in which man struggles in his losing battle against the Will is that of love. I have rather discounted Hardy's economic, social and 'Wessex' concerns, but now they can be introduced in their rightful place. Love is a subject that necessarily brings with it all the other relationships and situations that make up the significant side of a man's life. Writing of love enables Hardy to analyse the world and the workings of the Will in the right light. It is precisely in the matter of love that such manifestations of the Will as law, money, class, trade and education have their maximum impact. Tess Darbeyfield's smattering of education (a circumstance brought about by vast socio-economic causes) makes her the best candidate for the visit to the supposed d'Urberville relations; perhaps it is enough, too, to tip the balance of Angel Clare's scruples about marrying a milkmaid. The question of divorce is dealt with in the stories of Jude and Sue, Grace and Giles, not in that these are parables, dressed-up abstractions for the purpose of putting Hardy's point of view on divorce, but in that they isolate the critical point in the great chain of causes and effects at which man's deepest needs come into inevitable conflict with the nature of things. Love, therefore, is not only man's most serious concern in the world (an assumption, I should say, that Hardy makes throughout his work, but one that can, of course, be questioned), it is also the perfect illustration of man's situation in the world. This latter point can hold good even if we question the former.

Love has built into it certain features typical of man's position that makes it the perfect illustration. If a man loves a woman there is no guarantee that the woman will love the man. How is man to resolve the conflict between his desire for a physical relationship and his desire for spiritual communion? If this question seems old-fashioned, I would plead, first, that this is the very real situation of Jude vis-à-vis Sue and Arabella and, second, that it is still with us today in the work of Samuel Beckett, to mention no others. Then again, how is it that when a lover is unavailable, he or she is loved wildly, but when he or she is fully possessed, our interest diminishes?

9

These characteristics of love typify much in our lives, especially in this matter of things not living up to expectation. Who is ever as excited about something the tenth time it is encountered as the first time? As Hardy put it, 'Love thrives on proximity but dies on contact.' Man's loving conforms to the pattern laid down in Shakespeare's 129th sonnet – the sonnet on lust. Lust is

> Enjoy'd no sooner but despised straight;
> Past reason hunted; and no sooner had,
> Past reason hated, as a swallow'd bait,
> On purpose laid to make the taker mad.

Time and again Hardy's lovers are disappointed, but the disappointment of unrequited love, although painful, is in some ways less acute than the disillusionment of successful love. Eustacia Vye gets her much-desired Clym and finds life with him so tedious that she dies trying to escape with a former lover, Damon Wildeve, now become attractive again because he is barred to her. Fitzpiers soon tires of Grace Melbury, though not as quickly as Jude Fawley tires of Arabella. And always it is *too late*; the irrevocable step has been taken. Symbolic of all these lovers whose passion 'dies on contact' is Angel Clare, whose love is killed at a blow within hours of taking Tess for life. Clare is the archetype of this aspect of Hardy. He falls in love with Tess, who is his social inferior; after a considerable struggle he persuades himself that her purity and innocence make up for her social inferiority; she is beautiful and she is to be entirely and exclusively his. On their wedding night she confesses that she is not the virgin he has taken her for and he rejects her in an agony of mind that, even a permissive century later, we can still comprehend. Thus it is in the one vital area of innocence, in the very thing that conquers Clare's social scruples, that Tess proves to be deficient and he to have an uncontrollable aversion.

So the world goes; what we desired and got we desire no longer, what we still desire we cannot have. Bathsheba stirs Troy's emotions to the pitch of marrying her; they cool rapidly only to be awakened by the *dead* Fanny Robin, that is, by the girl he could have married when she was alive; he put a trifling point of pride before her when she could have been his (she was too *easy*) but now that she can never be his he declares total love for her. It seems that the fair 'maid from St Juliot' that Hardy himself married did not prove an exception to this law of love. He loved Emma Gifford in the days of their Cornish romance in the 1860s and again after her death in 1912, but the intervening years, the years of his actual possession of her, were largely without the magic of love. In December 1912 Hardy was able to write, among many other poems inspired by her death, 'The Voice', which opens:

> Woman much missed, how you call to me, call to me,
> Saying that now you are not as you were
> When you had changed from the one who was all to me,
> But as at first, when our day was fair.

When first seen, when married to another, when dead, women can be loved. But the spell won't survive nearer contact.

Although Hardy did not claim to have produced a system, he presents a remarkably consistent picture of the universe. It is exemplified in his treatment of love and constantly referred to throughout the novels and poems; we see a model of it in operation in *The Dynasts*. It is a picture which can hardly be said to have been contradicted in our own day. Hardy himself denied the charge of pessimism but admitted that his belief in 'evolutionary meliorism' (things may be bad, but they can and will get better) was shaken by the Boer and First World Wars. He was a true child of the faith-shaking advances of scientific knowledge that we associate particularly with Darwin and Huxley. Darwin's *The Origin of Species* appeared in 1859 when Hardy was nineteen, and all through his young manhood Hardy grappled with the questions posed by the theory of evolution. Was man only a higher sort of animal? Was man in no way exempt from the cruel laws of nature? Was there any reason to suppose that a God existed who cared specially about man when nature so obviously did not? Hardy's answers to these questions do not seem out of place in the days of the New Biology and the moon-landings. To give only one example: writing forty-five years after Hardy's death, and certainly without thinking of him, a modern scientist[2] proposes that we should try to arrest our civilization's headlong rush towards disaster but warns that whatever we do may prove useless, in which case 'man's place in nature will turn out to have been merely that of a fleeting episode of caring in the blind evolution of an uncaring universe'. This is pure Hardy.

[2] C. F. Hockett, *Man's Place in Nature*. New York: McGraw-Hill, 1973, p. 670.

2

Far from the Madding Crowd (1874)

In *Far from the Madding Crowd* Hardy finds his own voice for the first time. It was not, of course, his first novel. As early as 1868 he had completed a novel, *The Poor Man and the Lady*,[1] which was rejected by publishers who were looking for something more sensational. Hardy responded to this with *Desperate Remedies* (1871), which, although it certainly is sensational, has little else to recommend it. It is a strained novel, uncomfortable to read; too much of it comes from Hardy's own reading, and the characters are largely stock types, conventional villains, heroines and detectives from the ranks of minor Victorian fiction. It was suggested to him, however, that the rustic elements in both of these first novels were successful, and Hardy, taking the hint, produced *Under the Greenwood Tree* (1872).

In this work we can find in rudimentary form most of the elements of Hardy's major fiction, something we might expect from his having grouped it with the Novels of Character and Environment.

Under the Greenwood Tree is about love. It is about the love of more than one man for the same woman and it is about the winning of her by the poorest and least ostentatious of these men. This is an ordering of character and event that persists remarkably in Hardy. The characters bear a relationship to one another that will become familiar as the novels proceed. The men (usually two) who do not get our strongest sympathies (or the woman) are typically older, richer, better educated and of better class than the young lover who does get our sympathy. The woman has a hard time of it, for one reason or another, trying to resist the blandishments of the superior beings to whom her vanity attracts her. Thus Fancy Day is flattered by the attentions of Farmer Shiner (whose name has some connexion with his flashy appeal) and, later, she actually consents to marry Parson Maybold, such is the lure of social status. But the

---

[1] No longer extant but partially incorporated in the novella *An Indiscretion in the Life of an Heiress*, republished in 1976, and partially in *Under the Greenwood Tree*.

homely Dick Dewey wins through in the end, although even in this
'happy' story the winning is not without its irony, as the ending of
the novel indicates. The parson suggests that Fancy should admit
to Dick during their courtship that she has been betrothed to
another, but, *unlike Tess*, she says nothing and all is just about well.[2]

Then, *Under the Greenwood Tree* is set 'at home' in Hardy's Dorset.
The rustic community comes to life for us as the Mellstock Quire
sings its carols, holds its parties, visits the parson and comments on
the way of the world. There is an almost unbroken unity of place
here (Mellstock, with the odd excursion to Yalbury). The simplicity of the plot allows Hardy to develop his characters through
dialogue and small actions, and it is a very domestic novel pitched
at the 'normal' intensity of life. There is a nominal movement
through the book, as the titles of the parts imply, from winter to
spring to summer to autumn. But the rustic voice is not the only
one heard; already in chapter 1 the villagers are being compared
to Greek and Etruscan pottery figures, and the urban educated
reader is being invited not to immerse himself too deeply in the
pastoral.

But there is a lack of integration in *Under the Greenwood Tree*, a
sense that Hardy has made an arbitrary choice of actions and
motives, an artificiality in plotting and characterization similar to
that which mars *Adam Bede* as a novel of rustic life. There is not
much connexion between the activities of the choir and the main
action of love, nor much between the rural occupations we witness
and the conditions of the characters. The chapter 'Honey-Taking,
And Afterwards', for example, sounds promising, but, although it

---

[2] We can set out this constant scheme of Hardy's novels as follows. If UGT works
thus: Fancy – Dick/Shiner/Maybold, then FFMC can be seen to work: Bathsheba – Oak/Troy/Boldwood. The parallel is not exact, but the unsuccessful
suitors seem to have some combination of the following advantages: age, wealth,
glamour, class, education. In later novels there are sometimes only two men
involved, but they still fit into the same categories, thus:
>   in DR: Cytherea – Edward/Manston;
>   in PBE: Elfride – Stephen/Knight/Lord Luxellian;
>   in HE: Ethelberta – Petherwin/Mountclere/Julian;
>   in RN: Eustacia – Clym/Wildeve and Thomasin – Wildeve/Diggory;
>   in TM: Anne – Bob/John/Festus;
>   in LA: Paula – Somerset/de Stancy;
>   in TT: Lady Constantine – Swithin/Bishop/her brother (after a fashion);
>   in MC: Lucetta – Henchard/Farfrae;
>   in WL: Grace – Fitzpiers/Giles;
>   in TD: Tess – Alec/Angel;
>   in JO: Sue – Jude/Phillotson.

Only *The Well-Beloved* does not fit into this pattern, although even here Marcia
and Jocelyn are recognizable types.

is a lively and amusing scene with Keeper Day excelling himself as an apiarist, it is not integrated into the action, the drama, that is taking place by the hives. On the one hand we have the stoical keeper, taking little interest in the stings he is getting, and some good details of the hiving itself, while on the other hand we are trying to keep abreast of the struggle between Shiner and Dick for Fancy's attention. The minor, bucolic matter does not lend anything to the major, psychological movement. The subsequent scene, where the two men vie for the privilege of helping Fancy because she has been stung by a bee, goes some way towards drawing the two threads together, but even here we feel a slight awkwardness at the improbability to which Hardy has to resort to achieve this unity. Similarly, the drama of the Quire's dispersal connects with the main theme only in so far as it is Fancy, as organist, who is to replace the old string band. The Quire's visit to Maybold, good comedy though it is, has no particular relevance to the development of the emotions that are the plot. The result of the visit is a postponement of the date of the Quire's demise, but this is not allowed to impede the progress of the action, because Hardy simply skips over the intervening period and introduces Fancy to her job as organist without comment on the delay. In fact, *Under the Greenwood Tree* consists of two short stories loosely woven together.

In 1873 Hardy published *A Pair of Blue Eyes* (discussed with the other minor fiction in chapter 8 below). It is set in 'Off Wessex', Cornwall, and, although there is a small 'rustic chorus', there is a feeling that this airy land of sea and cliffs is a bit beyond Hardy's 'real' Wessex. Whether for this reason or because the action of the novel was so close to the events of his own life, *A Pair of Blue Eyes* does not show the integrated quality that seems to me to be Hardy's own voice. In general this is only consistently achieved in the Novels of Character and Environment, with the possible exception of *Under the Greenwood Tree*.

AN EPISODE FROM THE NOVEL IN DETAIL

Far from the Madding Crowd appeared at the end of a six-year apprenticeship (1874) and is Hardy's first major novel. Perhaps my first duty is to illustrate the quality that earns it this title by selecting an episode from it that compares significantly with the honey-taking episode from *Under the Greenwood Tree*. We can look at a section that amounts to half a chapter, Hardy's chapters being short; in this case chapter 18, 'Boldwood in Meditation – Regret'.

This is the point at which the novel turns. The earlier chapters have introduced us to the characters and their world, not in a static 'scene-setting' but as they are engaged in their daily lives. Nonetheless, as far as the main theme is concerned (the *raison d'être* of the novel, the loves of Bathsheba Everdene) we have only been given a general view of probable areas of conflict. Oak's fortunes have risen and fallen. Boldwood has received the Valentine, Troy has appeared, an ominous but as yet only slightly involved figure. But now spring comes suddenly and with it Boldwood's ardour increases to the point where he begins to seek Bathsheba out.

If we examine the second half of this chapter (from 'It was now early spring') we can see how much Hardy is keeping in play and how rich his resonances are.

'It was now early spring' and the year has suddenly and unexpectedly melted, like Boldwood's wintry reserve; the new season arrives 'abruptly'. Hardy mentions that 'we may suppose the Dryads to be waking for the season' as a kind of Jeevesian discreet cough to remind us of a whole area of polite pastoral literature that we, as educated people, may be keeping in mind while reading a novel with this title.[3] But the Dryads are Hardy's joke, of course. It is one of his little ironies that this reference to classical wood-spirits is at once swamped by a quite unclassical but very powerful description of the coming of spring.

The vegetable world begins to move and swell and the saps to rise, till in the completest silence of lone gardens and trackless plantations, where everything seems helpless and still after the bond and slavery of frost, there are bustlings, strainings, united thrusts, and pulls-all-together, in comparison with which the powerful tugs of cranes and pulleys in a noisy city are but pigmy efforts.

---

[3] I shall ignore the possible pun implicit in the fact that the Dryads were *oak* nymphs and instead quote in full the stanza from Gray's *Elegy* that contains the novel's title.

> Far from the madding crowd's ignoble strife,
>   Their sober wishes never learn'd to stray;
> Along the cool sequester'd vale of life
>   They kept the noiseless tenor of their way.

Is the irony intentional? The irony, I mean, of suggesting peace and quiet and pastoral seclusion by quoting only the first line of this as a title to a novel in which the 'wishes' of the characters are hardly 'sober' and certainly 'stray' too far for their own comfort. At all events, Hardy never subscribes to this eighteenth-century 'God made the country and man made the town' idealism.

There is no labouring of the symbols here. The description can stand perfectly well on its own, but it *can* be seen as analogous to the stirring forces rising in Boldwood. Further analysis underlines this possibility. Shortly after this description of spring we read that 'A man's body is as the shell, or the tablet, of his soul . . . There was a change in Boldwood's exterior from its former impassibleness'; then that 'The insulation of his heart by reserve during these many years, without a channel of any kind for disposable emotion, had worked its effect.' There is at least a subconscious connexion here between the seasons and the man. And again, nature may symbolize man when we read of the 'foisting' of the lamb on to its foster-ewe. We may even think of Boldwood when we learn that ewe and lamb are put in close proximity 'where they would remain till the old sheep conceived an affection for the young one'.

Bathsheba looks up and sees 'the farmer by the gate, where he was overhung by a willow tree in full bloom'. We feel a vague unease about this, perhaps because we know of the death-associations of the willow tree or perhaps because we know that the willow branch was traditionally worn in the hat by rejected lovers. Hardy, a self-made classicist and a man aware of country traditions, must have known both these associations.[4]

In looking up, of course, Bathsheba reveals her face. To Gabriel it is 'as the uncertain glory of an April day'. We might simply pass this over as a Shakespearian synonym for 'youthful and changeable', but Proteus' speech in *The Two Gentlemen of Verona* (I. iii. 83–6) from which this quotation comes, and of which the general emotional tone must have been in Hardy's mind, is more specifically relevant:

> O! how this spring of love resembleth
> The uncertain glory of an April day,
> Which now shows all the beauty of the sun,
> And by and by a cloud takes all away!

So 'the uncertain glory' refers specifically to the changeableness of *love*. Even for those who are not well versed in tree-lore or Shakespeare these resonances penetrate, and with them Hardy establishes an undertow in his prose that keeps us emotionally and morally moving in the right direction, wherever the surface action may appear to be going. When we notice this undertow we also

---

[4] Cf. Robert Graves, *The White Goddess*, 3rd edn (London: Faber, 1959), pp. 172–3. Persian carpet-makers, in their designs, use a tree that is clearly intended to be a willow to represent death.

notice that it is not arbitrary but appears to be an inevitable element underlying the action.

Enough has been said to establish the principle that there is a deliberating mind at work behind Hardy's prose; that it is not whimsical, freakish or arbitrary. At least in the major novels, starting with *Far from the Madding Crowd*, Hardy integrates action and symbol almost miraculously.

HARDY'S AUTHORIAL INTERVENTIONS

Hardy's commentary on the events as they take place might appear to be an exception to this integration and homogeneity in his best work. As this is something which persists through all the novels and which is disliked by most critics, it may be as well to examine its purpose at the outset. J. I. M. Stewart, for example, argues that *Far from the Madding Crowd* is flawed by this 'element of generalized reflection to which the action prompts the writer'. The great majority of these general reflections turn out to be on the subject of love, and I would defend them on the grounds that Hardy's views on this subject are idiosyncratic, ironic and certainly unusual in the eyes of his presumed readers; and that they therefore call for a special expression that will also explain the motivation of the lovers.

Examples appear early in the book. Chapter 4 opens with an aphorism and continues with further general comments:

The only superiority in women that is tolerable to the rival sex is, as a rule, that of the unconscious kind; but a superiority which recognizes itself may sometimes please by suggesting possibilities of capture to the subordinated man . . .

Love being an extremely exacting usurer (a sense of exorbitant profit, spiritually, by an exchange of hearts, being at the bottom of pure passions, as that of exorbitant profit, bodily or materially, is at the bottom of those of lower atmosphere), every morning Oak's feelings were as sensitive as the money market in calculations upon his chances.

Hardy can only express these ideas in this direct way. These complicated sentences, hard to fathom at first, are a bid to explain the subtle chemistry of love. It is an evasion of his function if a novelist simply relies on our own emotional education by presenting the *fact* of love. Hardy is an analyst, not a mere yarn-spinner. And the analysis is largely successful; the first of the sentences above invites us to consider the question raised and to apply our considerations to Bathsheba and Oak; it provides us, as it were, with a weapon, a tool for analysis. The second sentence, opening with one of the most pregnant metaphors in Hardy, develops a sort of discomfort in the reader that forces him to consider closely the question of who 'love' is, who lends to whom, who gains, who pays. In other words, Hardy offers open-ended comments, not gospel pronouncements. We are not told what to think about the action commented on, but are asked to think about it with the aid of a penetrating suggestion.

A little later in chapter 4 we come across the *dicta* that 'Love is a possible strength in an actual weakness. Marriage transforms a distraction into a support . . .' These represent the wisdom to which Oak and Bathsheba are gradually going to awaken.[5] And with them *we* are enlightened and edified.

This method continues throughout the novel. Chapter 5 teaches us 'that there is no regular path for getting out of love as there is for getting in'; chapter 18 that 'The causes of love are chiefly subjective'; chapter 19 that 'The great aids to idealization in love' of a woman are 'occasional observance of her from a distance, and the absence of social intercourse with her – visual familiarity, oral strangeness'; chapter 20 that 'The rarest offerings of the purest loves are but a self-indulgence, and no generosity at all'; and so on. Hardy is here working out the nature of love as the most important thing a man can be engaged in. Morally, the novel is concerned with selfishness and unselfishness in love. Oak's love, in spite of the aphorism just quoted, is not only steady and faithful but, compared with Boldwood's, relatively selfless. Boldwood concentrates so exclusively on his own feelings that he does his cause a disservice. Oak can 'rise above his own grief in noticing Boldwood's' (chapter 35).

Throughout the book there is a tension between Hardy's 'educated' views and the more limited opinions of his Wessex characters. But Oak and Bathsheba, at least, among the inhabitants of Weatherbury, come to learn something of their creator's wisdom. By the end they have learnt the stoical lessons that life teaches; in chapter 57, for instance, we learn that Bathsheba 'never laughed readily now'. While they are still untamed by misfortune, however, and thus not yet wise, we *need* Hardy's authorial commentary. I shall give two examples of this.

First there is the description, in chapter 4, of Oak putting oil on

---

[5] 'Marriage transforms a distraction into a support, the power of which should be, and happily often is, in direct proportion to the degree of imbecility it supplants. Oak began now to see light in this direction, and said to himself, "I'll make her my wife, or upon my soul I shall be good for nothing!"'

his hair to smarten himself up before going to ask for Bathsheba's hand.

[He] used all the hair-oil he possessed upon his usually dry, sandy, and inextricably curly hair, till he had deepened it to a splendidly novel colour, between that of guano and Roman cement, making it stick to his head like mace round a nutmeg, or wet seaweed round a boulder after the ebb.

Here we are looking at a man who is the unconscious object of these comparisons; this does not make them any the less apt or amusing, and it helps to keep him at arm's length in a way that is necessary to Hardy's purpose. It is essential that we see the follies of love, great and small, with an objective eye (though not a cold one; we feel an affection for Oak's bizarre attempts to make himself sexually attractive). This objectivity was a psychological necessity to Hardy, who needed to be detached from, even aloof from, his environment. In the *Life* (p. 131) he mentions how unpleasant he found crowds, and there is a well-known passage (p. 25) where he describes his dislike of being touched. But the 'superior' view taken of Oak or of village customs or a dozen other things is not merely a psychological quirk: it is an artistic device to reveal character and situation to us more fully, and a philosophical weapon for revealing the workings of the Immanent Will. Without Hardy's authorial interventions we would be struggling in the dark.

This parenthesis comes a few paragraphs later in chapter 4:

Calling oneself merely Somebody, without giving a name, is not to be taken as an example of the ill-breeding of the rural world: it springs from a refined modesty of which townspeople, with their cards and announcements, have no notion whatever.

This comment does not spring tautologically from the event it refers to; it is a relevant, explicatory, socially interesting aside that establishes the exact spirit in which we are to read Gabriel's behaviour, and preserves the tone of necessary distance while endearing him to us.

This novel moves towards its own moral, generalized conclusion as its plot moves towards its ending. Thus, if we take the very last chapter as a tail-piece – a final tableau in which we are satisfied by *seeing* Bathsheba and Gabriel married – the general moral conclusion comes at the end of the real action, that is, at the end of the penultimate chapter. Here we have the view of love that we have learnt is the only practical one, and it is Bathsheba's and Gabriel's:

Theirs was that substantial affection which arises (if any arises at all) when the two who are thrown together begin first by knowing the rougher sides of each other's character, and not the best till further on, the romance growing up in the interstices of a mass of hard prosaic reality. This good-fellowship – *camaraderie* – usually occurring through similarity of pursuits, it is unfortunately seldom superadded to love between the sexes, because men and women associate, not in their labours, but in their pleasures merely. Where, however, happy circumstance permits its development, the compounded feeling proves itself to be the only love which is as strong as death – that love which many waters cannot quench, nor the floods drown, beside which the passion usually called by the name is evanescent as steam.[6]

Here Hardy achieves an integration between generalized reflection and the particular story he is telling. His comments apply equally to his characters and to all mankind.

THE INTEGRATED STRUCTURE OF 'FAR FROM THE MADDING CROWD'

Far from the Madding Crowd opens with a description that shows Hardy at his best (we can compare it with the opening of *Under the Greenwood Tree*, whose first paragraphs fully repay close analysis). Oak and Bathsheba are presented at their most normal, at their most basic and ordinary. In the six pages of chapter 1 we learn a remarkable amount about them: the key to their personalities is given to us, as it were, so that we can 'read' them with greater ease later. Oak, who in certain fundamental ways will not change throughout the novel, is given a solid description from the points of view of the narrator, his neighbours and himself. Bathsheba, who is perforce to change, is more lightly sketched and presented from an external point of view only.

In this first chapter Hardy constantly shifts from the particular to the universal, intervening and commenting in the way we have discussed. Here he limits himself to a comment or two: when Oak pays the tuppence for Bathsheba to pass through the turnpike,

She might have looked her thanks to Gabriel on a minute scale, but she did not speak them; more probably she felt none, for in gaining her a passage he had lost her point, and we know how women take a favour of that kind.

[6] This is reminiscent of the first of the 'She, to Him' sonnets. In the poem the view is gloomier but the thought is the same when 'She' asks for 'The hand of friend-ship down Life's sunless hill' (CP p. 14).

20

But in chapter 2 this technique is expanded almost to its limits. We are presented with a description of Norcombe Hill at a specific time of night, and Hardy sets it, literally, beside the universe. First we feel the wind sweeping over the hill, and 'the instinctive act of human kind was to stand and listen'. So there we are – Hardy, the narrator, ourselves, Oak – standing and listening to the wind on Norcombe Hill. And we look upwards, of course, to see the clear sky and learn the names of some of the stars, and we can imagine the earth's roll beneath us as 'almost a palpable movement'. Having reached this highest point in the universalizing process, Hardy finds it hard to reconcile the sensation of the earth's swing through space with the tiny dimensions of the being who feels the sensation, man. As he says, 'it is hard to get back to earth', but we are brought down by the sound of Oak playing his flute. This opens for us in time a perspective similar to that just opened in space. Oak is the Arcadian shepherd with his pipe, while his lambing hut is compared to 'a small Noah's ark on a small Ararat'.[7] These depths established, Hardy swings round with the local, particularizing sentence 'It was only latterly that people had begun to call Gabriel "Farmer" Oak.'

The prose of a passage such as this in chapter 2 positively simmers. When mankind has obeyed the 'instinct' to 'stand and listen', for example, it learns

how the trees on the right and the trees on the left wailed or chaunted to each other in the regular antiphonies of a cathedral choir; how hedges and other shapes to leeward then caught the note, lowering it to the tenderest sob; and how the hurrying gust then plunged into the south, to be heard no more.

This sentence is balanced in a way that reflects the meaning of its central image; after the first semicolon, the image is prolonged and developed so that the wind at first becomes more human (the impersonal 'choir' has become able to make the 'tenderest sob') and is then impatiently torn away from the association with puny mankind and rushed into the darkness.

Gabriel first sees Bathsheba on 'a December morning' and the windy night is Midwinter Night. The hiring-fair which Gabriel attends in Casterbridge after the loss of his flock is most probably a Lady-Day fair (2 February) and the Valentine is, of course, sent on 14 February. Its effect on Boldwood is described in a chapter

[7] In chapter 6 he is a 'pastoral king' who sinks 'into the very slime-pits of Siddim' (again, a vaguely classical allusion is juxtaposed to a biblical one).

entitled 'Effect of the Letter – Sunrise'; as Boldwood's sun starts to rise, so does Fanny's, though both suns are deceptive. Chapter 18 shows us Boldwood 'in meditation' in 'early spring'. As I have indicated, this is the point at which Boldwood, the spring and the novel itself 'wake up'. From here on a close relationship is established between the seasons (both directly and in the shape of the events of the farming year that accompany them) and the development of plot and character. The rather arbitrary choice of a seasonal time-scale in *Under the Greenwood Tree* has given place to a thoroughly planned progress through the year.

Chapter 19 is set in May, when sweet lovers may well love the spring but honest farmers wash their sheep. Our interest in the sheep-washing pool is real enough: we are fascinated (as Hardy's metropolitan readers would also have been) to learn the details of its use; but underlying our interest is a special kind of suspense, since we read the description of the washing realizing that Hardy is filling in the time it takes Boldwood to cross the fields and to get his boots streaked with pollen from the buttercups. The whole approach to the tremulous moment when Boldwood, we know, is to declare his love shows us Hardy's 'cinema' technique (a description suggested by John Wain in his introduction to *The Dynasts*). We see the pool from the point of view of a bird, 'a glistening Cyclops' eye in a face of green'. This is followed by a 'close-up' of the grasses at the pool's edge and a more general view of the surrounding pastures and the river sliding along 'noiselessly as a shade'. We hear a cuckoo, see Boldwood walking 'meditatively down the slopes'. look at his boots and then cut to Oak, Coggan and the others engaged in washing the sheep, closing in on them until we can see that 'every protuberance and angle of their clothes [was] dribbling forth a small rill'. There is a satisfying integration of the movements, noises and emotions here which is developed further as Bathsheba moves away to find that Boldwood is following her and she has 'a consciousness that love [is] encircling her like a perfume'. The rich May air is charged with Boldwood's hot-house passion and loud with the cries of the washers who are not unconscious of what their employers are doing. The conversation that follows is painful to read as the infatuated Boldwood pours out his heart; it feels unhealthy, like the symptoms of a disease, in contrast to the bucolic occupations by the pool. The chapter ends with a characteristically perceptive simile: 'Realities then returned upon [Boldwood] like the pain of a wound received in an excitement which eclipses it, and he, too, went on'.

In chapter 20, the sheep having been washed, preparations are being made to shear them. Oak is grinding shears and Hardy is again at pains to broaden, even to universalize, this humble task. 'All the surrounding cottages were more or less scenes of the same operation', and this puts him in mind of the preparations for war: 'sickles, scythes, shears, and pruning-hooks ranking with swords, bayonets, and lances, in their common necessity for point and edge'. Cainy Ball turns the handle of the grindstone like a mindless Fortuna while Oak stands in the attitude of Eros sharpening his arrows. Bathsheba replaces Cainy and the turning becomes for her like an 'attenuated variety of Ixion's punishment'. Ixion was punished for seducing Hera, and there is something very Hardyan about the fact that although Ixion *thought* he was making love to that goddess, Zeus had in fact substituted a cloud in her shape. Such are the deceptions of love. Bathsheba swaps jobs with Gabriel, and there is a moment of physical contact when he shows her how to hold the shears – the sense of touch is always dangerous magic in Hardy. The action with the shears here may be a parallel with the scene of Troy's swordsmanship later. As they talk (about Bathsheba and her love life) they are performing complementary actions, working together in the most natural way, and Bathsheba's dismissal of her devoted servant at the end of the conversation is deliberately made to seem an impossible folly, almost something unnatural.

In chapter 21 the season has advanced to the point where the new clover is in the fields, tempting the sheep. The agricultural disaster now threatened (only possible at this one point in the year) forces Bathsheba to rescind her order of dismissal. Oak's skill is essential to her, and we see him bending over the sheep, saving them with his special skill and thus establishing himself as a pastoral king with a special relationship to nature.

In chapter 22 the sheep, having been washed and saved from death, are sheared in the Great Barn. It is 1 June, and we are told that 'every stalk was swollen with racing currents of juice'. Gabriel shears well, of course, but, in his anxiety to watch his mistress with Boldwood, he snips one of the ewes, significantly, in the groin. She reprimands him, and Hardy comments,

To an outsider there was not much to complain of in [the reprimand]; but to Oak, who knew Bathsheba to be well aware that she herself was the cause of the poor ewe's wound, because she had wounded the ewe's shearer in a still more vital part, it had a sting which the abiding sense of his inferiority to both herself and Boldwood was not calculated to heal. But a

23

manly resolve to recognize boldly that he had no longer a lover's interest in her, helped him occasionally to conceal a feeling.

This little drama takes place at a number of levels of implication or involvement, as Hardy indicates. There is the typically Hardyan figure of the 'outsider', who is one of us readers, admiring the picturesque scene, unaware of the passions at work in the June sunlight. Then there is Boldwood, watching but unaware of Gabriel's feelings; then Bathsheba's cruelty in speaking to Gabriel with 'severe remonstrance'; then the fact that she is herself 'well aware' of her own cruelty; then the fact that Bathsheba, Gabriel and the reader are all aware of the extra edge this cruelty has because of the social difference between mistress and man; then another 'edge' beyond this in that Gabriel is also inferior to Boldwood; then, to return to base, the fact that it is just this social difference that enables the two farmers to go off riding while the shepherd must work on. But it does not stop here. *We* know (though Gabriel can only guess) that Bathsheba does not relish this courtship by her neighbour and that her cruelty may mean that she still has some feelings left for her first suitor. We see Oak *enduring*, going on working in spite of love, a fact we shall remember when we see Boldwood ruining himself by neglecting his farm. It is almost as if one must fight not to give in to love if one does not want one's life to be destroyed.

Thus the analogy between the sheep's wound and Gabriel's (in a 'still more vital part' than the groin) is an elegant matrix for these ironic levels, and it is no arbitrary matrix: there is a weight of tradition behind the wounding potential of love. To give only one illustration: Oberon describes the flower that Puck is to fetch ('Love-in-idleness') as having been white until Cupid's shaft made it 'Purple with love's wound'.

The shearing is followed by the shearing supper (chapter 23), an event again universalized by reference to the ancient world. Jacob Smallbury's ballad is 'as inclusive and interminable as that with which the worthy toper old Silenus amused on a similar occasion the swains Chromis and Mnasylus, and other jolly dogs of his day'. The half-ironic vocabulary connects these classical figures with their Wessex counterparts – they too are topers and swains and would be thought jolly dogs. Soon they grow 'as merry as the gods in Homer's heaven', an ambiguous enough merriness, as a moment's thought must reveal. But the important point is that Hardy not only succeeds in associating this bucolic event with the thousands of years of shearing celebrations that have preceded it, but also weaves into it an appropriate development of the main action. There is a sense of relaxation and satisfaction – of the task well done – on an occasion like this which makes Gabriel's unease stand out by contrast. There is the necessary social decorum that dictates that Boldwood can oust Gabriel from the foot of the table and that he can visit Bathsheba inside the house after the meal. And all is carried on in the June sunset and dusk, a magic time of toned-down colours, quiet and peace, in which we rather want Bathsheba to have done with her feelings and simply accept Boldwood so as to prevent any more of these painful scenes.

This very night, within minutes of making her half-promise to Boldwood, she makes her regular tour of inspection of the farm and becomes, literally, entangled with Troy (chapter 24). The next chapter is an interlude in which time does not move forward but Troy is described, so that now, half-way through the book, we have a complete picture of the dramatis personae. But with chapter 26 we are back in the swing of the year – it is hay-making time (a process traditionally best carried out before midsummer if the 'goodness' is not to go out of the grass). Troy seizes his opportunity to flatter Bathsheba, both here and in the bee-hiving episode that follows (chapter 27). The hiving operations of late June are followed by the sword-exercise scene which takes place among the fully grown ferns of a Wessex hillside (chapter 28). Troy's lightning courtship arouses a summer love in Bathsheba that we cannot help contrasting with the longer passions of Boldwood and Oak. Midsummer itself sees the rejection of Boldwood and the secret marriage to Troy. This climax (apparently final) is situated just after the middle of the novel and certainly in the middle of the year. When the wheat is full and ripe, Bathsheba abandons herself to her passion for the soldier in spite of Oak's advice (chapter 29) and in the next chapter she is ominously the possessor of 'hot cheeks and tearful eyes'. Boldwood, too, is presented in the midst of omens of rage and fury in chapter 31; a 'timely thunder-shower' has 'refined the air, and daintily bathed the coat of the land' when Bathsheba sets out to visit Liddy's sister at Talbury, but

Before her, among the clouds, there [is] a contrast in the shape of lairs of fierce light which showed themselves in the neighbourhood of a hidden sun, lingering on to the farthest north-west corner of the heavens that this midsummer season allowed.

And standing before her is Boldwood, suffering the 'torture' of having been 'fooled to utter heartburning' by her rejection of him. He storms at her, and at Troy, leaving her faint and full of dread under an unseen but magnificent sky.

Because of the lightness of this night, Maryann sees someone apparently stealing a horse; because of the earlier thundershower Oak and Coggan are able to follow the tracks of Bathsheba's gig in the softened ground (chapter 32). We learn that it *is* Bathsheba in the gig only when her pursuers do, some distance along the road to Bath. But we turn back with them, too. This is a deliberate self-limiting device on Hardy's part. We learn of events outside the immediate scene of the drama only at second hand: Cainy Ball slowly and painfully reveals that his mistress has been seen with Troy in 'the Kingdom of Bath' in chapter 33; and when Troy and Bathsheba come home again (chapter 34) we learn that they are certainly married only when Boldwood does. This method of presentation is cumulative and highly effective. We are kept in a certain suspense and each revelation breeds a new suspense – it *is* Bathsheba in the gig at Sherton Turnpike, but where is she going? It *is* she whom Cainy has seen in Bath, but what has she been up to there? She *has* married Troy, but what will become of her (and Oak) now? So that what might seem the high-summer climax of the book in fact leaves us more anxious than ever.[8] The guardian angel Gabriel watches on. Boldwood lours and the tricky Troy seems permanently but somehow uncertainly master of a woman and a domain in neither of which has he the right sort of interest.

For a brief chapter nature holds its breath, and we with it. Chapter 35 opens 'It was very early the next morning – a time of sun and dew', and Boldwood, who has not slept, rides past the early rising Oak who has seen Troy[9] leaning from one of Bathsheba's upstairs windows. This summer's day starts with everyone finally certain that Bathsheba has married Troy; and the temperature rises steadily. We are not surprised, then, by the thunderstorm that follows or, to emphasize Hardy's careful choice of setting, by being asked to pass over the two hottest months and move straight to 'the end of August'. The opening paragraphs of this next chapter (36) show Hardy at his most powerful. As we, and Gabriel, wait for a dénouement of some kind, the power of his writing depends first on the atmosphere of palpitating emotion built up in

[8] The same technique is used for Boldwood's reprieve at the end of the novel. We wait with Gabriel and the men for Laban to tell *us* the news too.

[9] From behind 'an elder bush, now beginning to be enriched with black bunches of fruit'. For the ominousness of this cf. Graves, *The White Goddess*, p. 183. .

earlier chapters and, second, on the brilliant observation of natural phenomena:

The fields were sallow with the impure light, and all were tinged in monochrome, as if beheld through stained glass. The same evening the sheep had trailed homeward head to tail, the behaviour of the rooks had been confused, and the horses had moved with timidity and caution.

While Troy has refused to believe in the coming storm, all nature seems to be preparing for a catastrophe. The toad (feeling to Oak's foot 'like a boxing glove') is a 'direct message from the Great Mother'. So are the slugs, the spiders, the sheep. But this is not all. The catastrophe that threatens is a late-August storm, and August is the harvest month. The catastrophe becomes possible because this is the season in which we are least inclined to believe in bad weather, because harvest suppers are great times for merrymaking and because such merrymaking under Troy's guidance becomes a drunken revel which renders the farm hands incapable of taking the simple steps necessary to avert calamity. This interweaving of cause and irony can perhaps go some way towards countering the charge that Hardy relies too heavily on contrived coincidence. In keeping with the natural background to the drama of this chapter, it is the 'natural' Oak who resolves to save the wheat and barley ricks if he can (as he saved the hayricks in February when they were most needed – a rare example of a recurring motif in Hardy). His motivation is transparently sentimental; of course, Oak presents it to himself as economic, but then they are Bathsheba's ricks and we know Oak's heart. Hardy adds a comment that could also be applied to his own style: 'man, even to himself, is a palimpsest, having an ostensible writing, and another beneath the lines'.

The catastrophe brings the two good-hearted, intelligent people together; their qualities display themselves as stoicism and a capacity for faithful love. Bathsheba talks honestly about herself as they work on the ricks, but then honesty is simply another of the moral qualities required for endurance in Hardy's world. Illusions are dangerous.

The chapter ends with another omen – the swinging of the weather-vane – that disturbs Gabriel's work and shows us how Hardy prefers to present things from a point of view within the novel; not coldly and objectively, but through the eyes of a participant. In the rain Oak meets Boldwood, who bares the depths of his suffering for a moment (chapter 38); and almost at once we learn that there are rifts in the lute of Bathsheba's marriage (chapter 39).

The rift that will finally 'silence all' – Fanny Robin – appears, comparable in her misery to a more courageous Boldwood, as she drags herself towards death in the Casterbridge workhouse (chapter 40) with a painful and bizarre motion that we find again in the grotesque thrashings of Beckett's Molloy. The dog that helps her gets the traditional reward of the selfless friend.

Fanny is to be buried on a day that brings the first fog of autumn and this, melancholy enough in itself, is also what prompts the saintly Joseph Poorgrass to fortify himself at the Buck's Head en route between the Union and the graveyard (chapter 42). Hardy, as ever, has chosen his moment; and this early autumn season is also the setting for Bathsheba's night by the sinister pool and for Troy's planting (correctly, the gardeners will say) bulbs that will flower in the spring and summer. But the autumn brings rain too, and the 'gurgoyle' concentrates this on Fanny's grave in an ironic version of the 'watering-in' of new bulbs, a process that also 'waters-in' the new corpse. The year is not so far advanced, however, that it has finished with warm days on which long walks might prompt a man to have a swim, and Troy swims at Lulworth, with purgatorial symbolism, nearly dying. From this point (chapter 47) onwards there is an open tension in the novel – we know Troy to be alive, and the others suppose him dead. 'The later autumn and the winter drew on apace.' It is hard to believe that it is only a year since we stood on Norcombe Hill and listened to the wind. Hardy moves over the following nine months without difficulty, and we find ourselves at the Greenhill sheep fair which takes place in 'the autumn sun'. Again, Hardy has chosen the moment and the venue for his action with great care; there is an intrinsic interest in the spectacle of the rustics at the fair that supports our interest in the episode as critical to the plot. We feel retrospectively that Bathsheba has been living in suspense during the missing nine months and that as autumn comes round again a new crisis will be reached in her affairs. And so it is. Boldwood, riding home beside her, makes her promise to marry him at Christmas. We slide into winter, hastened into the cold season by Bathsheba's anxiety. Chapter 52 ('Converging Courses') is divided into seven brief sections, showing that although Hardy can dispense with unnecessary time (the nine months) he can also descend to minute detail when it is needed and dwell for pages on the actions of one evening. Hardy's camera swings restlessly from one actor to another as the climax approaches. The sense of simultaneous action, of coincidence, here obviously fascinates him. This is one of the webs woven by the Will, an artistry in circumstance, of which a vaster and simpler example appears in 'The Convergence of the Twain' (CP, p. 306) where the iceberg is slowly preparing to meet the *Titanic* until 'The spinner of the years' says 'Now!'; chapter 53 of *Far from the Madding Crowd* is entitled 'Concurritur – Horae Momento'.

Troy dies, and Boldwood puts himself away; Bathsheba collapeses while Gabriel still waits, reinforcing his claim to moral strength by his visit to Boldwood in prison. Bathsheba remains prostrated during the winter, but chapter 56 opens 'Bathsheba revived with the spring', and we learn that 'As summer drew on she passed more of her time in the open air.' Thus nature is woven in to these developments. She meets Gabriel in August, but it is not until after Christmas that she learns that he means to leave her. She now courts him – she has learned the lesson of the drama, and the stoical survivor, Gabriel, is at last recognized and given his reward. As early as chapter 49 Bathsheba is described as having been 'pruned down' – a suitably rural metaphor. In her new state she marries her first lover, quietly, as they say, in what must be January. The year has turned again; midwinter is past but spring is still distant – a modest hope is all that man can entertain.

Weatherbury Farm is going to continue its immemorial round as long as there are good men and women to run it. The destructive forces that are ranged against it parallel those of *As You Like It*: foul weather and man's ingratitude. The first is beyond man's moral competence but it can be dealt with by care, patience and faith. The second, in Hardy, is not a matter of courts and kings but, in the cool, sequestered vales of Wessex, a matter of love. Love, faithful love, keeps Gabriel by Bathsheba's side and thus on the farm. Misplaced love (Bathsheba's for Troy) almost destroys the farm, just as excessive and irrational love destroys Boldwood (and his farming). Oak remains to save the day, and the end of the novel is precisely a compromise between the forces of agriculture and the forces of love – only where nature's will (the Immanent Will) and man's will (Bathsheba's desires, Oak's desires) coincide can man even begin to consider the possibility of happiness.

MOMENTS OF VISION

In this account of *Far from the Madding Crowd* I have tried to stress the extraordinary success of Hardy's attempt to weave together the natural progress of the seasons and the development of the plot.

There is an absolute integration between agricultural events and emotional developments, between time, place and feeling. This is the backbone of the novel. But when we think about it, we soon realize that there is a priority to be given to the human side of this process. In other words, however lovingly and brilliantly Hardy handles bee-hiving or the Wessex sky, he is first interested in human beings and their emotions.

Reading Hardy's poetry makes one realize that he is particularly interested in moments of intense emotion. We can say that his concern is based on the perception that love is the most intense experience man is capable of. Certainly a great number of his short lyrics, describing and exploring moments of intensity, involve a love experience of some kind. In his novels, too, Hardy frequently catches at a moment of intensity, and frequently it involves love. It is often said that he spoils his fiction by these vivid evocations, that the moments are melodramatic, the incidents contrived. But if we look into our own memories we can easily see that life is not perceived as an even surface under which all events have an equal value – on the contrary, we remember significant moments 'as if they happened yesterday' and others not at all. So it is with Hardy.

Thus, throughout *Far from the Madding Crowd*, at just the points where the process of interweaving and integration is at its most successful, there is a series of climaxes, intense 'moments of vision', usually concerned with love. These are dangerous, exciting, dramatic moments that crystallize or bring to a head the forces and emotions latent in the situation which they crown. They obviously fascinate Hardy in their own right as well as being essential to his vision of the world. Several are associated with Troy.

We first meet him properly at the moment when Bathsheba does; the first dramatic scene in which he is involved is that where he gets his spur entangled in her dress in the darkness of the fir plantation. The intensity, the breathlessness of the description are entirely appropriate to the vivid memory the scene itself would have created; Hardy makes us aware that a turning-point has come, a new element has erupted into Bathsheba's life, one of love's arrows has struck:

The man to whom she was hooked was brilliant in brass and scarlet. He was a soldier. His sudden appearance was to darkness what the sound of a trumpet is to silence. Gloom, the *genius loci* at all times hitherto, was now totally overthrown, less by the lantern-light than by what the lantern lighted. The contrast of this revelation with her anticipations of some sinister figure in sombre garb was so great that it had upon her the effect of a fairy transformation.

This is not melodrama; once again Hardy has subtly integrated symbol and reality. The physical intrusion of Troy into Bathsheba's life exactly parallels the emotional effect he is going to have on her. She is surprised and dazzled by him physically in the dark lane just as her heart will become surprised and dazzled by him emotionally within a few pages.

Then there is the famous episode of the sword exercise in the 'hollow amid the ferns' where again what we are witnessing is a perfect symbol for Troy's dazzling sexual attraction (his sword) and its effect on Bathsheba. That he is powerful and dangerous is implicit in his action; that he is not to be trusted is implicit in his lie that the sword is not sharp; that he has lured Bathsheba from the steady course of her life is implicit in the slightly guilty isolation of their meeting-place, and so the resonances go on.

There are other intense moments, too: the fire, the storm, Fanny's last journey, Fanny's coffin being opened by Bathsheba and many others. In every case our interest is concentrated on the human emotion involved and in every case symbol and reality become one, so that, for instance, as Fanny nears the end of her *via dolorosa*, about to give birth to Troy's child, we can hardly distinguish between the physical and psychological bases of her suffering: is her tormented journey towards death in the workhouse a symbol for her hopeless love of Troy, or is her hopeless love a symbol for her tormented condition as one example of 'poor, hard-run humanity'?

It is worth remarking here how rare Bathsheba is among Hardy's characters in that she gets very close indeed to the dangerous machinery of intense passion but survives.

Finally, over and above all the other claims I have made for this novel, I think that it must be admitted that *Far from the Madding Crowd* also succeeds at the humbler level of straightforward concrete description. Among the rustics, and especially with Gabriel Oak, we get a strong sense of the actuality of daily rural life. Hardy is second to none in his ability to bring the country to life before us. We know, after reading this novel, what it feels like to be a shepherd under a winter sky, to shear sheep, to jostle at a sheep fair. We know what it feels like to stamp in from the snow and feel the warmth of a good fire. Hardy never stays at this level for long (the shepherd uses the stars to tell the time, so we start thinking about time and the cosmos), but, wherever his head and heart go, his feet are on the ground.

3
The Return of the Native (1878)

THE 'RUSTIC CHORUS' AND ENVIRONMENT

In discussing *Far from the Madding Crowd* I said little about the 'rustic chorus' (Poorgrass, Coggan, Fraye and the others) which contributes enormously to that novel's accessibility. This group provides the humour and the 'humanity' of the book – one thinks of Poorgrass' difficulties in finding Ephesians in a Bible obstinately full of Colossians – and it fulfils, with irony, of course, the commentatorial function of the Greek chorus – one can ponder the significance, for example, of Poorgrass' being given the last word in the novel. Hardy had been advised that his forte was rural description and character, and these homely characters come to life to prove it. More importantly, they provide a living continuity that is not merely a 'background' to the main action but is integrated into it, as the analysis of the procession of the seasons has shown.

In the early chapters of *The Return of the Native* it seems as if Hardy is going to follow the same method again. However, as the novel proceeds it changes direction and it is in this shift of emphasis away from the 'rustic chorus' that we can look for a clue to Hardy's new concerns. None of the later novels, after all, has so large or so active a 'chorus' as *Far from the Madding Crowd*, and in *The Return of the Native* we can watch the chorus starting to wither away. Increasing attention is paid (in *Tess*, say, or *The Woodlanders*) to the main characters and to the play of emotions between them; Hardy seems to have less time for the large leisurely groups of rustics and their simple humour. Indeed he seems to have found it necessary to spend more time on fewer characters altogether. There is far more concentration on Tess herself than there was on Henchard and more on Henchard than there was on Bathsheba. By the time of *Jude* the minor characters appear only rarely and the chorus has virtually disappeared.

This picture of Hardy's development, however, is inadequate in so far as it stresses the relationship of individuals to one another but ignores their relationship to their physical, 'natural' environment.

My analysis of *Far from the Madding Crowd* in terms of the integration of action, commentary and environment showed the special importance of this last, but we have not yet considered it sufficiently. It is almost never the case that the setting in Hardy is mere 'scenery'. The environment of *Far from the Madding Crowd* is the living force of nature as manifested at the spot on the map named Weatherbury, a name with relevant overtones. Environment is conceived in dynamic terms – the rush of the rising sap, the bustle of sheep-washing, the violence of the storm-wind, the slow plodding of horse and man. Even the manmade elements are worked into this integrated, dynamic world. Warren's Malthouse, for instance, is an ancient and, as it were, naturalized part of the environment; it forms a focal point; to it the rustics come to provide each other (and us) with opinions concerning their employers; and to it are brought the new-born lambs to warm by the fire among the boots and the beer mugs. At the Malthouse, Oak acts as intermediary between the workmen and the world of the lovers; from its comforting warmth the chorus emerges to witness, on our behalf, the actions preliminary to the fatal encounter at Boldwood's hopeless party.

To put it simply, in *Far from the Madding Crowd* we have a mixture of individuals, chorus and environment. In *The Return of the Native* the chorus element in the mixture shows signs of weakening, while the environmental element is strengthened. The inhabitants of Egdon react individually with one another and directly with the heath. We soon come to realize that the furze of which the bonfires are made at the beginning of the novel is of more significance than those who carry and light it. As signals and symbols the bonfires outlast their makers.

One might say, ironically, that here we have Hardy employing *people* as mere 'scenery'; the 'Dorsetshire Labourer', personified as a Cantle or a Fairway, however picturesque, is not of the emotional stuff to hold Hardy's attention. Egdon Heath, on the other hand, is raised to a human – even a divine – status for which it would be hard to find parallels in the history of the novel.[1]

The heath is established from the first page as an environment larger, older and stronger than its inhabitants. Hardy was constantly concerned to present mankind against a background of vast impersonal forces (the indifferent universe), and Egdon was a superb opportunity. We can compare the triviality of man on the

---

[1] A possible parallel is the description of London fog that opens *Bleak House*, but the differences are more instructive than the similarities even here.

heath with a series of other vignettes: Oak against the night sky on Norcombe Hill in *Far from the Madding Crowd*, Swithin St Cleeve against the astronomical immensities seen through his telescope in *Two on a Tower*, Tess walking to Talbothays through the fields 'like a fly on a billiard table', Jude in the huge cornfield. But nowhere does Hardy make this point so forcibly as in his handling of Egdon.

THE FIRST CHAPTER

It is worth examining the opening chapter of Book First in some detail. It consists of twelve paragraphs and is entitled 'A Face on Which Time Makes but Little Impression'. We are told that it is a Saturday afternoon in November towards dusk; very ordinary, this, and human, and exact. But we are not told *which* November. Egdon Heath 'Embrowned itself moment by moment': already we see that it has power over itself; it is not 'embrowned' by any external agency; at least in the grammar of this sentence it embrowns itself. Overhead, the sky is sinister, its blue shut out by a 'hollow stretch of whitish cloud'. Both hollowness and the uncomfortable indefiniteness of 'whitish' have unpleasant connotations. We are in a 'tent' of heath and cloud, on 'Egdon Heath', now defined for us as a 'vast tract of unenclosed wild'. This unenclosedness of the heath, like the Saturdayness of the afternoon, locates not Egdon, but *us*. We are not rabbits or heath-ponies, we are intelligent urbanites to whom the days of the week matter and who know what the Enclosures were. So here is Hardy's old trick again, the balancing trick between visceral involvement in nature and intellectual detachment from it; he is going to bring us into as close a contact with Egdon as he possibly can, while at the same time holding us at arm's length by reminding us of purely intellectual aspects of his subject.

It is no use pretending that 'unenclosed' simply means 'unfenced'; the connotations of the word sound at least as loudly as its denotation. Thus we learn that Egdon is free, like common land; old, in that it antedates the Enclosures; untamed by landlord; unlimited by man.

Because of the whitish cloud and the dark heath, the exact time of day, this Saturday twilight, becomes hard to determine. Moving into the second paragraph, Hardy chooses his words with care: 'the heath wore the appearance of an instalment of night which had taken up its place before its astronomical hour was come'. What is an 'instalment'? Primarily the part-payment of money due, figuratively the delivery of any part of anything, particularly of a novel for serial publication such as *The Return of the Native*. The deliberate inappropriateness of the word throws us back to ourselves, to our minds that have been trained elsewhere than on Egdon. Meanwhile 'astronomical' opens up the vast spaces all around man by proposing the true, though unusual, view that the sun is a star and that solar time is really stellar time. Surprise words such as these show us that we are not going to be allowed to drowse over the heath as over, say, Macpherson's *Ossian*: there is no incantation in Hardy.

We find, almost without noticing it, that we are not alone. There are furze-cutters here. Later they are going to become important; for the moment they are only putative. 'Looking upwards, a furze-cutter would have been inclined to continue work.' Who is telling us about furze-cutters and unobtrusively feeding us the necessary information as to the likely occupation of the inhabitants of Egdon? An omniscient narrator, an educated one at least, a countryman too; Mr Hardy, evidently.

This second paragraph ends with another of Hardy's disturbing oscillations – this time from the near-flippant to the awe-inspiring. He takes the anthropomorphic conceit that the 'complexion' of the heath's 'face' can alter the apparent time of day and works it out to a climax as he discovers that, like so many other natural phenomena, Egdon's colouring is more to be feared than enjoyed:

It could . . . retard the dawn, sadden noon, anticipate the frowning of storms scarcely generated, and intensify the opacity of a moonless midnight to a cause of shaking and dread.

We notice that the heath at no point enlivens or improves. The faintly biblical tone of this passage, its careful alliteration, its change of pace ('sadden noon' can only be said slowly) and its splendid rhythm work on us, so that our approach to the heath cannot be anything but wary.

With another change of tone, Hardy lets us off, as it were. 'In fact', he says, and explains in a matter-of-fact way that we are to be initiated into 'the great and particular glory of the Egdon waste' because we are privileged to be there now, at just this moment of dusk when we can hear (or rather feel) Egdon's 'true tale', to wit, that it is a 'near relation of night'. Thus, just as Clym cutting furze in the half-darkness is foreshadowed by the putative furze-cutter of this opening section, Eustacia is also foreshadowed in that she, too, has a close relationship with night.

35

This 'in fact' paragraph (the third of the chapter), also builds up to a sonorous, biblical climax. Hardy establishes his conceit (Egdon = night) and works it out, developing it to its dramatic maximum and ending with

And so the obscurity in the air and the obscurity in the land closed together in a black fraternization towards which each advanced half-way.

The fourth paragraph begins 'The place became full of a watchful intentness now', and we can here uncover yet another of Hardy's 'balancings' or 'oscillations' by asking ourselves what time 'now' refers to exactly. Of course, it is the moment when night falls, any night; but we cannot help also locating this 'now' at that very moment of nightfall on that Saturday during that November. It is, for instance, the very moment at which we are about to meet Captain Vye. But Hardy deliberately omits any way of choosing between these alternatives. We are intended to accept both the universal and the immediate 'now' merely on hearing that word.

The immensely impressive image that follows, of Egdon appearing 'slowly to awake and listen' is for Hardy a way into the widest possible reflections. The heath wakes, listens, seems to be waiting for something. And what is this thing for which the massive patience of Earth, the planet as personified by Egdon, gears itself to wait? 'The final overthrow', a nebulous but ominous notion, at once religious and scientific, that puts into perspective all the vain strugglings of man, including those about to ensue on this November day.

From this broadest possible reference to 'the final overthrow' Hardy moves back into his familiar position beside us and beside his characters. Egdon is 'a spot which returned upon the memory of those who loved it with an aspect of peculiar and kindly congruity', and again we are in that curious position of not quite knowing what Hardy is talking about: 'those who loved it' must include this narrator at our elbow, and the 'furze-cutter' whom we have already met perhaps, and people yet unmentioned who will walk Egdon in the ensuing pages, the 'native', no doubt, who returns. But we cannot be sure *exactly* who is meant. And below this we must sense the irony of anybody's feeling that sinister Egdon has a 'kindly congruity' with his memory.

Having thus returned to our sides in his guide-book rôle, Hardy at once sets out again for the universal. Why should people feel at home in so sinister an environment? Why not in prettier surroundings? The answer is supplied: 'Fair prospects wed happily with fair times; but alas, if times be not fair!' Egdon is the key to a symphony, we realize, and it is going to be a sombre one. Hardy wants the widest possible reference to be established, however, and he cannot resist drawing the most ominous conclusions from his observations:

> Indeed, it is a question if the exclusive reign of . . . orthodox beauty is not approaching its last quarter. The new Vale of Tempe may be a gaunt waste in Thule: human souls may find themselves in closer and closer harmony with external things wearing a sombreness distasteful to our race when it was young.

Not a bad guess – little more than a quarter of a century was to elapse before *The Waste Land* appeared.

Having already met two 'pseudo-characters' (the furze-cutter and 'those who loved' Egdon) and perhaps a third in the narrator–guide at our elbows (Hardy), we now meet another, 'the most thorough-going ascetic'. He is a generalization, of course, but he just slightly foreshadows Clym's puritanism and he could be you or me, or even Hardy himself, the thoughtful young man from Bockhampton, a village a few miles away. But the *real* personality present among these 'pseudo-characters' is the heath itself, thoroughly anthropomorphized with its slumbers, wakings and moods: 'the storm was its lover and the wind its friend'. We feel an uncomfortable familiarity with this personality which seems to have something in common with the dark places of our dreams.

The eighth paragraph of this section ('It was at present . . .') is a summary of the riches that have gone before, a synthesis of what we have already learnt. It brings together the heath's appearance, the suggestion that such a place is in keeping with modern man's feelings, and a fusion of the lonely faces of the pseudo-characters we have met. The heath takes on moral qualities in connexion with its physical ones; it is 'neither commonplace, unmeaning, nor tame; but, like man, slighted and enduring'. It is hard to say whether we first think of Egdon, the pseudo-characters or Hardy himself when he concludes, 'It had a lonely face, suggesting tragical possibilities.'

From this exposed and speculative position we once more return to safe home ground, this time to the area of an antiquarian interest in the heath in history: 'Bruaria', says Domesday Book, and so on. But we still cannot rest – the reference to Domesday awakens perspectives of time down all of which we see Egdon as an unchanging monster: 'Civilization was its enemy.' And, just as Hardy must always move from the particular to the general, so he must always include the element that is necessary for anything whatever to appear interesting – man. Thus he moves from the antiquarian to the general or universal (from Domesday Book to 'Civilization') and thence to a human, individual perspective of the sort that confronts Lear on *his* heath in the shape of the 'poor, bare, forked animal', Edgar representing humanity. 'A person on a heath in raiment of modern cut and colours has more or less an anomalous look' follows immediately from the description of the heath's 'one coat'. Hardy cannot keep mankind from the scene. Almost nowhere in his work is there a 'pure' description of unpersonified, ungeneralized, unanthropomorphized nature.

The penultimate paragraph starts with Hardy's 'trick' again: another pseudo-character appears, this time one 'reclining on a stump of thorn in the central valley of Egdon'. This is clearly a description of the narrator's position, of Hardy on the heath pondering, as we learn he did in the *Life*, on the relative antiquity of things. The claim is made not just that Egdon is old but that it is *especially* old, older than the seas. This is because age is a function of change – the seas are 'renewed in a year, in a day, in an hour', but Egdon does not change and so it can be said to be older. What is interesting here is what Hardy says about this absence of change; Egdon does not alter because it has nothing *excessive* about it. 'Those surfaces were neither so steep as to be destructible by weather, nor so flat as to be the victims of floods and deposits . . .' Like Gabriel Oak the heath may be 'slighted' but it is 'enduring'; without the steep passions of a Boldwood it survives and wins through. The parallel with classical tragedy is clear: the great are cut down by the vengeance of the jealous gods, the unknown and unimportant survive. Like Oak, Egdon will remain unchanged while the 'tragical possibilities' it suggests are realized by its passionate but insignificant inhabitants.

There is nothing manmade on the heath except the road and Rainbarrow. The former is particularly noticeable at this time of night, still glowing whitely in the dusk. As educated people, standing looking at the road 'on the evening under consideration' we can observe how parts of it are reconstructions of 'the Via Iceniana, or Ikenild Street', a touch of pedantry that keeps us alive to the real situation we are in – *we* are never going to be heath-dwellers and there will always be a limit to the involvement we can feel with their tragedies, except, of course, in so far as that beneath the indifferent stars we, and Egdon, are all involved in the same cosmic calamity.

THE NOVEL'S ACTION

What happens on the heath? Does the action of the novel live up to Hardy's overwhelming description of its environment?

The passionate Eustacia Vye, living sullenly with her grandfather on the heath, where 'kisses are at famine prices', has some sort of an affair with Damon Wildeve, who, although educated and a gentleman, keeps the Egdon inn, the Quiet Woman. She transfers her allegiance to Clym, the son of another heath-dweller, Mrs Yeobright, when he returns from the glamour of Paris. In revenge Wildeve marries Mrs Yeobright's niece, Thomasin; Eustacia marries Clym. Neither marriage is happy. Because Wildeve is now inaccessible to her, Eustacia starts to desire him again and she leaves her husband. The same cause works the same effect on Wildeve: Eustacia's 'preciousness in his eyes' increases 'in geometrical progression with each new incident that remind[s] him of their hopeless division' (III, 8). Finally she and Wildeve decide to escape from their marriages together. They are drowned as they attempt this, one rainy winter's night. Such is the main plot. The heath creates the conditions of its possibility. Eustacia's frustration is exacerbated by her isolation: she yearns to escape from Egdon, feels herself to be its prisoner. Damon seems especially glamorous in the limited environment in which she meets him. Clym, coming from Paris, seems yet more glamorous, but the heath, his native heath, has drawn him away from worldly success and soon stamps him as its own; he becomes almost literally engulfed by it.

The point is that Clym *is* a native of Egdon – literally one born there. So is Thomasin. And these two tie their unhappy partners to the heath. In escaping from Clym, Eustacia escapes from Egdon: in leaving Thomasin, Wildeve leaves the heath. Neither Eustacia nor Wildeve is a native of Egdon; both die trying to leave it. Of course, Eustacia, almost against her will, is utterly bound up with the heath. But she hates it.

Old Mrs Yeobright also dies, on the heath, because of the heath, bitten by a snake. The heath kills her although Clym feels, with some slight justification, that he is responsible for her death, albeit unwittingly.

Besides the two couples and Mrs Yeobright the action involves the 'reddleman', Diggory Venn. More even than the Yeobrights, he is intimately related to the heath, sometimes appearing to be its very spirit. Hardy had two possible endings for Venn in the novel, and his inability finally to discard either indicates the importance of Venn's relationship to the heath. In one ending Venn was to have vanished mysteriously into the heath; in the extant ending, of course, he marries the most natural native of the heath – Thomasin. Both endings stress the reddleman's intimacy with his environment.

Even from this bald summary it can be seen that our question, whether the action of *The Return of the Native* is worthy of or appropriate to the heath on which it takes place, is not really applicable. The action is inseparable from its environment.

'THE RETURN OF THE NATIVE' AS TRAGEDY

Hardy's novels seem at times to be trying to conform to Aristotle's definition of tragedy. In *Far from the Madding Crowd*, for example, there is a conscious attempt to limit time and place. The main movement (chapters 1–49) occupies a whole year, from Oak's first sight of Bathsheba to Troy's disappearance. The two brief movements that follow occupy another year each (chapters 49–54 and 54–6), and the last chapter (57) acts as a coda in which we see Bathsheba and Oak married in the story's fourth spring. The action nearly all takes place at Weatherbury although it can go as far afield as Casterbridge and Greenhill Fair. But the town of Bath, for instance, lies outside the book's world and is only presented indirectly. This is hardly Aristotle's ideal of one day and one place, but a comparison with Dickens or George Eliot or even with Jane Austen soon reveals how exceptional it is that Hardy limited himself so strictly.

In *The Return of the Native* this limiting and 'tragic' tendency is somewhat developed. The action is limited (in Books First to Fifth) to a year and a day, from 5 November one year to 6 November the next. And we do not move off the heath *at all*. When Thomasin and later Eustacia go to get married, we feel that they have, in cinema terms, 'gone out of the picture'. Thomasin is married in *Wildeve's* parish church – where would that be? Eustacia is married at the nearest church, as we are specifically told, but it is outside our ken and the closest we are allowed to get to the ceremony is when we hear the bells pealing faintly in the distance (III, 7).

Unity of place is maintained in *The Return of the Native*, then, and there is a gesture towards unity of time. What of the third Aristotelian category, unity of action? Here matters are not at all clear. Who, for example, is our protagonist? The 'native' Clym, as the book's title implies? Eustacia, perhaps? Wildeve? Venn? Thomasin? Compared with his confident handling of the heath, Hardy's unsureness as to which character he is most interested in and which plot he is going to adopt is quite striking. This impression of unsureness is confirmed by the publishing history of the novel. There is, for instance, the famous note at the end of VI, 3, in which Hardy suggests a possible alternative ending, the simple disappearance of Diggory Venn into the heath. The note implies that he would have preferred this ending but that it was impossible for a novel published as a serial. His preference, however, cannot have been very strong, because he did not take the opportunity of including it either in the first book version of the novel, published in 1878, or in the revised versions of 1895 and 1912. On the other hand, there is the curious fact that when, in the 1895 version, Hardy did try to clear up one of the novel's most important uncertainties (whether Eustacia and Wildeve were lovers before the story opens) and made it plain that Eustacia is *not* a virgin when we first meet her, he lost his nerve and in the final revision of 1912 obfuscated the matter once again. I adduce these points as evidence of Hardy's difficulty in deciding how his novel should develop and quite where its emphases should lie.[2]

More important than these historical considerations, however, are the purely aesthetic problems posed by the story itself. Perhaps we can get back to these by referring again to Hardy's 'tragic' intentions. The 1895 edition included a Preface in which the possibility is mentioned that Egdon may be King Lear's heath. Is it *that* class of tragic hero that Hardy wants us to have in mind? If so, which of his characters can possibly come within hailing distance of the 'very foolish, fond old man'? Put in these terms, none of them can, of course, although there is a theme of filial loyalty and disloyalty in the novel in the relationship between Clym and his mother and in that between Eustacia and Captain Vye. But if we examine the Lear of the heath scene we find well-known elements of his madness that are close to Hardy's heart. Lear's mind, for instance, is inclined to dwell on the intimate relationship between the storm and the people upon whom it indifferently beats. He wants it to drown the world, to burn it, to crush it, so that man will be unable to reproduce: he rejoices above all in nature's indifference:

---

[2] A full discussion of these issues can be found in J. Paterson, *The Making of 'The Return of the Native'*. Berkeley: University of California Press, 1960.

> I tax you not, you elements, with unkindness;
> I never gave you kingdom, call'd you children,
> You owe me no subscription: then let fall
> Your horrible pleasure . . .
>
> (III.ii.16–19)

The storm falls from a heaven that is Hardyan in its indifference, and it lashes the defenceless as hard as anyone else, though of course they suffer more. In this scene, and in the later scene between Lear, Edgar and the Fool (III.iv) there is a constant harping on things sexual. Somehow the force of the storm can only be associated with violent sexuality. The Fool refers to cod-pieces, bawds, lechers; Edgar describes himself at length as 'one that slept in the contriving of lust, and wak'd to do it'; Lear himself strays in his talk to whipping whores and incest and thence to an extraordinary concentration on flesh, flesh that is to be punished for begetting ungrateful daughters, the flesh of the 'poor, bare, forked animal'. This is the element in *Lear*, it seems to me, that Hardy is pointing to: this tremendous, tearing sexual energy appears, palely loitering through this Victorian drama, in Eustacia, virgin or not.

Is Eustacia our protagonist, then? She is intimate with the heath as Lear is with the elements, defenceless and passionate, defenceless *because* passionate, an ancient mystery in young flesh. When she appears on Rainbarrow, almost as the priestess of the immemorial rite we are about to witness, a sense of antique mystery is generated. Hardy's immediate analysis of the bonfire-lighting (1, 3) reinforces this. He opens his usual perspectives in time:

It was as if these men and boys had suddenly dived into past ages, and fetched therefrom an hour and deed which had before been familiar with this spot. The ashes of the original British pyre which blazed from that summit lay fresh and undisturbed in the barrow beneath their tread.

He extends this to include references to Thor and Woden, to 'Druidical rites and Saxon ceremonies' and to the Gunpowder Plot. And he adds a psychologist's insight:

To light a fire is the instinctive and resistant act of man when, at the winter ingress, the curfew is sounded throughout Nature.

But, having moved from the perspectives of time and mythology to a simple piece of country psychology, he now moves out again to the widest horizons in that intensifying method of generalization that we saw at work in the opening description of the heath. Lighting a fire, we learn, indicates a spontaneous, Promethean rebelliousness against the fiat that this recurrent season shall bring foul times, cold darkness, misery and death. Black chaos comes, and the fettered gods of the earth say, let there be light.

This passage is cast in brilliant and sonorous language entirely suitable to its function. But we cannot avoid asking, in the context of the novel, whose is this Promethean rebellion? Eustacia's, to be sure; but it is also Clym's. Hence we have the dichotomy of Hardy's point of view, his unsureness about *The Return of the Native*, neatly symbolized. The light of Promethean rebellion that Eustacia represents is the fire of passion: the light Clym stands for, like Prometheus in the myth, is the light of learning. Both lights are to be dimmed, as they will be for Jude Fawley. In the dimming lies the tragedy.

EUSTACIA VYE

Can I still maintain that it is Eustacia's tragedy? Perhaps we should compare her stature to that of Clym. In the eyes of the Egdon work-folk, for instance, his stature is great but mundane. He does not live up to the early glamour given him by his return from Paris: his nature is too mild and reasonable. As Eustacia recognizes, Wildeve is a more exciting person. Eustacia herself, on the other hand, is a queen. She is 'Queen of Night' as the title of 1, 7 tells us. That whole chapter is an interlude of description, after the manner of the interlude that describes Sergeant Troy in *Far from the Madding Crowd* (chapter 25, 'The New Acquaintance Described'). What does it tell us and how does it work?

'Queen of Night' is Hardy's clear but unsuccessful bid to give Eustacia the tragic stature suggested by the references to Lear and Prometheus. Just as tragic pride (*hubris*) swells the hero to the level of the gods, so this section claims that 'Eustacia Vye was the raw material of a divinity. On Olympus she would have done well with a little preparation.' Hardy even goes on to picture how the world would be if Eustacia were fate itself.[3]

[3] It is interesting to consider this picture for the light it throws on Hardy's world view. He suggests that the world would be very little altered if Eustacia were its ruler: we would see 'the same captious alteration of caresses and blows that we endure now'. Here is an instance of Hardy's 'pessimism' that we can examine. He appears fair in his equal presentation of 'caresses' and 'blows', but there is the matter of the word 'endure'. What do we endure? The 'captious alteration' of pleasant and unpleasant. Why should this need to be 'endured'? Because an alteration, especially an alteration over which we have no control, between pain

Of course, Eustacia is not inflated thus quite uncritically. There is humour and irony in that 'with a little preparation'. There is also a touch of class-consciousness. Hardy himself did well at the dinner tables of the London season, after a little preparation. There are other good things in this description too. The passage on Eustacia's hair and its sensitivity to brushing is one, and there is a serious attempt to convey the subtleties and profundities of her eyes. But Hardy's idiosyncrasy overcomes him when he gets to the mouth, whose curve resembles that 'so well known in the arts of design as the cima-recta or ogee'. What seems to be wrong here is that his undeniable talent for detail has led him to unearth the most esoteric detail possible in order to convey the *exact* curve of Eustacia's mouth. Alas, the detail is too remote and it conveys nothing. On the other hand the very next sentences propose metaphors that are within our common knowledge, so that they work excellently:

It was felt at once that that mouth did not come over from Sleswig with a band of Saxon pirates whose lips met like the two halves of a muffin.

(I, 7)

From this homeliness Hardy again pushes off out into the romantic deep where he is less at home. The paragraph after the one about muffins opens

Her presence brought memories of such things as Bourbon roses, rubies, and tropical midnights; her moods recalled lotus-eaters and the march in 'Athalie'.

I do not offer a close criticism of the half-dozen pages of this chapter, although that would be a profitable exercise, but simply point out some of Hardy's different attempts to get Eustacia on to paper. I have said that his description of her fails, but it also succeeds. We get a strong enough impression of the girl once we have fought our way through the Bourbon roses. And in a sense the very failure is in a good cause. When the rubies and tropical mid-

---

and pleasure renders pleasure uncertain while not materially altering the status of pain. Furthermore, 'captious' means 'apt to take one in' and 'disposed to find fault'. Thus the agent responsible for the alterations (God) not only carries them out as a game in which man is deliberately 'taken in' or deluded but also has a predisposition to blame and punish. 'Captious' has the same etymology as 'captive'. So the whole phrase, far from being objective and 'fair', is heavily loaded with pessimistic assumptions. This is not intended as a criticism of Hardy, but people sometimes try to defend him by maintaining that he was not a pessimist. This is not the best defence.

nights appear, they are not simply romantic clichés. Hardy is attempting here two new and difficult tasks.

First, he is striving for a vocabulary and a style that will convey immediately and excitingly the subtle emotional effect of a woman like Eustacia on a sensitive observer. (Here he is again, this presumed sensitive observer of Hardy's who is simultaneously Hardy and ourselves: 'Her presence brought memories' – to whom?) A 'simple' psychological description that attempted to capture the magic of Eustacia's presence would be impossibly complex and infinitely longwinded. Hardy's method is bold, dangerous, and clearly the work of a poet. It is a method that was taken over and developed by Lawrence, whose descriptions of emotion and its causes are also criticized for being overwritten.

The second thing that Hardy is attempting in passages such as this is to strike a novel balance between nature and art. There is a deliberately fragile artificiality about the roses and the rubies, an 'artiness' about the lotus-eaters and the viola. So much the better. It is a deliberately contrived picture that Hardy is presenting, as we see from this: 'In a dim light, and with a slight rearrangement of her hair, her general figure might have stood for that of either of the higher female deities.' As we gaze at Eustacia, we are being asked to remember pictures and statues of goddesses that we have seen. The paragraph ends with the word 'canvases'. There is a curious movement here as Hardy suggests pictures: 'The new moon behind her head, an old helmet upon it, a diadem of accidental dewdrops round her brow, would have been adjuncts sufficient to strike the note of Artemis, Athena or Hera respectively.' We are being asked to see Eustacia as a fake goddess of the sort that Victorian painters were apt sometimes to produce. I think Hardy's purpose here is very modern. The immediate, vigorous classicism of the seventeenth and eighteenth centuries has been left far behind and here we have the attenuated classicism of the nineteenth century, the sort that seems to leave the original untouched. Hardy is deliberately employing this fake classicism to undermine Eustacia's status, the very status which he is trying simultaneously to establish. This is the final effect of Hardy's division into an 'educated' and an 'uneducated' half. The uneducated Hardy is aware of Eustacia's power and unerringly associates it with the power of Egdon and the night; the educated Hardy tries to express this awareness through metaphors and similes that will evoke appropriate emotions, but the artificiality of this endeavour is apparent to him, so he incorporates the artificiality into his prose, lets us know that he knows its falseness ('a diadem of *accidental* dew-drops') and creates a tension between the 'natural' and 'artificial' Eustacias. The ironic possibilities of this tension are not missed; the next paragraph begins 'But celestial imperiousness, love, wrath, and fervour had proved to be somewhat thrown away on Nether-ward Egdon.'

The same process is apparent a few lines further on, where Hardy solemnly quotes from the aesthetician Richter's code that 'Nothing can embellish a beautiful face more than a narrow band drawn over the brow' and at once deflates this pomposity with the mundane dismissiveness of 'but if anyone suggested coloured ribbon and metallic ornaments to Eustacia Vye she laughed and went on'.

None of this is intended to detract from our sympathy for Eustacia. Quite the reverse. She is a poor, trapped bird like so many of Hardy's heroines, a queen 'without realms or hearts to queen it over'. Too passionate for her own good, she is forced to live on Egdon where 'coldest and meanest kisses were at famine prices'. So she is at once our tragic goddess and a trapped bird. 'To be loved to madness – such was her great desire. Love was to her the one cordial that could drive away the eating loneliness of her days', but, on Egdon, 'where was a mouth matching hers to be found?'

Hardy's novels are about love. We have seen the 'resolution' of love adopted in *Far from the Madding Crowd*, where the practical, down-to-earth love of Gabriel and Bathsheba is seen as safer, stronger and better than the excesses of the other loves in the story. In *The Return of the Native* there is, not surprisingly, a revolt against this solution. From the standpoint of the later novels we shall be able to look back at Eustacia and see that perhaps Hardy is speaking for his other major characters when he says of her that

She could show a most reproachful look at times, but it was directed less against human beings than against certain creatures of her mind, the chief of these being Destiny, through whose interference she dimly fancied it arose that love alighted only on gliding youth – that any love she might win would sink simultaneously with the sand in the glass.

POSITIVE AND NEGATIVE CHARACTERS

It becomes apparent that Hardy's characters fall into two groups which we can roughly call 'productive' and 'non-productive' or 'positive' and 'negative'. Belonging to one of these depends on a character's moral relationship to his environment.[4]

When Gabriel Oak, by thatching the ricks against the coming storm, saves for Bathsheba '£750 in the divinest form that money can wear – that of necessary food for man and beast' (FFMC, 36), it is clear that his resourcefulness and tenacity qualify him as having a productive relationship with Weatherbury Farm. Indeed, Gabriel is the archetype of the positive character in Hardy: he is a man, if not in control of his environment, then at least concerned to make the best of it, certainly to encourage the land to yield all it can. Troy, who will pick up a pitchfork or a bee-keeper's net only to be near a woman, represents the opposite type. He stands out from the environment in his red uniform where Oak blends in; he allows crops to be spoiled while Oak preserves them. Bathsheba, at heart, is on Oak's side – literally at his side as he thatches the ricks. Boldwood moves from being productive, a good farmer, to being non-productive when he falls in love and lets his farming slide. Herein lies one of the dangers of excessive passion.

In *The Return of the Native*, Wildeve is clearly negative in the same way as Troy. Just as Troy only receives the benefits of Weatherbury Farm and puts nothing into it, so Wildeve merely reaps the reward of faithful work carried out by others.

Wildeve's Patch, as it was called, was a plot of land redeemed from the heath, and after long and laborious years brought into cultivation. The man who had discovered that it could be tilled died of the labour: the man who succeeded him in possession ruined himself in fertilizing it. Wildeve came like Amerigo Vespucci, and received the honours due to those who had gone before.

(I, 4)

Wildeve is constantly presented as rootless and uncommitted – not necessarily evil, but negative and non-productive, not in a working relationship with his environment. Clym Yeobright, obviously, is the opposite of Wildeve and is something of an Oak figure. In his desire to escape from a world of vanity (represented by his having been a jeweller in Paris) and in his acceptance of humble employment in the very bosom of the heath, he represents the sensible, stoical, productive theme in Hardy which is clearly given a moral value. The remarkable portrait of Clym, as he works half-blind at his furze-cutting, makes it quite clear that this value derives from or depends on a relationship with nature:

---

[4] This model of Hardy's novels can be put alongside the model given in note 2, chapter 2 above.

His daily life was of a curious microscopic sort, his whole world being limited to a circuit of a few feet from his person. His familiars were creeping and winged things, and they seemed to enroll him in their band. Bees hummed around his ears with an intimate air . . .

(IV, 2)

It is well worth pondering the entire paragraph of which this is the opening. And there is an earlier passage that makes the point even more strongly:

If anyone knew the heath well it was Clym. He was permeated with its scenes, with its substance and with its odours. He might be said to be its product.

This is as strongly put as any other description in Hardy of the relationship between man and nature.

What are we to say of Eustacia in this context? We first see her, 'a Figure against the Sky', on Rainbarrow, mystically caught up in the wind in a way that even Gabriel Oak wasn't on Norcombe Hill. The wind of Egdon is the voice of a pagan past, older and stronger than man. It blows through the dead 'heath-bells', and of the resulting noise Hardy says, 'The spirit moved them' and explains this as indicating that 'it was the single person of something else speaking through each at once' (I, 6). And Eustacia joins in: 'the heather-bells had broken silence; at last, so did the woman; and her articulation was but as another phrase of the same discourse as theirs' (I, 6). So she, too, is deeply associated with the heath, sharing its wild and passionate nature, without at all being a productive character. Like Boldwood, Eustacia is made unproductive by passion; the heath, for example, produces little enough firewood, but what her grandfather has collected she can waste on a fire that signals her presence to a man she is interested in. She may blend into the heath well enough, echo its moods, appear as the queen of its dark soul; but she has none of the care, responsibility or feeling for the place that could make her identification with it something productive. This is why she is so strange and interesting a character. She is of the heath but she bears it no love; she is 'a creature of light surrounded by an area of darkness' (V, 8). Her whole attitude is that of love–hatred; when Clym suggests that she should hate not people but what produces them, she replies, 'Do you mean Nature? I hate her already' (III, 3). And in the same conversation she admits, 'I cannot endure the heath, except in its purple season. The heath is a cruel taskmaster to me.' This is how

Eustacia becomes a tragic figure; she is the heath's alter ego, but she loathes it.

Eustacia sees this tension in her life as being that between her aspirations and her environment, and so it is. But the tension is not really *outside* her in the shape of simple external forces that keep her bound to Egdon when she aspires to Paris, it is *inside* her in that she is possessed by the elemental passions of the heath which nothing, certainly not Paris, can assuage. The perfect image for this is found by Hardy in the last scene in which she appears. She leaves Captain Vye's house in the rain at half-past eleven at night. As she walks towards Rainbarrow she stumbles over a few poor products of the heath about whose function as omens we are left in no doubt: 'twisted furze-roots, tufts of rushes, or oozing lumps of fleshy fungi, which at this season lay scattered about the heath like the rotten liver and lungs of some colossal animal' (v, 7). When she reaches the Rainbarrow (= 'rain-grave', appropriately enough on this November night) her long, unwilling identification with nature reaches its climax. 'Never was harmony more perfect than that between the chaos of her mind and the chaos of the world without' (v, 7). As she stands, 'slightly rocking' in her unhappiness, we learn that 'Between the drippings of the rain from her umbrella to her mantle, from her mantle to the heather, from the heather to the earth, very similar sounds could be heard coming from her lips' (v, 7). The identification between Eustacia and the heath is complete. What is so impressive is that Hardy is here able to overcome the distinction between outer and inner. When he hints at his favourite bird image for poor hard-run women ('The wings of her soul were broken by the cruel obstructiveness of all about her') we realize that we do not make a distinction in our reading between the physical and mental 'obstructiveness' of her surroundings. Her limitations are social, psychological, financial and physical, but as the novel nears its climax these become fused into the single dark work of an unseeing destiny. The last we see of Eustacia alive is in the situation of King Lear, in a storm on a heath, and in the mood of Prometheus, in bitter revolt against heaven:

O, the cruelty of putting me into this ill-conceived world! I was capable of much; but I have been injured and blighted and crushed by things beyond my control! O, how hard it is of Heaven to devise such tortures for me, who have done no harm to Heaven at all!

(v, 7)

So Eustacia is perhaps greater than the categories 'negative' and 'positive' can comprehend in the special meaning we gave them. She is identified with nature but does not have a productive relationship with it; and her greatness of soul is in opposition to nature's forces. There is wisdom in acceptance, in stoic good sense, as we see in Gabriel Oak and Clym, and there is danger in passion. Bathsheba learns this lesson in time; Eustacia does not.

NATURE AND MAN

In discussing *Far from the Madding Crowd* I stressed Hardy's ability to integrate the elements in his work into a natural, agricultural, biological, seasonal background. The 'gurgoyle', for example, 'waters-in' the body of the newly buried Fanny in an elaborate though unexpressed planting metaphor that casts an ironic light on Troy's attempts to put flowers on her grave. In *The Return of the Native* we find the same integration; there is a concentration on the heath itself that should warn us that Hardy is once again working natural and human courses in the same crucible. I have pointed to those places where, describing Eustacia, he abolishes the distinction between 'outer' and 'inner', and there are further examples to show this integration between man and nature.

Diggory Venn illustrates this in his own weird manner.[5] His relationship to the heath is made strikingly clear when he actually covers himself with turf to eavesdrop on the conversation between Wildeve and Eustacia (1, 9). He crawls along, a bizarre piece of moving earth, listening as though he were the heather itself. If this seems improbable it is worth asking what else there is on Egdon to hide behind or under in order to watch people or listen unobserved. For it is precisely Venn's character to *observe*, and he must be physically permitted to do this; moreover, he is the son of the heath and his place is close to it. He limits and controls the action in much the same way as the heath itself does.

Clym's interpenetration with the heath reminds us of one of the conditions for 'integrated existence' in Hardy – the condition of knowledge, awareness, consciousness. 'If anyone knew the heath well it was Clym.' This intelligent young man is not an unthinking

---

[5] To use the categories we have so far employed, Venn is positive and productive; his trade is useful and he easily becomes a successful dairy farmer. He is also, for most of the book, the 'poor man' who aspires to the 'lady' (Thomasin) in rivalry with Wildeve, who is relatively richer and of a better class. Venn is also the 'outsider', the 'mephisphelean visitant', something like Sergeant Troy and Alec d'Urberville in his devilish redness.

part of the Egdon landscape; there would be no drama in that. He must *know* his heath: 'He gazed upon the wide prospect as he walked, and was glad.' This integration is not just a matter of literary style. Hardy develops it so strongly that it comes to absorb the moral and aesthetic values in the work. Nature, in some sense, becomes a touchstone for humanity to live by and to make judgements by.

Hardy provides himself with several incidents and set-pieces in the novel that permit him to exercise his talent for integrating man and nature, weaving them together with his own strange brand of symbolic realism. There is, for example, the dance at 'the gipsying' where Wildeve and Eustacia come together again. The dancing continues until the couples are illuminated by rays from 'the disc of the moon'. Two pieces of weaving together of man and nature take place simultaneously here. First, there is the direct effect of the natural phenomenon of moonlight on the dancers:

All the dancing girls felt the symptoms, but Eustacia most of all. The grass under their feet became trodden away, and the hard, beaten surface of the sod, when viewed aslant towards the moonlight, shone like a polished table . . . The pretty dresses of the maids lost their subtler day colours and showed more or less of a misty white. Eustacia floated round and round on Wildeve's arm . . .

(IV, 3)

Here the dancers become part of the moonlight. Besides this there are the connotations of the moon already established in the story: Eustacia is the 'Queen of Night'; when Clym and Eustacia arrange to meet, it is during an eclipse; and so on.

It is perhaps worth observing that the way in which Hardy 'works up' an incident like this one of the dancing leads him into realms that anticipate D. H. Lawrence: Eustacia floats on Wildeve's arm, 'her face rapt and statuesque; her soul had passed away from and forgotten her features, which were left empty and quiescent, as they always are when feeling goes beyond their register' (IV, 3). It is almost as if this were Hardy's version of an 'epiphany' (to move from Lawrence to Joyce). His 'epiphanies', if we can use that word, are always based on an intense experience, usually of love, in which the natural surroundings of the characters, the natural symbols associated with them, and even their cultural associations, are united in a flowering of their souls. We have seen some examples of this in *Far from the Madding Crowd*, notably in the analysis of Boldwood's first amorous approach to Bathsheba at the sheep-washing. This dancing in *The Return of the Native* is another example, and it adds a slight mystical touch. When Eustacia and Wildeve next meet, Hardy comments,

Nobody could have imagined from her bearing now that here stood the woman who had joined with him in the impassioned dance of the week before, unless indeed he could have penetrated below the surface and gauged the real depth of that still stream.

(IV, 6)

It is a conventional enough sentence, but it keeps us aware of Eustacia's continuing potential while again associating her with nature's 'stream'.

Sometimes moments of integration between the doings of the characters and their environment (between man and nature) fall rather flat. The 'moth-signal', used by Wildeve to attract Eustacia's attention without arousing Clym's suspicions, is original, but it seems rather laboured as an attempt to bring the life of the heath into the lives of the characters. On the other hand, the snake-bite that Mrs Yeobright suffers is highly appropriate. Altogether, as my analysis of the opening description of the heath was intended to show, there is underlying the novel a sense of vast natural forces, indifferent to but not unrelated to man. Man tries to come to terms with them, but can only be partially successful. The whole range of Hardy's style, from its most whimsically idiosyncratic to its most powerful, is a struggle to express this intimate relationship between nature and man. When I have spoken of integration, homogeneity and interpenetration in discussing these first two novels I have been trying to establish a vocabulary that will cope with the relationship.

In *The Rise of the Novel* Ian Watt suggests that *Robinson Crusoe* is the best work from which to date the development of modern fiction. He says, 'Just as the modern study of society only began once individualism had focused attention on man's apparent disjunctions from his fellows, so the novel could only begin its study of personal relationships once *Robinson Crusoe* had revealed a solitude that cried aloud for them.'[6]

This solitude, in Watt's eyes, was a matter of the social and economic individualization attendant on the growth of Calvinism and capitalism as well as an expression of the ontological loneliness of man. I would associate this with one level of Hardy's attempt at 'integration': his picture of Wessex life becomes possible only when the old, homogeneous, mutually dependent society has star-

[6] (Harmondsworth: Penguin, 1963), p. 95.

ted to break up and to throw up 'individuals' such as Clym. In this light we can best see Hardy as the chronicler of the impact of nineteenth-century industrial life on primitive Wessex agricultural life. The 'sick hurry' and 'divided aims' of those who arrive in Wessex, or return to it, from the 'modern' world (Troy, Clym, Eustacia, Farfrae, Fitzpiers, Mrs Charmond, Angel Clare) create or at least exacerbate the tragic situations. Hardy reveals these types as either not sufficiently rooted in nature to survive (Troy, Mrs Charmond) or rooted in nature but not prepared to be contented with this (Eustacia). On the other hand, those who are merely content to remain embedded in the old ways of Wessex life and thought may be safe, but they are never able to attain a full individuality (they remain the rustic chorus). This dilemma, solved in *Far from the Madding Crowd* by positioning Gabriel strategically on the fence so that he is neither a member of the rustic chorus nor an individualistic modern man, became more acute as the nineteenth century progressed and both Hardy's consciousness and Dorset became increasingly invaded by the modern world. If Hardy has established natural integration as a value, and if the modern world is characterized by disintegration and individualism as Watt says, then Hardy must move towards tragedy as time goes by and nature recedes. As the old world becomes a weaker and weaker opponent of the new, it is inevitable that Hardy should find himself pitting ever weaker heroes and heroines against ever stronger forces.

MRS YEOBRIGHT

Like most discussions of *The Return of the Native*, mine has paid scant attention to Mrs Yeobright. Hardy must have seen her story as an important part of the novel, and she has her own tragedy, but she is a difficult character for the reader to grasp. She is not very sympathetic, nor can she very easily be associated with themes of amorous love or integration with the environment. I have two points to make about her and one question to ask.

First, Hardy does give her a tragic status of some sort. He writes as if he assumes that the reader will feel pity for her and, just possibly, terror at her estrangement from her son. This may be a typically Victorian emphasis, but I think not. There is, surely, between all generations, a tension in which impatience with the old world of the parents is at odds in the children's minds with their need for parental love. *Lear*, after all, is a parents' tragedy.

This leads to my second point. Like Mayor Henchard, Mrs Yeobright has feelings for her only child which are suspiciously strong. Perhaps this is a theme worth looking at in Hardy. I am not suggesting incest, but it almost seems as if Hardy found the passion of sexual love so absorbing that other strong relationships in his novels get drawn towards it, as for example in the case of Lady Constantine's brother in *Two on a Tower* (cf. note 2, chapter 2 above) or in the lesbian case of Miss Aldclyffe and Cytherea in *Desperate Remedies*. It is no coincidence that Henchard, like Melbury in *The Woodlanders*, has a daughter, while Mrs Yeobright has a son.

My question about Mrs Yeobright concerns the heath and takes us back to several earlier points. Why does the heath kill her? Is she not a native too? Is it enough of an answer to say that, in her own way, she commits the tragic error of loving not wisely but too well? Does the heath, as the representative of fate, deal out retribution to her for her possessiveness and her lack of self-effacement? Even if we can accept this reading of her death intellectually, it is hard to be convinced by it emotionally.

4
The Mayor of Casterbridge (1886)

A bald synopsis of the plot of *The Mayor of Casterbridge* might surprise us if we had read only Hardy's other novels. We might well
feel less attracted to this novel than to the others. After all, if we
have been impressed by Hardy's treatment of the land and landscape of Wessex and by his presentation of the ways of love (the two
elements I have most stressed in the preceding chapters), we may
well wonder where these elements have disappeared to in Henchard's story.

Young Henchard, depressed and drunk and out of work, sells his
wife at a country fair, and with her their baby daughter, Elizabeth-
Jane. Sober the next morning, he searches for her but cannot find
her; he vows to abstain from drink for twenty-one years and goes
to find work in Casterbridge. Twenty years later his wife, who
thinks that her purchaser, the sailor Newson, is drowned, reappears
with the grown-up Elizabeth-Jane. Out of a sense of duty and
reparation Henchard, now mayor of Casterbridge and a well-to-do
corn merchant, remarries his wife, who later dies. Another woman,
one Lucetta, whom Henchard has in some way compromised when
they were together in Jersey, arrives in Casterbridge and, in her
turn, claims reparation in the shape of marriage from the mayor.
But before he can take any steps in this direction Lucetta has fallen
in love with Donald Farfrae. Farfrae is a Scotsman who, by accident more than by design on his own part, has become Henchard's
manager and assistant in his corn business. Henchard and he have
quarrelled, and he has set up on his own account. Gradually the
Scotsman prospers and Henchard declines, so that at one point in
the novel their rôles have become reversed and Farfrae has
married Henchard's Lucetta, taken Henchard's house, bought his
business and become mayor. This leaves Henchard only with his
daughter, Elizabeth-Jane. But he has learnt that she is not in fact
his daughter: the baby sold with the mother died, and Newson
agreed to call the child he then had by Henchard's wife Elizabeth-
Jane as well. Worse still, Newson himself now reappears, having
only feigned death after the shipwreck. At first Henchard manages

to convince him that Elizabeth-Jane is dead, but eventually Newson learns the truth and returns to see his daughter. She, meanwhile, has married Farfrae after the death of Lucetta. The final situation of the characters when Henchard has crept out into the country to die is that Farfrae has added to his other trophies Henchard's supposed daughter and is playing host to Newson. It is as if there is no room left anywhere in life for Henchard, and his death seems to follow naturally as the consequence.

Most of the action thus recounted takes place in the town of Casterbridge, which sounds an unpromisingly urban environment, and little of the action has to do with love. This needs some explanation.

First, Casterbridge is not really a town in the modern sense or even in the Victorian-industrialized sense. It is almost as far removed from Dickens' London, say, as the smallest villages of Wessex.

Casterbridge was the complement of the rural life around; not its urban opposite. Bees and butterflies in the cornfields at the top of the town, who desired to get to the meads at the bottom, took no circuitous course, but flew straight down High Street without any apparent consciousness that they were traversing strange latitudes.

(chapter 9)

In fact, Casterbridge (mid-nineteenth-century Dorchester modified by Hardy's imagination) is in spirit a village, or perhaps a marketplace with some villages attached. Hardy's insistence on its integration into the life of the surrounding country is very marked, and parallels his attempts to integrate man and nature in other novels.

Casterbridge was in most respects but the pole, focus, or nerve-knot of the surrounding country life; differing from the many manufacturing towns which are as foreign bodies set down, like boulders on a plain, in a green world with which they have nothing in common.

(chapter 9)

Casterbridge has everything in common with the 'wide fertile land adjoining', and Hardy finds some striking ways of expressing its proximity to the fields: it is 'like a chess-board on a green table-cloth'; 'the farmer's boy could sit under his barley-mow and pitch a stone into the office-window of the town clerk' (chapter 14).

Even this, however, is not quite the same thing as the strong natural background that Weatherbury Farm provides in *Far from the Madding Crowd* or Egdon Heath provides in *The Return of the*

56

Native. Casterbridge is as nearly part of the country as a town can be; the talk there is all of sowing, reaping and farm work; the shops are full of agricultural equipment; the inhabitants are country-men; but the sense of space that belongs to the country proper is missing, and the relationships of the characters to the land are more tenuous and less important than in Hardy's other major novels, except perhaps *Jude*. There is certainly great concern about the weather in this novel and there are one or two points at which Hardy comments on the relationship between man and nature in the style of the earlier novels. There is the famous passage, for instance, describing young Henchard looking out of the furmity tent after he has sold his wife (chapter 1). At first a contrast is drawn between 'the peacefulness of inferior nature', as exemplified by the horses 'rubbing each other lovingly' with their necks, and 'the wilful hostilities of mankind', as exemplified by the wife-selling just witnessed. But then the point is made, presumably by Hardy as much as by Henchard, that 'all terrestrial conditions are intermittent' and that nature can sometimes be cruel just as man can sometimes be innocent. Then there is the example of the 'long-tied espaliers' in Henchard's garden that have 'pulled their stakes out of the ground' and stand 'distorted and writhing in vegetable agony, like leafy Laocoöns' (chapter 12). This is Hardy's characteristic association of suffering nature with suffering man that we shall meet again, especially in *The Woodlanders* and *Tess*. And towards the end of the novel we learn that part of Henchard's 'wish to wash his hands of life' arises from 'his perception of its contrarious inconsistencies – of Nature's jaunty readiness to support unorthodox social principles' (chapter 44). Besides these, we might feel that the Roman amphitheatre goes some way towards supply-ing natural grandeur, but these examples do not add up to a state-ment of a main theme.

My second point is closely connected with this. I have suggested that the central concern in Hardy is with love, and if it is true that his rural interest is partially suppressed in *The Mayor of Casterbridge*, we might expect that the exploration of love would therefore be carried on with greater intensity. In fact it is not. When we first meet Henchard he has clearly already lost interest in his wife, as his sale of her confirms. When she reappears he marries her out of a sense of duty. When Lucetta appears, her affair with Henchard is also well in the past; her love letters are now a source of shame and embarrassment. Henchard again proposes marriage out of a sense of duty and is goaded into a short period of the passionate concern typical in Hardy only when Lucetta falls in love with Farfrae. The Scotsman, however, is no Don Juan either. His love is real enough, but it flows in a safe, orderly channel: neither of his marriages is upset by a storm of passion. Elizabeth-Jane loves Farfrae from an early stage in the novel, but she learns the lesson of renunciation and knows how to hold her heart in check.

However, as with the issue of the 'urban' setting of Casterbridge, our first assumptions (our unease at the thought of Hardy handling town life; our surprise that love does not loom larger) are proved to be partially false. Hardy does introduce a love theme in *The Mayor of Casterbridge*, but he does so covertly, under the guise of parental feeling. Henchard's relationship with Elizabeth-Jane, without being for a moment sexual, has a lot of the characteristics of a love affair. They both blow hot and cold, they both think about their relationship and suffer over it. The last time they are together (chapter 44) is a painful scene: the pain we feel in witnessing it touches exactly that part of our emotional make-up usually reserved for our reactions to the sufferings of lovers. Henchard arrives at the house in Casterbridge just when Elizabeth-Jane's wedding celebrations are in full swing, just when she has given herself to his rival for ever. He sits in a little parlour getting occasional agonizing glimpses of his beloved's dress. He feels real jealousy when he sees her dancing with Newson. He meets her, she speaks harshly to him, he stumbles away in despair and dies.

Now, of course, Henchard's sufferings over Elizabeth-Jane are only the final blows that crush this already much-abused man and, of course, his relationship with her is *not* that of a lover. But, as I suggested earlier, for Hardy passionate love has such a magnetic attraction that it tends to absorb into itself other relationships of a different sort.

One of the ways in which we can see the shift in Hardy's interests is by comparing the frequent asides on the subject of love in *Far from the Madding Crowd* with the very few in *The Mayor of Casterbridge*. Those that we do find in the later novel, however, are exactly of a piece with Hardy's usual views on the subject. For instance, when Farfrae has turned his attentions from Elizabeth-Jane to Lucetta, Hardy remarks (on behalf of Elizabeth-Jane) that Farfrae hardly seems the same man as the one who had 'walked with her in a delicate poise between love and friendship', and he glosses this poise as 'that period in the history of a love when alone it can be said to be unalloyed with pain' (chapter 25).

So, in spite of first appearances, there is something in this novel of Hardy's interest in the country and something of his interest in love. But neither of these is the main motivation of the work, and clearly Hardy is concentrating here on something rather different. I suggest that what he is concentrating on is writing a special sort of tragical biblical parable in novel form.

TRAGEDY AND 'THE MAYOR OF CASTERBRIDGE'

Several critics have pointed to the classical tragic shape of *The Mayor of Casterbridge*.[1] It is the story of the rise and fall of a 'man of character', a man flawed in certain self-destructive ways; his story is confined in space and time; there are clear echoes of Greek tragedy and of *King Lear*. I think that this account of the novel is useful and interesting, and it is hard to believe that it was not part of Hardy's intention to imitate tragedy to some extent. However, I do not think that this is the whole story. Henchard feels much more like a character from the Old Testament than a character from Sophocles. This, too, has been noted by a number of critics, and parallels have been drawn between Henchard on the one hand and Job, Saul, Samson and Cain on the other. But, again, this is not the whole story.

I suggest that Hardy uses these elements simply as pointers to the sort of seriousness he is attempting. He is an immensely ambitious writer, and he wants to give an account of the human condition that will work on the cosmic level as well as on an intensely local, detailed level. This ambition is what fires his major novels and separates them from the minor work. It produces an account of the human condition that is *like* that of the Book of Job or of Sophocles or of Shakespeare, but it is something new, something entirely nineteenth-century. At this level, where Hardy is coming to grips with the universe and its relationship to man, he creates parables, allegories, living stories whose burden is cosmic.

In *Far from the Madding Crowd* Hardy found his own voice for the first time. In that novel he fully recognized the seriousness of the theme that most attracted him, and managed to integrate the movements of love into the landscape, into the movements of nature, and even into the intellectual information expected of the reader. This stress on love and this integration are maintained in different degrees in most of his later novels, but from *The Return of*

[1] For instance, John Paterson, '*The Mayor of Casterbridge* as Tragedy', *Victorian Studies*, III (Dec. 1959), 151–72. Reprinted in A. J. Guerard (ed.), *Hardy*, pp. 91–112 (see Reading List).

the Native onwards a new element appears. This is the ambitious, cosmic element I am discussing. Eustacia is no mere individual woman, as Bathsheba was. She *is* individual, of course, but she is also symbolic of passion, frustration, loneliness, ambition and desire; she is the 'raw material of a divinity'. Clym *is* Clym Yeobright, but he is also man turning his back on the artificial and involving himself once more in nature. Diggory, as we saw, is the spirit of Egdon Heath. The heath itself is the enduring, dangerous, indifferent Earth, symbol of the indifferent universe.

When we come to *The Mayor of Casterbridge* it is obvious that this cosmic tendency in Hardy has come to outweigh his earlier concerns, and he naturally turns to the most 'cosmic' areas of earlier literature to find parallels. In my opinion he loses something by this extreme application of a method. He knew instinctively that love was the area which most obviously revealed to man his true relationship to the universe and, in Henchard's story, this great exemplar love is not sufficiently present. In *Tess* Hardy managed once again to combine his universal ambitions with his knowledge of love, as he had done in *The Return of the Native*; *Tess* is his masterpiece because it achieves a perfect integration between the cosmic parable of life on a 'blighted' planet with the story of Tess Darbeyfield's life and love and death. How far does Hardy succeed in *The Mayor of Casterbridge*, then, considering the disadvantage he gives himself by not focussing on love?

Most of the answer to this depends on what we learn about Henchard. His character is the clue to the parable, his life reflects the aspect of the cosmic struggle that Hardy is pointing to.

When he first appears, Henchard has a 'dogged, cynical indifference personal to himself' (chapter 1). He gets drunk, he sells his wife. Already he seems to care very little about himself and, in so far as his wife is *his*, he does not care much about her either. Further into the novel, when we have learnt of his success, we are surprised, in spite of these opening pages, to find Henchard saying to Farfrae that he sometimes sinks into 'gloomy fits' when 'the world seems to have the blackness of hell'. On these occasions, he says, 'like Job, I could curse the day that gave me birth' (chapter 12). The mention of Job universalizes this tendency to depression in the mayor and leads us quite naturally into Henchard's permanent undertow of pessimism. He is telling Farfrae of the past, a time years before when he was gloomy (it was the time in Jersey when Lucetta nursed him), but now, telling his story in the present, he exclaims that he does not know why Lucetta bothered to look after him:

'Heavens knows why, for I wasn't worth it.' A few lines later he adds, 'For myself I don't care – 'twill all end one way.' Much later in the novel we learn that Henchard would hardly defend himself against accusations, 'so little did he value himself or his good name' (chapter 43).

Our impression of Henchard's extreme indifference to himself is frequently reinforced as the novel proceeds – for instance, when Hardy offers us three reasons why Henchard presses on with his plans to remarry his own wife. They are: to make amends to her, to provide a home for Elizabeth-Jane and 'to castigate himself with the thorns which these restitutory acts brought in their train' (chapter 13). Later, when one of the many blows that fall upon him has just struck, we are told,

His usual habit was not to consider whether destiny were hard upon him or not – the shape of his ideas in cases of affliction being simply a moody, 'I am to suffer, I perceive.' 'Thus much scourging, then, is it for me?' But now through his passionate head there stormed this thought – that the blasting disclosure was what he had deserved.

(chapter 19)

For this man there is nothing beyond suffering to learn; for this Lear there is no reconciliation with Cordelia (his last words from Elizabeth-Jane are harsh); and for this Oedipus there is no Colonus. But we have gone beyond Job, too, for Henchard has no God to turn to in his suffering. When goaded beyond endurance his cynical indifference turns into the speculation that there might exist supernatural beings positively hostile to him; these two levels of his reaction to his fate are summed up thus:

Misery taught him nothing more than defiant endurance of it . . . He looked out at the night as at a fiend. Henchard, like all his kind, was superstitious, and he could not help thinking that the concatenation of events this evening had produced was the scheme of some sinister intelligence bent on punishing him.

(chapter 19)

The sentence which follows this should be set against our claims that Hardy is a pessimist. It reads, 'Yet they [the events] had developed naturally.' There is no malign intelligence controlling our affairs; things simply are as they are. Alas, they are not conducive to man's happiness, but it is nobody's fault. As the passage implies, it is superstition to look for some power to blame for the way things are. That would be of a piece with going to a weather prophet to ascertain the market prospects in corn.

So the universe is indifferent, and it is superstitious to look for any divine or malign interference with it, but Hardy is acutely conscious of the power of that superstition. He recognizes the value of the myths of divine antagonism to man. Oedipus battling against the decrees of the gods symbolizes a truth, as does Job in his confrontation with Jehovah, and to this Hardy adds a Christian dimension. This is only going to appear fully recognizable in *Jude*, where the parallels between Jude and Jesus cannot be accidental and where the inference must be drawn that Hardy offers Christ sympathy for his bitter sharing of man's bitter lot. But, meanwhile, there are Christian elements in Hardy's audacious bid to universalize *The Mayor of Casterbridge*. First there is the matter of the 'scourging' of Henchard – the word is used several times – which must be reminiscent of the scourging of Christ before the Crucifixion; then there is the fact that Elizabeth-Jane's earlier life is referred to as a 'Capharnaum' in contrast to the peace of her maturer age. And it is Elizabeth-Jane who decides not to dress too brightly because 'It would be tempting Providence to hurl mother and me down, and afflict us again as He used to do' (chapter 14). In this example are brought together the Greek notion of *hubris* (pride which goes before a fall) bringing an inevitable abasement, an Old Testament notion of a vengeful God and, perhaps with irony, the New Testament notion of God's 'providential' concern for man.

Behind all these notions is Hardy's simple recognition that they are only symbols and that things are not controlled by men or gods but just *are* as they are. Events occur because of a concatenation of circumstances. One of the circumstances is the personality of the person concerned in the event: 'Character is Fate' as Hardy puts it, quoting George Eliot's version of Novalis. There are endless other circumstances that contribute towards fate (we may personalize it with a capital letter, or with names like Nemesis or God, but that is metaphorical: the literal meaning of fate is 'fact', the way things are).

The part of the weather in Henchard's disastrous speculations in corn affords a perfect example. Hardy describes Britons anxiously awaiting the harvest in the years before the repeal of the Corn Laws:

Their impulse was well-nigh to prostrate themselves in lamentation before untimely rains and tempests, which came as the Alastor of those households whose crime it was to be poor.

(chapter 26)

Here we are given a possible personification of divine malignity: Alastor, Vengeance; but even the poorest Wessex peasant does not imagine that there is really anything personal behind bad weather. His impulse is only '*well-nigh* to prostrate' himself.

Under these circumstances, with destiny weaving our fates blindly, character is obviously an important element in the material that destiny works with, and certainly we can say of Henchard at every turn that if his character had not been as it was things would have turned out differently. His 'sledge-hammer directness', his lack of patience and finesse, all his qualities – even the most admirable (such as his honesty when he is accused by the old furmity-woman) – make for his undoing. Hardy's realism here is a sort of amoralism: he rejects the convention that good qualities will lead to prosperity and bad ones to ruin;[2] it would be a brave man who tried to make the case that Farfrae is Henchard's moral superior. Character is fate, but not in the Christian sense that people 'get what they deserve'.

There is an interesting variation on this theme at the point in the novel where Farfrae is told that he is likely to be made mayor. Before he learns the news that he may be elected, Lucetta has been urging him to leave Casterbridge. Her view is unchanged by the announcement that he could become mayor, but the Scotsman is obviously well pleased and wants to accept. There is a clear clash of personalities between them, but, without a doubt, it is Farfrae's character that determines that they should stay in Casterbridge and that he should accept election. His ambition, his tendency to put his business before his love life (we remember that he stopped to do business on his wedding day) are aspects of his character that make it inevitable that he will want to remain in the town. The results of this are numerous – among them is Lucetta's death. Farfrae's character is Lucetta's fate. Of course, it is Lucetta's character to love ardently and, therefore, to remain with Farfrae; so her own character is her fate, too. However, Farfrae's reaction to the news that he is to be mayor makes no allowance for this, and he says:

See how it's ourselves that are ruled by the Powers above us! We plan this, but we do that. If they want to make me Mayor I will stay.

(chapter 34)

---

[2] This may sound so naïve, expressed thus baldly, that we may want to reject it as a summary of what is 'conventional', at least in the novel. But it is a moral naïveté that has absolute sway in even the best of Hardy's English predecessors. To see this point one only has to think of *Tom Jones* or *Bleak House* or *Middlemarch*. Almost everyone in these novels gets what he or she 'deserves'. Life, of course, is not like that.

There is a fine ironic counterpoint here: Farfrae's disingenuous blaming of 'the Powers' for giving him something that he wanted reminds us that, with Henchard, we know that blaming 'the Powers' is mere superstition. Yet it is equally true that when we 'plan this' we *do* 'do that'.

Like Farfrae, Hardy himself is able to bring in 'the Powers' when he needs to, again with a host of ironies. Among the complexities of Henchard's character, for instance, is a deep need for the solace of music: 'high harmonies transubstantiated him'. Having dropped a religious clue in that verb, Hardy goes on, 'But hard fate had ordained that he should be unable to call up this Divine spirit in his need' (chapter 41). Here we find that 'fate' is able to 'ordain' things, something which, in the context of the novel, we have to take ironically. On the other hand we have *seen* the power of music at work in the story (Farfrae's singing, the psalm sung in the Three Mariners for Henchard), and although we must take the 'Divine spirit' of music metaphorically, we must also take it seriously. This is something that is always happening in Hardy: the bent of his mind is towards supernatural explanations, but he keeps remembering that those explanations are valueless. Thus it is the agnostic Hardy who, of all Victorian writers, uses the Bible most frequently. These ironies tell us a lot about the division between the intellectual and the emotional: Hardy described himself as 'churchy', and certainly attended church long after he had lost his faith. The loss of the intellectual conviction did not remove the emotional need.

THE BIBLE AND THE MAYOR OF CASTERBRIDGE

'Who is such a reprobate as I! And yet it seems that even I be in Somebody's hand!' With this exclamation (which concludes chapter 41) Henchard reacts to being saved from suicide: for us it can serve as a summary of the points I have been making. Henchard is always depreciating himself and blaming himself in a way that has *some* truth in it, although not very much, and he is superstitiously inclined to seek supernatural reasons for his successes and failures. We know, and Hardy means us to know, that Henchard is not a 'reprobate'. At the same time, we know that his rise and fall are a direct consequence of his character. In this he is like all men. We also know that he is not in 'Somebody's' hand, that the image of himself floating in the pool came there by the most natural means, and that a man with a character only slightly different from his would have gone ahead and committed suicide anyway. It is precisely the superstitious part of his nature as revealed in his reaction to the image of himself that explains his feeling about the Providence that looks after him.

By playing with religious concepts like this, Hardy achieves something extraordinary. He manages to present man as struggling against a power beyond his comprehension and control – something like a malign deity – while at the same time demonstrating that things are as they are because there is no deity, malign or otherwise. Man's fate is not willed by any power except, of course, the power of man himself, whose very will forms part of the scheme within which he is entrapped.

The Mayor of Casterbridge is studded with more or less overt Christian and biblical references that form a curious ground-bass to this tragic and agnostic novel. When Henchard and Farfrae have tea together at Lucetta's, for instance, Hardy says,

They sat stiffly side by side at the darkening table, like some Tuscan painting of the two disciples supping at Emmaus. Lucetta, forming the third and haloed figure, was opposite them; Elizabeth-Jane, being out of the game, and out of the group, could observe all from afar, like the evangelist who had to write it down.

(chapter 26)

Hardy is actually comparing that passionate lightweight Lucetta to Christ, the desired and feared apparition at Emmaus. She too is desired and feared, and she too has returned from a past life. A similar reference to the New Testament appears after Henchard's fall when he says of Lucetta's choice of Farfrae, 'She was wise, she was wise in her generation!' (chapter 32).

References to the Old Testament are frequent: Henchard visiting the weather prophet 'felt like Saul at his reception by Samuel'; stock-breeding is carried on about Casterbridge 'with Abrahamic success'; Elizabeth-Jane cries out at one point 'in Nathan tones' and her 'upper room' is 'no larger than the Prophet's chamber'; the church choir play and sing a psalm to Henchard at the Three Mariners and he comments, 'Don't you blame David.' Then again Mixen Lane is described as the 'Adullam' of the area and Henchard sees himself as 'a Samson shorn'. Besides these there is the Job parallel, already mentioned, and to it can be added a Samuel-and-David parallel and perhaps a Cain-and-Abel parallel.

In addition to this there is a tendency for Hardy's prose to catch biblical tones and phrases that lend a portentous air to Henchard's story and give it a dignity that is somehow hardly diminished by the author's religious scepticism. The following phrases and sentences, for instance, all owe something to the Authorized Version. The echoes become stronger in each example.

And thus the once flourishing merchant and mayor and what not stood as a day-labourer in the barns and granaries he formerly had owned.

(chapter 32)

She has supplicated to mé in her time; and now her tongue won't own me nor her eyes see me!

(chapter 38)

He might possibly have to linger on earth another thirty or forty years – scoffed at.

(chapter 41)

Thus she assured him, and arranged their plans for reunion; and at length each went home. Then Henchard shaved for the first time during many days, and put on clean linen, and combed his hair; and was as a man resuscitated thenceforward.

(chapter 41)

And then he would say of himself, 'O you fool! All this about a daughter who is no daughter of thine!'

(chapter 44)

Then, before she could collect her thoughts, Henchard went out from her rooms, and departed from the house by the back way as he had come; and she saw him no more.

(chapter 44)

Most of these examples come from the last part of the novel (it has forty-five chapters). All the examples I have given (that is to say the New Testament and Old Testament references as well as the language echoes) come from the second half of the novel. The reason for this seems to me to be that Hardy's ambitious attempt to write a novel which would include cosmic significance as well as merely social or psychological significance only comes alive once the consequences of the past start to catch up with Henchard. The workings of fate (the blind weavings of destiny) only become apparent once the tragic reversal of fortune has begun, so only then does Hardy need to work up the Christian and biblical counterpoint that simultaneously dignifies Henchard and ironically underlines his plight.

It is interesting that towards the end of the novel Henchard himself starts to make comparisons with biblical figures, for instance when he calls himself 'Cain' (chapter 43). Before that it is Hardy who draws the parallels. It is as if he is leading Henchard towards a certain view of man's relationship to the universe; Henchard learns the lesson, but it is opposite to the lesson of most tragic heroes. Oedipus, Job, even Lear, seem to find some sort of peace; they learn the folly of pride, power and wealth, and something else appears to be given to them in place of these, a touch of divine pity. Henchard, on the other hand, looks into the darkness and learns only that it *is* dark and that beyond it there is only more darkness.

TIME. ELIZABETH-JANE

I shall return to the question of the sort of stature Henchard achieves at the end of the novel. Meanwhile there are two important aspects of *The Mayor of Casterbridge* which deserve attention. The first of these concerns time, and the second concerns Elizabeth-Jane. The former has been dealt with by critics in some detail; the latter seems to have been curiously neglected.

In one of the best general studies of Hardy,[3] J. Hillis Miller sums up the 'time' aspect of the novel thus:

> *The Mayor of Casterbridge* may be defined as a demonstration of the impossibility of escaping from the past. Though Henchard tries to free himself, his own past actions, as well as the universal patterns he unwittingly incarnates, come back to destroy him.

> (pp. 100–1)

This typically tragic theme of the rising up of the past against the protagonist is handled unequivocally by Hardy. The reappearances of Susan Henchard, of Elizabeth-Jane, of Lucetta and of Newson make this clear enough, and it is underlined by the highly dramatic appearance in front of Henchard of the old furmity-woman at the magistrate's court. If ever an accusing and avenging voice rose from the past, it is hers. In different ways this rôle is also played by Jopp and Abel Whittle: the former's rough treatment by Henchard and later by Lucetta brings belated and disproportionate vengeance, while Henchard's kindness to Whittle's mother brings that poor young man to Henchard's deathbed as his former employer's only companion.

At this level, the level of Henchard's personal past, there is a constant interchange between what was and what is. When Susan and Elizabeth-Jane returns to Weydon-Priors, after the 'long

[3] *Thomas Hardy: Distance and Desire* (see Reading List).

procession of years' has passed since the wife-selling, Hardy comments that the 'spring-like specialities' of the mother have been

transferred so dexterously by Time to the second figure, her child, that the absence of certain facts within her mother's knowledge from the girl's mind would have seemed for the moment . . . to be a curious imperfection in Nature's powers of continuity.

(chapter 3)

Here the identification of past and present is so complete that the observer is almost taken in by it, although he knows that nearly twenty years have elapsed and that mother and daughter are separate individuals.[4]

In the same way, when Lucetta appears at the Roman amphitheatre (chapter 35) to appeal to Henchard for the return of her letters, Henchard is disarmed by the similarity of time and place to those of the incident 'in bygone days' when Susan had stood there and Henchard had decided to make amends to her for what he had done. Even Lucetta's unusually plain dress reminds him of Susan's widow's attire, and this detail alone wins half her battle for her.

Then again, because character is fate, and because character does not change greatly, history is inclined to repeat itself. Thus the 'simple faith' of the sailor Newson when he buys Susan, 'on the spur of the moment and on the faith of a glance at her face', reappears when Henchard tells him that Elizabeth-Jane is dead. He does not for an instant suspect Henchard of telling him a lie and he leaves Casterbridge without so much as turning his head. As Hardy comments, the 'young sailor' of the earlier episode 'was still living and acting under the form of the grizzled traveller who had taken Henchard's words on trust,' (chapter 41). The past is inside us; we carry it with us in our characters as in our memories.

Time, as Hardy frequently observes, leaves its mark upon inanimate objects in a way that humanizes them. One of his clearest expressions of this comes in the poem 'Old Furniture' (CP p. 485), the second stanza of which runs:

> I see the hands of the generations
>   That owned each shiny familiar thing
> In play on its knobs and indentations,
>   And with its ancient fashioning
>   Still dallying.

---

[4] This situation reappears in Hardy's last-published novel *The Well-Beloved* (1897) where the hero falls in love with the 'same' face as it appears in three generations of women separated by twenty-year intervals.

So it is for Henchard in his fall:

> The ring of the bell spoke to him like the voice of a familiar drudge who had been bribed to forsake him; the movements of the doors were revivals of dead days.
>
> (chapter 34)[5]

As he walks out of the novel towards his death, Henchard makes a ritual gesture of recognition towards the past and its power. He journeys to Weydon-Priors and revisits the scene of the wife-sale, an episode in his life which he now remembers in surprising detail. His wheel has come full circle and he has rejoined his past: time has almost literally caught up with him.

> And thus Henchard found himself again on the precise standing which he had occupied a quarter of a century before.
>
> (chapter 44)

Henchard's personal past is not the only important function of time in the novel, however. We are also presented with the vast impersonal past which Hardy so frequently sees in the environments of his novels. In the case of Casterbridge this impersonal past is largely symbolized by Roman remains, notably the amphitheatre. The sense of man's insignificance is stressed by the perspective in time opened by the references to Hadrian's soldiery and to the mummified corpses found buried around the town. Hardy's attitude to this is summarized in his comment on the view from the cottage that Henchard takes for his returned wife:

> Beneath these sycamores on the town walls could be seen from the sitting-room the tumuli and earth forts of the distant uplands; making it altogether a pleasant spot, with the usual touch of melancholy that a past-marked prospect lends.
>
> (chapter 13)

Hardy is always conscious of 'past-marking' and seems rather to relish the sadness of it: for him, nostalgia is already built into the environment.

Henchard, then, is on fortune's wheel and the motive force that drives it round is circumstance, but circumstance includes Henchard's own character and his own past. When he recognizes the

---

[5] Besides functioning as reminders of the past, inanimate objects often come alive for other reasons in Hardy. In *The Mayor of Casterbridge*, for instance, when Lucetta is declining to see Henchard, 'her windows gleamed as if they did not want him; her curtains seemed to hang slily, as if they screened an ousting presence' (chapter 26).

mutability of fortune in a conversation with Farfrae ('' 'Tis turn and turn about, isn't it! . . . Up and down!') the Scotsman comments, 'It's the way o' the Warrld' (chapter 32), and in the context we feel both that it *is* 'the way of the world' and that it is so only because 'the world' is an entity that includes headstrong Henchards and prudent Scots. This implies that Hardy is not altogether a fatalist: it is presumably possible to develop an attitude to the world more like Farfrae's and less like Henchard's, to become less vulnerable, by changing one's character to change one's fate. Perhaps this cannot be done simply by taking thought, but a certain number of hard knocks might encourage a more reserved view of the world than Henchard has. So it is, anyway, with Elizabeth-Jane.

It is hard to remember that Elizabeth-Jane plays almost as large a part in Henchard's story as he does himself: almost as many pages are devoted to her as to her step-father. The fact that we think about her much less than about him establishes the point about her reserved outlook: she does not attract disaster, she does not hold herself up as a target for the slings and arrows of outrageous fortune, she has learnt the lesson of renunciation, she has developed a certain spiritual conservatism which minimizes her vulnerability. Interestingly, she comes at times to speak for the narrator, and the narrator comes to speak for her, so that her wisdom seems very like Hardy's own: of all Hardy's characters, I would hazard, she comes the closest to a direct expression of his views.

When we first really get to know Elizabeth-Jane it is in a context of indecision between knowledge and ignorance. Susan, her mother, is happy with Newson while ignorant that the 'marriage' by purchase may not be binding; but once a 'friend' has 'ridiculed' her on this subject it is 'all over with her peace of mind' (chapter 4). For Susan, ignorance was bliss. Newson solves the problem posed by her new knowledge by giving it out that he has been drowned. Almost at once we learn that Elizabeth-Jane has become a source of worry to her mother, because it seems impossible, given their poverty, that she will ever be able to receive the education for which she is beginning to thirst. Rather like Tess after her, Elizabeth-Jane has an intellect that wants to rise above her humble surroundings: 'She sought further into things than other girls in her position ever did' (chapter 4). We immediately suspect that this searching into things will not increase her chances of happiness. In the present context, for instance, her mother has refrained from telling Elizabeth-Jane of the true relations of her parents, and

Hardy comments that it has seemed to her to be 'folly to think of making Elizabeth-Jane wise'.

Elizabeth-Jane's perceptiveness, however, revealing to her the dark and bitter side of existence, also arms her against that darkness and bitterness. Hardy remarks rather scornfully of Lucetta that she finds Henchard unattractive in his shabby old clothes because 'a woman's eye' is 'ruled . . . so largely by the superficies of things' (chapter 37). Elizabeth-Jane, on the other hand, can see the truth, the reality, the 'real man' for instance, under the externals. Similarly she can see the reality under the surface of optimisms and aspirations:

She had learnt the lesson of renunciation, and was as familiar with the wreck of each day's wishes as with the diurnal setting of the sun. If her earthly career had taught her few book philosophies it had at least well practised her in this.

(chapter 25)

I think that this is Hardy's own voice. The second of these sentences, especially, seems to come from somewhere outside the girl's mind; it seems to be a comment that sums up her experience for us just as the first sentence sums up her experience for herself. And, above all, Hardy does not deny the validity of the experience. He even expresses it universally: she is not merely familiar with the wreck of her own wishes but with the wreck of 'each day's' wishes – the phrase can apply to everyone as much as to her alone.

Elizabeth-Jane bears her disappointments stoically (cf. for instance the opening paragraphs of chapter 25) but her stoicism is not selfishness; it is tempered with love. She can be harsh; and certainly her concern with doing the right thing and behaving with propriety is the self-protective reaction of an insecure personality. But, once again, her perceptiveness makes her aware of, even vulnerable to, the sufferings of others. Visiting Henchard towards the end of the novel, she says,

'I thought you seemed very sad this morning . . . so I have come again to see you. Not that I am anything but sad myself. But everybody and everything seem against you so: and I know you must be suffering.'
How this woman divined things!

(chapter 41)

To Henchard she seems to be a 'pin-point of light' (chapter 40) and generally a source of hope and of love; to Hardy she is 'our poor only heroine' (chapter 43), and if we try to cast Lucetta or Susan

71

in that rôle we soon discover what Hardy means. His heroine must be more than merely an attractive woman and more than merely a wronged and suffering woman; she must be one who has suffered and has then seen through her suffering to the inherent nature of things. She must be one whose attractiveness is of mind as much as of body. As such she must be a resigned figure, one tending towards the sacrificial, faintly Christ-like. The last two paragraphs of the novel bear this out: what Elizabeth-Jane has grown into, what she has learnt, is the lesson taught by Henchard's life as much as by her own. This lesson is the Stoic philosophy of endurance, of making the best of the small opportunities life offers for satisfaction, of not aspiring too high or expecting positive happiness during the 'doubtful honour of a brief transit through a sorry world'.

THE CLIMAX

Immediately before the final paragraphs of the novel that discuss Elizabeth-Jane comes the climax of Henchard's story, the description of his death given by Abel Whittle and the reading of his will. By common critical consent[6] Whittle's speech shows Hardy at his most successfully Shakespearean: it is a masterpiece of tragic reported action (the convention in Greek tragedy is that death and violence should not be seen on stage; instead, messengers and others recount such actions at some length). Whittle can be seen as the Fool to Henchard's Lear. As in *The Return of the Native*, we find ourselves on a heath, in fact part of Egdon Heath again, Lear's heath. In the company of Farfrae and Elizabeth-Jane we find Whittle shambling about outside a hut beneath a hill crowned with 'blasted' fir trees. Elizabeth-Jane is a Cordelia come too late; she seems to understand Henchard's death and is ready to respect the difficult conditions of his will:

She knew the directions to be a piece of the same stuff that his whole life was made of, and hence not to be tampered with.

(chapter 45)

The will directs that Henchard should not be mourned and not be remembered – like Job before him and Jude after him he wishes to sink into oblivion and be utterly forgotten. This is of a piece with his earlier self-contempt and is one man's version of what Hardy called 'the coming universal will not to live'.

[6] E.g. Laurence Lerner in *Thomas Hardy's 'The Mayor of Casterbridge'*, p. 66 (see Reading List).

Besides suggesting tragic parallels of this sort, Hardy enhances the grandeur of his climax in other ways. Henchard is referred to as a 'netted lion', for instance (chapter 42), and he sees himself as becoming a 'fangless lion' (chapter 43). When he faces Elizabeth-Jane for the last time, he stands 'like a dark ruin' obscured by 'the shade from his own soul upthrown' (chapter 44). Such details, together with the biblical sonorities already mentioned and the suggestions of tragic death, combine to elevate the end of the novel to a point where we can hardly continue to imagine that this is a story of the Wessex countryside, of trade rivalry or even of paternal love. It *is* these things, of course, but it is much more. What is so particularly striking is that Hardy achieves a sense of grandeur, synonymous here with a sense of Henchard's stature, at the same time as showing us Henchard chastened, softened and humanized. At Elizabeth-Jane's wedding party Henchard's stoical indifference to his own suffering has begun to melt ('He was no longer the man to stand these reverses unmoved') and he begs his step-daughter to 'save a little room' for him in her heart. He keeps a few things about him to remember her by – gloves, even shoes. At the end he tries to chase poor Whittle away, but is unable to do it. This is clearly the same man as the one we met at the outset of the novel, and again as mayor, but it is a weaker version of him. By just the same paradox Lear weakens and softens at the end of his story and *thereby* achieves a greater tragic stature.

Before leaving the question of the ending of the novel, it might be of value to ponder the significance of the caged goldfinch that Henchard brings to Elizabeth-Jane as a wedding present. The unfortunate bird seems so obviously to be a symbol that we read about it with extra care. Hardy gives few clues, simply narrating Henchard's purchase of the cage, his leaving it outside the house where the wedding party is being held, its discovery by 'Mrs Donald Farfrae' and her reaction to the bird's death. Most significant, perhaps, is this last point. Elizabeth-Jane is affected by the starvation of the 'poor little songster' thus:

She went out, looked at the cage, buried the starved little singer, and from that hour her heart softened towards the self-alienated man.

(chapter 45)

From that hour, we feel, Elizabeth-Jane has made her final estimate of Henchard: her wisdom is now such that she can see him for the suffering creature he really is and can make common cause with him (the common cause of all humanity) against a capricious if not malignant fate. In that case the goldfinch perhaps symbolizes Henchard's soul, his will to endure terrestrial conditions. The one thing that can help a sensitive soul to desire life is love, and for the goldfinch and for Henchard Elizabeth-Jane's love comes too late, when they are both dead. Both were imprisoned in their fates, both could have endured them with her assistance. There is that much consolation in this story of the life and death of a man of character.

5

The Woodlanders (1887)

The Woodlanders does not completely abandon the mythical and 'cosmic' elements that we found to be so important in *The Mayor of Casterbridge* but it does show Hardy in retreat from his 'ambitious' position (the position in which Eustacia Vye is a goddess and Henchard is King Lear). In *The Woodlanders* the other side of Hardy predominates, the side of him that weaves together so brilliantly a story of love with the parallel movements of the rustic setting in which that story takes place. None of Hardy's major novels is purely one or the other of these things. As we saw, even in *The Mayor of Casterbridge* there are strong natural elements, and that novel is in part a love story; conversely, even *Far from the Madding Crowd* makes some attempt on the cosmic and universal.[1]

Hardy's interest in *The Woodlanders*, which was, incidentally, his favourite novel, centres once again on love and once again on the havoc that love creates in its capriciousness. Grace Melbury, the only daughter of a timber merchant in remote Little Hintock, is, as we can expect from what we have learnt of father–daughter relationships in *The Mayor of Casterbridge*, much beloved by her father. He has virtually promised her hand to a worthy woodlander, Giles Winterborne, but when she returns from boarding-school, educated and refined, her father aspires to a greater match for her. This is to Edred Fitzpiers, an impoverished but aristocratic young doctor who has settled in the village. Fitzpiers is never really faithful to her, and not long after their marriage he starts an affair with a local member of his own class, Mrs Charmond. Meanwhile we learn that Giles Winterborne is loved by a local member of *his* class, his companion tree-planter Marty South. Grace, 'belonging' to Giles on the one hand (her father's old promise) and to Fitzpiers on the other (by marriage), in fact belongs to the world of neither. Like other characters of Hardy's, including Tess, she has been

[1] We have to go outside the major novels to find 'pure' examples. *Under the Greenwood Tree* seems to have none of Hardy's more ambitious side in it, and *The Dynasts* is the best example I can give of a work entirely devoted to the cosmic significance of the events it deals with.

taken out of one class but not settled in another. Dissatisfaction is the result, and, at one point in the novel, we can summarize the situation by saying that Marty wants Giles who wants Grace who wants Fitzpiers who wants Mrs Charmond.

Giles dies of an illness exacerbated by staying out in the rain, virtually without shelter, to protect Grace's honour. She remains inside the hut to which she flees from Fitzpiers while Giles in effect kills himself outside. Mrs Charmond is shot by a jealous lover. (Love is a lethal business, we see.) Marty and Grace mourn Giles, the former with greater tenacity, the latter with a calm devotion that is overshadowed by her eventual reconciliation with a now humbled and chastened Fitzpiers.

What I have described here, the main action of *The Woodlanders*, is certainly a love story. It is set in an intensely realized natural environment. It is also studded with references and associations that remind us occasionally of possible cosmic significances. In the first chapter Hardy compares the dramas that take place in the woodlands with those of Sophocles; in the second chapter Marty compares Barber Percomb's asking for her hair to the devil's tempting Faustus; in the third chapter Marty is credited with being the descendant of the Scandinavian goddess Sif, and so on. These hints, however, are not really taken up and worked out as they are in *The Return of the Native* and *The Mayor of Casterbridge*, or as they will be, with a vengeance, in *Tess* and *Jude*.

THE FIRST CHAPTER

In the first lines, in the leisurely tones of a guide book, the narrator, blessed as ever with absolute freedom in choosing his point of view, shows us the South-West of England as it might appear on a map.

The rambler, who, for old association's sake, should trace the forsaken coach-road running in an almost meridional line from Bristol to the South shore of England, would find himself during the latter half of his journey in the vicinity of some extensive woodlands.

(chapter 1)

Having entered the woods, he describes them in tones that are almost neutral except for the slight ominousness of the fact that the trees 'make the wayside hedges ragged by their drip and shade' (chapter 1). This neutrality will not last, as we might guess from the conclusion of the first paragraph. The narrator fixes our attention on one particular spot along the road through the woodlands:

The spot is lonely, and when the days are darkening the many gay charioteers now perished who have rolled along the way, the blistered soles that have trodden it, and the tears that have wetted it, return upon the mind of the loiterer.

(chapter 1)

This spot where the leaves lie thick is within a mile or two of the setting of the ensuing drama, Little Hintock, and our expectations of the drama are conditioned here by the gloomy tone; Hardy is the loiterer, the narrator is the loiterer, we are the loiterers, and if we are capable of the light irony of 'the gay charioteers' it is only because the events about to be narrated are events of long ago.

If there is any doubt as to Hardy's attitude, the next paragraph dispels it. It describes the deserted highway and the feelings it arouses – loneliness and an awareness of the disparity between the possible and the actual. The 'tomb-like' stillness of empty roads is accounted for, 'probably', by 'the contrast of what is with what might be'. We remember this when we hear of the 'Unfulfilled Intention' (chapter 7; Hardy's capitals). And we think of it again when Grace first visits Fitzpiers and he sums up his feelings by saying, 'I thought, what a lovely creature! The design is for once carried out. Nature has at last recovered her lost Union with the Idea!' (chapter 18). This is the theme of the novel and Hardy has set the mood in the earliest paragraphs.

Nature remains unfulfilled. Her intentions are thwarted in town and country; in Hintock especially

the leaf was deformed, the curve was crippled, the taper was interrupted; the lichen ate the vigour of the stalk, and the ivy slowly strangled to death the promising sapling.

(chapter 7)

This is the background against which the intention that Giles should marry Grace is frustrated; it is a simple enough intention and, fulfilled, would have prevented the whole tragedy. What is more, the union of Grace and Giles is specifically *nature*'s intention. For example, Giles describes Melbury's efforts to secure a divorce for Grace as leaving the old man 'on tenterhooks of anxiety to repair the almost irreparable error of dividing two whom nature had striven to join together' (chapter 38). But it is incorrect to say that the 'natural union' of Grace and Giles is impeded by the 'social', 'extraneous', 'cultural' forces which make her Fitzpiers' wife. After all, Giles is at least as naturally suited to Marty South as to Grace, as Grace realizes:

77

[She] was abased when, by degrees, she found that she had never under-
stood Giles as Marty had done. Marty South alone, of all the women in
Hintock and the world, had approximated to Winterborne's level of
intelligent intercourse with Nature. In that respect she had formed his
true complement in the other sex.

(chapter 44)

The Immanent Will ('nature' if you like) knows no distinction
between what we call 'natural' forces and what we call 'social'
forces; Melbury's schemes for Grace's social advancement are as
much part of the order of things as her attraction to Giles and his
to her. This view is underlined by the early sonnet 'At a Bridal'
(CP p. 10) which is subtitled 'Nature's Indifference'. The poet is
watching a wedding and dreaming of the fine children that 'Love
designed' he and the bride should have. 'Mode' decrees otherwise.
But nature (the 'Great Dame') 'does not care/If the race all such
sovereign types unknows'. Here Hardy carries the fire into the heart
of the enemy's camp; even over questions of heredity nature is
indifferent.

The loiterer of chapter 1 turns out to be someone who has lost his
way, and there we have Hardy's favourite picture of the figure in the
scene – the solitary on the empty road. The figure in this case turns
out to be that of the aptly named Barber Percomb, who hardly
appears again in the novel but whose actions here have remote and
devastating consequences, in a way which underlines Hardy's conception of the multitude and variety of causes from which action
springs. We travel with Percomb along the road and learn that
Little Hintock is a place so remote that a town man would need 'a
candle and a lantern' to find it. And it is generalized as 'one of those
sequestered spots outside the gates of the world', neither busy nor
intellectually impressive,

yet where, from time to time, dramas of grandeur and unity truly
Sophoclean are enacted in the real, by virtue of the concentrated passions
and closely-knit interdependence of the lives therein.

(chapter 1)

Hardy's generalization about Hintock's remoteness and its apt-
ness as a setting to a drama can be seen as a model of the whole
novel. The narrator's calm foreknowledge of events and his ability
to compare them with the elevated sufferings of Greek tragedy
show the gap between his educated consciousness and the 'Imper-
cipience' of the actors in the story. This is not to accuse Hardy of
superior callousness. *Hardy* is both the narrator and all the characters; the intellectual objectivity of the one increases our sympathy

with the others. This gap between the educated narrator and the country folk is mirrored within the novel. Between all the main characters there are distances, and it is the function of these distances to increase desire by preventing satisfaction. This is the kind of simple 'natural' law that Hardy sees as operating throughout the world, to the inevitable dissatisfaction of all. We want what we cannot have, and what we can have we do not want. Marty feels Giles to be superior to herself, a better woodsman; Giles knows Grace to be educated, almost a lady, superior to him; Grace knows Fitzpiers to be a gentleman, distinctly an educated one; and Fitzpiers' attitude to Mrs Charmond is not uninfluenced by her social position and cosmopolitan aura.

And in so far as the tables are turned and we look *down* the social scale, in so far as Grace loves Giles or Fitzpiers loves Grace or Mrs Charmond loves Fitzpiers, it coincides with the apparent opening of other gaps. Grace is won by Giles's moral strength and his extreme considerateness but also by the fact that she is married to another and, later, by Giles's death, the greatest gap of all. Fitzpiers is won by Grace's angelic beauty and quotes Shelley to that effect. The whole stanza that he quotes (chapter 16) establishes above all the celestial quality of the 'shape' addressed; Fitzpiers, as lover, is of 'this earth' while Grace merely moves upon it, a visitor from a higher region. Mrs Charmond is won by the piquancy of Fitzpiers' position as her former wooer but also by the gap imposed by his marriage to another.

These distances that generate desire are no coincidence; they constitute a law of nature for Hardy. This law states, among other things, the simple commonplace that the grass always seems greener on the other side of the hill. Man does not know his fellow men adequately and can always delude himself that others are fulfilled in a way that he is not. Jude does not simply want an education in the abstract, he wants to go to Christminster where, he believes, the students are fulfilled as scholars. The possible, 'what might be', becomes identified with the actual of other people. There is thus a double irony at work behind the main theme of the Unfulfilled Intention. Not only are hopes thwarted, they are based on misconceptions anyway; Giles is not a better worker than Marty; Grace has really lost as much as she had gained by her education; Fitzpiers may be a gentleman but he is penniless (and by no means as spiritual as his intellectuality suggests to Grace); Mrs Charmond's hair is Marty's. The circle thus established is a deluded extension of the eternal triangle.

TIME AND PLACE

In *The Woodlanders*, as much as in *Far from the Madding Crowd* and *The Return of the Native*, Hardy is concerned to associate his story with its setting. There is a deliberate limitation of the action to Little Hintock, and the 'unity truly Sophoclean' is almost achieved in respect of the unity of place. Except for the occasional scenes in Sherton Abbas, nowhere is described directly except Hintock and its woods. We know that Melbury goes to London and that Fitzpiers goes to Europe twice (once with Grace and once with Mrs Charmond). He also goes to Middleton Abbas, and Giles travels in his trade. But we never see these places directly. There is a strong sense that they are 'away out there', beyond the lives, and usually beyond the thoughts, of the woodlanders. Place, and the developments within that place, are closely associated with time. As in *Far from the Madding Crowd* and *Tess of the d'Urbervilles* the seasons form a backcloth against which we watch the action.

The novel opens on 'the louring evening of a byegone winter's day' (chapter 1) in 1876 or so,[2] and proceeds through the two following years into the third spring. Apart from the indirectly described and rapid visits to the 'outer world', Hardy moves along the road to Hintock (Marty's house, Melbury's), and along the still-winterbound road to Sherton to collect Grace, and back (Melbury's, the woods, Hintock House). With the spring Fitzpiers materializes in Grace's life: 'a delicate understanding now existed between two who in the winter had been strangers . . . Spring weather came on rather suddenly . . .' (chapter 19). Their love grows, to the point where on Midsummer Eve Fitzpiers can seize Grace during the village girls' 'nocturnal experiment' with old love and 'claim' her as his own. Ironically, it is during that same pagan night that Fitzpiers and Suke Damson first make love – ironically, but somehow appropriately, a combination frequent in Hardy. And the later summer brings Grace's marriage and honeymoon. On their return, in the autumn, Grace sits in the window of the Earl of Wessex and calls to the cider-maker below – Giles *Winterborne*, 'autumn's very brother'.

Back at Hintock, Fitzpiers grows restless and during the winter he courts Mrs Charmond. In the spring the woods act their usual indifferent part when Grace and Mrs Charmond lose their way and are forced into confidences they both find painful, and

---

[2] Cf. the note on the time scheme at the end of the New Wessex Edition of the novel.

Spring had not merged in summer when a clinching rumour, founded on the best of evidence, reached the parish and neighbourhood. Mrs Charmond and Fitzpiers had been seen together in Baden, in a relation which set at rest the question that had agitated the little community ever since the winter.

(chapter 37)

When that summer does come it brings with it the illusory hope that Giles may get his Grace after all; it is 'a fair green afternoon in June' when we see Grace in Giles's arms and see them kiss for the first time. And we know, and Giles knows, and only Grace does not, that this first kiss will be their last and that she cannot divorce Fitzpiers. The same summer, a few weeks later, brings heavy rain: enough to finish a sick man without a roof over his head; Giles dies in the *summer*, a point easy to miss. Nature is completely inconsistent; her ironies are the result of accident; she does not know what she does. Inevitably, neither because of the human suffering we are witnessing nor in spite of it, autumn comes again and winter lays its blight on the woods.

Fitzpiers spends this winter penitentially in the Midlands and starts his approach to Grace again with a letter on St Valentine's day. Grace and Marty visit Giles's grave 'for the purpose of putting snowdrops, primroses, and other vernal flowers thereon as they came' (chapter 45). But come May (and the incident of the Man-Trap) only Marty is at the graveside; Grace is in the Earl of Wessex again with Fitzpiers and will stay with him in spite of her father's forebodings.

THE TREES. NATURE

Through the seasons, then, within the woods, and virtually within the village, the scene is laid. The title of the novel conjures up sunlight through beech leaves, a sylvan idyll, the forest of Arden, the sappy, leafy glades of a Wessex wood. The Hintock woods, however, are not described as green, fresh and growing but as sinister, hostile and dark. They decay and fall so much more readily than they grow. Their commentary on the action that takes place beneath their boughs varies from the ironic to the hostile. When Grace and Giles meet in the marketplace at Sherton Abbas it is under an *uprooted* tree. Their love will suffer the fate of that tree. Such commentary as nature offers (necessarily inferred by Hardy or by a character) is of a piece with this. For instance, there is this unequivocal episode:

A diversion was created by the accident of two large birds, that had either been roosting above their heads or nesting there, tumbling one over the other into the hot ashes at their feet, apparently engrossed in a desperate quarrel that prevented the use of their wings. They speedily parted, however, and flew up with a singed smell, and were seen no more. 'That's the end of what is called love,' said someone.

(chapter 19)

Another example of the direct commentary of nature upon human action comes when Grace watches Fitzpiers ride away through the 'gorgeous autumn landscape of White-Hart Vale'. The earth is in 'the supremest moment of her bounty', but even now, Grace's musings bring blighted nature and blighted man together:

In all this proud show some kernels were unsound as her own situation, and she wondered if there were one world in the universe where the fruit had no worm, and marriage no sorrow.

(chapter 28)

We can follow Hardy's use of natural forms in this description of the work of Melbury's men during the 'barking season'. It is a good example, incidentally, of Hardy's detailed knowledge of country work. The italics are mine.

Each tree *doomed* to the *flaying* process was first *attacked* by Upjohn. With a small bill-hook he carefully freed the *collar* of the tree from twigs and patches of moss which encrusted it to a height of a foot or two above the ground, an *operation* comparable to the *'little toilette' of the executioner's victim*. After this it was barked in its erect position to a point as high as a man could reach. If a fine product of vegetable nature could ever be said to look *ridiculous* it was the case now, when the oak stood *naked-legged*, and as if *ashamed*, till the *axe-man* came and cut a ring round it, and the two Timothys *finished the work* with the cross-cut saw.

As soon as it had fallen the barkers *attacked it like locusts* and in a short time not a particle of rind was left on the trunk and larger *limbs*. Marty South was an adept at peeling the upper parts; and there she stood encaged amid the mass of twigs and buds like a great bird, running her *ripping-tool* into the smallest branches, beyond the furthest points to which the skill and patience of the men enabled them to proceed – branches which, in their lifetime, had swayed high above the bulk of the wood, and caught the earliest rays of the sun and moon while the lower part of the forest was still in darkness.

(chapter 19)

Images of torture and execution predominate. The tree is spoken of as though it were human. The barkers attack it, hurt it, kill it, as though they were the ministers of some hideously cruel justice.

Man's inhumanity to man is implied in this passage simultaneously with man's inhumanity to nature. Marty is 'encaged' among the branches like a bird: the marriage of man and nature is complete and each comments on the other. Perhaps it will be objected that in this example I have merely illustrated *man's* destructive and cruel relationship with his fellow man and with nature, and that *nature's* cruelty is not involved; but the same cannot be said of Hardy's description of

> the creaking sound of two over-crowded branches in the neighbouring wood, which were rubbing each other into wounds, and other vocalized sorrows of the trees.

> (chapter 3)

Or of this:

> Next were more trees close together wrestling for existence, their branches disfigured with wounds resulting from their mutual rubbings and blows ... Beneath them were the rotting stumps of those of the group that had been vanquished long ago.

> (chapter 42)

Here it is nature's own cruelty unaided by man that we are witnessing – the cruelty of 'Nature red in tooth and claw' brought home to the later nineteenth century by Darwin's formulation of the inexorable laws governing survival. Hardy was a pure Darwinist. His poem 'The Ivy-Wife' speaks for itself:

> I longed to love a full-boughed beech
>   And be as high as he:
> I stretched an arm within his reach,
>   And signalled unity.
> But with his drip he forced a breach,
>   And tried to poison me.
>
> I gave the grasp of partnership
>   To one of other race –
> A plane: he barked him strip by strip
>   From upper bough to base;
> And me therewith: for gone my grip
>   My arms could not enlace.
>
> In new affection next I strove
>   To coll an ash I saw,
> And he in trust received my love;
>   Till with my soft green claw
> I cramped and bound him as I wove ...
>   Such was my love: ha-ha!

By this I gained his strength and height
　　Without his rivalry.
But in my triumph I lost sight
　　Of afterhaps. Soon he,
Being bark-bound, flagged, snapped, fell outright,
　　And in his fall felled me!

(CP p. 59)

But if man can be cruel to man, and to nature, and nature can
be cruel to nature, nature can also be cruel to man. The poem
'In a Wood', subtitled 'See "The Woodlanders"', makes
it clear that man cannot expect to learn pity or loyalty from
nature:

　　　　Heart-halt and spirit-lame,
　　　　　　City-opprest,
　　　　Unto this wood I came
　　　　　　As to a nest;
　　　　Dreaming that sylvan peace
　　　　Offered the harrowed ease –
　　　　Nature a soft release
　　　　　　From men's unrest.

　　　　But having entered in,
　　　　　　Great growths and small
　　　　Show them to men akin –
　　　　　　Combatants all! . . .

　　　　Touches from ash, O wych,
　　　　　　Sting you like scorn!
　　　　You, too, brave hollies, twitch
　　　　　　Sidelong from thorn.
　　　　Even the rank poplars bear
　　　　Lothly a rival's air,
　　　　Cankering in black despair
　　　　　　If overborne.

　　　　Since, then, no grace I find
　　　　　　Taught me of trees,
　　　　Turn I back to my kind,
　　　　　　Worthy as these.
　　　　There at least smiles abound,
　　　　There discourse trills around,
　　　　There, now and then, are found
　　　　　　Life-loyalties.

(CP p. 64)

On the evening when Grace leaves home because she cannot bear to meet the penitent Fitzpiers, she passes through the autumn woods on her way to Giles's hut, and we read:

The plantations were always weird at this hour of eve – more spectral far than in the leafless season, when they were fewer masses and more minute lineality. The smooth surfaces of glossy plants came out like weak, lidless eyes; there were strange faces and figures from expiring lights that had somehow wandered into the canopied obscurity; while now and then low peeps of the sky between the trunks were like sheeted shapes, and on the tips on boughs sat faint cloven tongues.

(chapter 40)

Admittedly, Grace is seen passing through this ghostliness unheeding; she is a child of the woods and anyway very upset. But by this time our overall impression of the trees has been subtly manipulated so that we feel them to be a sinister force. When Barber Percomb arrives at Little Hintock, for instance, he paces cautiously over the dead leaves which 'nearly buried the road or street of the hamlet' (chapter 1) and he smells cider in the air, the smell mingling 'with the scent of decay from the perishing leaves underfoot' (chapter 1). Old John South is terrified that the tree outside his cottage will fall and kill him. And when it does fall, he dies. His irrational obsession with the tree is one of the most disturbing parts of the novel. Giles Winterborne has 'a marvellous power of making trees grow' (chapter 8) and is throughout associated with nature's fecundity, but when he plants a sapling it starts to 'breathe' in the wind –a sound which will not 'cease night or day till the grown tree [is] felled – probably long after the two planters [are] felled themselves' (8). And Marty comments, 'It seems to me . . . as if they sigh because they are very sorry to begin life in earnest – just as we be' (8). Grace's apprehension of danger when she is in her father's gig and the horse threatens to bolt is limited to the possibility that the horse might have 'run under the trees where the boughs are low enough to hit my head' (chapter 19). With the coming of spring we find the woodland green for once, but even now we are not to enjoy it:

The boughs cast green shades, which disagreed with the complexion of the girls who walked there; and a fringe of the same boughs which overhung Mr Melbury's garden dripped on his seed-plots when it rained, pitting their surface all over as with pock-marks, till Melbury declared that gardens in such a place were no good at all.

(chapter 20)

In the autumn we have a description of the largest, remotest old trees in the park, where slimy streams of fresh moisture, exuding from decayed holes caused by old amputations, ran down the bark of the oaks and elms, the rind below being coated with a lichenous wash as green as emerald. They were stout-trunked trees, that never rocked their stems in the fiercest gale, responding to it only by crooking their limbs. Wrinkled like an old crone's face, and antlered with dead branches that rose above the foliage of their summits, they were nevertheless still green – though yellow had invaded the leaves of other trees.

(chapter 27)

When Grace and Melbury go out to wait for Fitzpiers (absent so long because he is visiting Mrs Charmond), 'They halted beneath a half-dead oak, hollow and disfigured with white tumours, its roots spreading out like claws grasping the ground (chapter 29). When Melbury sets out to look for Giles in his greatest disturbance of mind it is

on a rimy evening when the woods seemed to be in a cold sweat; beads of perspiration hung from every bare twig; the sky had no colour, and the trees rose before him as haggard, grey phantoms whose days of substantiality were passed.

(chapter 21)

Because of the changing outlines of the wood Grace and Mrs Charmond are lost together almost as if they have been bewitched: the branches are dark sentinels everywhere –

The breeze was oozing through the network of boughs as through a strainer; the trunks and larger branches stood against the light of the sky in the forms of sentinels, gigantic candelabra, pikes, halberds, lances, and whatever else the fancy chose to make of them.

(chapter 35)

Perhaps the hostility of the woods is finally and most firmly established in the dreadful scenes of Giles's martyrdom. The effect of the wind on the woods is terrifying and Grace suffers because of it:

No sooner had she retired to rest that night than the wind began to rise, and after a few prefatory blasts to be accompanied by rain. The wind grew more violent, and as the storm went on it was difficult to believe that no opaque body, but only an invisible colourless thing, was trampling and climbing over the roof, making the branches creak, springing out of the trees upon the chimney, popping its head into the flue, and shrieking and blaspheming at every corner of the walls. As in the grisly story, the assailant was a spectre which could be felt but not seen. She had never before been so struck with the devilry of a gusty night in a wood, because she had never been so entirely alone in spirit as she was now. She seemed

almost to be apart from herself – a vacuous duplicate only. The recent
self of physical animation and clear intentions was not there.

(chapter 41)

The culminating image is particularly violent:

Sometimes a bough from an adjoining tree was swayed so low as to smite
the roof in the manner of a gigantic hand smiting the mouth of an adver-
sary, to be followed by a trickle of rain, as blood from the wound.

(chapter 41)

This is the climax of the book: it is the night that seals Giles's fate;
when he is dead, 'The whole wood seemed to be a house of death'
(chapter 43). We do not expect much mercy from the Hintock
trees.

There are moments, however, at which nature seems in kinder
mood. When Grace and Fitzpiers meet in the woods before break-
fast on the day that she has seen Suke Damson leave Fitzpiers'
house, he is entranced by her beauty among the trees:

His remote gaze at her had been one of mild interest rather than of
rapture. But she looked so lovely in the green world about her; her pink
cheeks, her simple white dress, and the delicate flexibility of her movements acquired such rarity from their wild-wood setting that his eyes
kindled as he drew near.

(chapter 24)

Of course, our appreciation of this momentary unbending on the
part of nature is considerably qualified by the fact that we know
of Fitzpiers' infidelity and are aware that the result of Grace's
beauty and its new effect on him will be the certainty of their
marriage and simultaneously the near certainty of its failure.

For Hardy, nature is not a malign trickster, merely indifferent;
but it so happens that man is intimately involved in nature and
that this involvement is frequently painful. In the novels and
poems there are almost no 'pure' descriptions of nature: they are
always directly related to the human participants, as we have seen
in the case of the Hintock woods.

Thus all forms of relationship are possible. Nature is unques-
tionably beautiful, but her beauty, like all her moods, is irrelevant,
or at least so unpredictably relevant that it might as well be
irrelevant. The morning sunshine may smile on a scene of treachery,
or the rain may ruin Mayor Henchard's crops at just the moment
to do him most damage. There is *no* correlation between man's
desire and nature's law. In general nature thwarts more than she

aids, but this is the purest chance – it is 'the nature of things', not design.

Take for example the opening of chapter 4 of *The Woodlanders*:

> There was now a distinct manifestation of morning in the air, and presently the bleared white visage of a sunless winter day emerged like a dead-born child. The woodlanders everywhere had already bestirred themselves, rising this month of the year at the far less dreary time of absolute darkness. It had been above an hour earlier, before a single bird had untucked his head, that twenty lights were struck in as many bedrooms, twenty pairs of shutters opened, and twenty pairs of eyes stretched to the sky to forecast the weather for the day.
>
> Owls that had been catching mice in the outhouses, rabbits that had been eating the winter-greens in the gardens, and stoats that had been sucking the blood of the rabbits, discerning that their human neighbours were on the move, discreetly withdrew from publicity, and were seen and heard no more till nightfall.

Nature is not seen here as very pleasant. But the important word is 'seen': nature is only perceived by man. Stoats suck the blood of rabbits however fair or foul the day; only man can attribute values, and here the narrator does so in his comparisons. Man is a conscious moral being. The Immanent Will (nature) is unconscious; Hardy is sure that it would 'fashion all things fair' if it became aware of itself (cf. the last lines of *The Dynasts*) but until then it must proceed without any reference to good or evil.

THE CHARACTERS

Hardy quite early established an elastic group of 'types', such that we recognize, from a synopsis of any of his novels, the approximate personality and fate of most of the characters.[3] When I say, for instance, that Edward Springrove in *Desperate Remedies* is the architect son of a farmer, I arouse expectations in those who have not read the novel that he is 'someone like' Stephen Smith in *A Pair of Blue Eyes*, or like Hardy himself; when I say that Lady Constantine in *Two on a Tower* is a passionate but bored and suffering aristocrat, you can expect 'someone like' Mrs Charmond in *The Woodlanders* or Cytherea Aldclyffe in *Desperate Remedies*. And the expectation thus aroused will be a useful and genuine insight into the new character. There is nothing better as a commentary on one Hardy novel than another Hardy novel.

In talking of *Far from the Madding Crowd*, *The Return of the Native*

[3] Cf. note 2, chapter 2 above.

and *The Mayor of Casterbridge*, we saw several of these types established. The Gabriel Oak–Diggory Venn type (the faithful watcher
and waiter attractively allied to the soil of Wessex) obviously reappears now as Giles Winterborne. Giles's fate, as his name
implies, is to be darker than that of his predecessors; on the other
hand, he has a closer alliance with nature than either of the others:

> He looked and smelt like Autumn's very brother, his face being sunburnt
> to wheat-colour, his eyes blue as corn-flowers, his sleeves and leggings
> dyed with fruit-stains, his hands clammy with the sweet juice of apples,
> his hat sprinkled with pips, and everywhere about him that atmosphere
> of cider which at its first return each season has such an indescribable
> fascination for those who have been born and bred among the orchards.
> [Grace's] heart rose from its late sadness like a released bough; her senses
> revelled in the sudden lapse back to Nature unadorned.
>
> (chapter 28)

Giles, she feels, has 'arisen out of the earth ready to her hand'. He
rises from the earth as Diggory Venn appears on the heath; but he
has none of the reddleman's capacity for manipulating events; he
is simplicity itself in an unpejorative sense of that word.

Mrs Charmond belongs to the group of almost neurotic older
women. Her name suggests charm and worldliness; her situation
in the big house relates her to all the 'ladies' that Hardy created
out of the impulse that produced his first novel *The Poor Man and
the Lady*. Women must be high, remote, different, difficult and
worth suffering for if Hardy's men are to become interested in
them. There is an interesting passage in the *Life*, echoed faithfully
in *A Pair of Blue Eyes* and probably in 'Beeny Cliff' (CP p. 350),
where Hardy is described as walking with Emma Gifford during
their courtship in Cornwall. It is a normal enough walk down to
the cliffs and the sea for Hardy, but Emma is not walking – she is
riding. In 'Beeny Cliff' she is 'the woman riding high above with
bright hair flapping free'. At all costs there must be distances and
barriers between the lovers. The distance of social position, barriers
such as death, another marriage, a previous liaison, an illegitimate
baby – or just a wall or a window; any of these is enough to thwart
love and at the same time, of course, to keep it alive. Mrs Charmond,
as a lady, exerts an automatic fascination over Hardy and over
Fitzpiers. She is a 'Soul of souls!' full of an emotional electricity
that she must discharge; she will grow tired of love only when she
is ninety or a hundred years old. She has the necessary deeply
set, mysterious eyes; she is 'Inconsequence' itself – that is, she is
capricious and thus doubly interesting.

Grace is almost Hardy's perfect woman: she has pride enough and modesty enough, she is passionate enough and reserved enough, she is beautiful. Above all, she is something precious, something worth suffering for. She is like Elizabeth-Jane in *The Mayor of Casterbridge* in her normality, like Thomasin in *The Return of the Native* in her *ingénue* simplicity. She is neither highly sexed like Eustacia Vye nor under-sexed like Sue Bridehead. Her name, with all its connotations, sums her up, and with her grace there goes the flesh-and-blood woman whom Giles loves.

Marty is one of Hardy's 'forsaken women'. She has the dogged faithfulness of Tess (which is also that of Oak, Venn and Giles himself) and something of Tess's purity. Some insight into Marty is provided by the poem 'The Pine-Planters' (CP p. 271), which corresponds to the section of the novel (in chapter 8) where we see Giles and Marty planting trees together. Chapter 8 is a superb piece of writing that leads us straight into the personalities of the characters and defines them for the rest of the novel. It is no accident that Marty has the last pages of the novel to herself. She is transfigured at the end, achieving thus the only sure reward of faithfulness in Hardy: memory, a little wisdom and the right to go on being faithful. Here we have Marty put into the 'memorious' position Hardy was to find himself in when his first wife died in 1912. More usually in *The Woodlanders* we find memory linked to the setting around the characters. Fitzpiers finds winter at Hintock tedious, for instance, because he lacks 'old association – an almost exhaustive biographical or historical acquaintance with every object, animate or inanimate, within the observer's horizon' (chapter 17). Marty has an emotional depth which Fitzpiers lacks because of her depths of 'old association'.

FITZPIERS AND HARDY'S GENTRY

We learn most about Hardy's assumptions and attitudes in this novel from a study of Fitzpiers. First, he belongs to the 'outsider' group that includes Sergeant Troy, Donald Farfrae, Parson Maybold, Clym Yeobright and Alec d'Urberville. He has something about him that arouses the rustic curiosity of the woodlanders; he is a scientist[4] and they think him a necromancer. He first appears

---

[4] G. S. Fayen, jun., in 'Hardy's *The Woodlanders*: Inwardness and Memory', *Studies in English Literature*, 1 (1961), pp. 81–100, suggests that Fitzpiers is a kind of Casaubon – a failed scientist and intellectual. David Lodge sees him as a 'third-rate Shelley' (cf. Introduction to New Wessex Edition).

as a light on the hillside – the bright light of a chemical experiment seen from Grace's bedroom window – we do not meet him face-to-face until chapter 14, when he appears good-looking, gentlemanly and 'undoubtedly a somewhat rare kind of gentleman and doctor to have descended, as from the clouds, on Little Hintock'. Thus at first he is hedged with some sort of divinity. It is ironic that by chapter 38 Grace will have come to see the new divorce law in its turn as 'a god-like entity lately descended upon earth'. When Fitzpiers seemed beyond a villager's reach he was divine; when a villager *has* reached and married him divinity is transferred to the one hope she has of being released from him.

Though Fitzpiers is, of course, not divine, he is separated off from the 'natural' world of Hintock. When Grace sees the light in his lodgings turn blue, violet, red, Hardy comments,

Almost every diurnal and nocturnal effect in this woodland place had hitherto been the direct result of the regular roll which produced the seasons' changes; but here was something dissociated from these normal sequences, and foreign to local knowledge.

(chapter 6)

These Faustus-like goings-on associate Fitzpiers with the devil in that playful but ominous way that heightens our awareness of the significance of Sergeant Troy with his red jacket and pitchfork; of Alec d'Urberville with his satanic face, his characteristic appearance through smoke and his real name (Stoke); and of Diggory Venn's redness. Fitzpiers, then, is at once divine and devilish *before* we meet him. When we do meet him we find him very normal, and have no trouble in placing his type accurately. But that is because we are educated, like Hardy, and like Fitzpiers himself, and we all three know our Shelley.

Fitzpiers 'much preferred the ideal world to the real' (chapter 16). In this he is like the young Hardy, who did not want to grow up, and the young Jude, who prefers to dream and muse. He can be in love with two women at once and can quote whole stanzas of Shelley, but he can also have the tree cut down that so disturbs old John South without caring a fig for Mrs Charmond's wrath. The point is that, like so many of the *gentlemen* in Hardy, Fitzpiers has an enviable command of himself and his environment. This may seem a strange thing to say of the man who can become as infatuated as Fitzpiers does with Mrs Charmond, and who rides miles night after night to see her at Middleton Abbey. There is no question, however, but that his superior education and intelligence give him an objectivity that Hardy admired, himself developed, and saw as both the birthright of the upper classes and a good shield against the buffets of existence.

There are remarkably few real gentry in Hardy and almost none in the major novels. Boldwood in *Far from the Madding Crowd*, for all his reserve and distinction, is clearly only a farmer. Alec d'Urberville is a usurper of that ancient and dangerous name. Perhaps Angel Clare is the only other person near Fitzpiers' class in the Novels of Character and Environment. In the other groups of novels we find a sprinkling of aristocrats whose intelligence and relative detachment enable Hardy to use them for wider ranges of association than the characters of lower class are suitable for. It is almost as if there is a four-way conspiracy between Hardy, his narrator, the gentleman character and the reader (assumed to be gentle, and thus educated). The intellectual Henry Knight in *A Pair of Blue Eyes*, for instance, is 'one of us', as is Fitzpiers; these characters are capable of passion, but they are possessed of Hardy's own ability to see things from a detached position as well as from a committed position. Jocelyn Pierston in *The Well-Beloved* is absurdly passionate, but his *consciousness* of what he is about keeps his head a little above water. There are women who are 'gentle' too. They have a natural inaccessibility, of course, which we have seen to be part and parcel of their desirability; and as aristocrats they are also in control of their actions, or at least conscious of them. Lady Constantine in *Two on a Tower* conceals her infatuation for Swithin St Cleeve until the last pages of the book. Miss Aldclyffe in *Desperate Remedies* knows precisely what she is about, even if her massive reserve once or twice breaks down late at night. Her view of the girlish heroine, Cytherea, is Hardy's view, the narrator's view, and *our* view because we are expected to share a common standard in questions of taste, culture, manners and morals.

So Fitzpiers, apparently the villain of the piece, is closer to us and to Hardy than might at first appear. The lines of Shelley struck *Hardy* as significant, beautiful, appropriate; and it is thus that they strike Fitzpiers. But not Giles. Giles 'could have declared with a contemporary poet' what is said in the stanzas from Edmund Gosse's 'Two Points of View' only if he had known them – or any other poetry. When Fitzpiers has married Grace and settled at Melbury's house, he realizes that he has lost some of the aura which his birth and education gave him: 'it was easy for so supersubtle an eye as his to discern, or to think he discerned, that he was no longer regarded as an extrinsic, unfathomed gentleman of limitless potentiality, scientific and social (chapter 25). This example appears qualified (Fitzpiers may only *think* he can discern the change) but Hardy is telling us that a change *has* taken place, and he explains precisely how and why; as so often, we are seeing a movement (in this case a movement of opinion, but it could as well be of the tide or the wind) from exactly the same point of view as the gentleman character. Often enough, of course, we get a 'worm's-eye view' of the goings-on of more important characters from the position of some uneducated rustic; but this is usually in the form of an ironic commentary, a piece of shrewd but homely perception that we know to be accurate but limited; we can judge of its truth just because we are 'above', looking down at the scene. And usually we *are* above. We are expected to have some acquaintance with, for example, Dumpy levels, Doctor Faustus, The Ginnung-Gap, Loke the Malicious, the Hapsburgs, Van Dyke, Olympus and the fabled Jarnvid Wood. These examples are taken from the first sixty pages of *The Woodlanders*.

The female aristocrats are adept at being cruel to their admirers, and Hardy seems almost to delight in the sufferings that female disdain or infidelity can inflict. This was particularly apparent in *Far from the Madding Crowd*, and in *The Woodlanders* we see it in constant operation. Grace causes Giles to suffer and yet will not apply the knife to his suffering but instead perversely 'entertain[s] a tender pity for the object of her own unnecessary coldness'. She *could* encourage him at this point but will not, preferring to pity him, something which can only increase his torment. Later she *will* encourage him, only to find herself irrevocably wed to another. She is literally the death of him. As we see in Hintock House when Mrs Charmond shows Grace some of her antiquities, women are man-traps: 'Man-traps are of rather ominous significance where a person of our sex lives, are they not?' (chapter 8).

Giles's appropriate poetry, we are told, is the deeply submissive 'Two Points of View', the second stanza of which runs:

> Though you forget,
> No word of mine shall mar your pleasure;
> Though you forget, –
> You filled my barren life with treasure;
> You may withdraw the gift you gave,
> You still are queen, I still am slave,
> Though you forget.

Giles does not forget and it costs him his life. His sufferings by the hut in the woods, described in chapters 41 and 42, are a taste of what love can bring about. Only for Grace, of all the people in the world, would Giles have insisted on staying out of the hut so long; and the irony is, of course, that Grace comes to abandon herself to her love for him at this very moment, but too late, too late. The consummation of their love is a fiction, a lie she tells her husband, since she punishes him by letting him believe that she and Giles have been lovers. During Grace's days in the hut, she communicates with Giles through a window – Hardy's favourite symbol of thwarted passion – and we are reminded of the scene where she calls down to him from the window of the Earl of Wessex, to his great pain.

Mrs Charmond's relationship with Fitzpiers also involves suffering; for example, 'He then raised her hand to his mouth, she still reclining passively, watching him as she might have watched a fly upon her dress. At last, she said, "Well, sir, what excuse for this disobedience?"' (chapter 30). Her independence and dominance stand out in this encounter and her whip puts the seal on this stage in their relationship.

The sufferings of the 'Italianized American' from South Carolina show how a beautiful woman can ruin a decent man. The episode can be compared with Boldwood's destruction by Bathsheba. Suke Damson's love for Fitzpiers creates a bitterness in young Tim Tangs that even the distance of twelve thousand miles seems unlikely to lessen: in love even the rustics suffer. When Fitzpiers is attempting to reinstate himself in Grace's favour towards the end of the book, he abases himself in a way that may be just, but that reminds us of the sufferings at the hands of women that we have witnessed earlier in the novel.

The boot can be on the male foot as well. Poor Marty suffers over Giles, and he seems to know it, but he is inevitably powerless to help the matter.

In some ways *The Woodlanders* is the most perfect of Hardy's novels – in its unity of place and its concentrated action, for instance. It also has a precision of style, a quality Hardy is not usually credited with. To give only two examples: when Fitzpiers goes away briefly during his first courtship of Grace she is described as awaiting his return in 'an excitement which was not love, not ambition, rather a fearful consciousness of hazard in the air' (chapter 23), a description of the finest accuracy. An early morning in Melbury's garden is described a few pages later:

The tones of morning were feeble and wan, and it was long before the sun would be perceptible in this overshadowed vale. Not a sound came from any of the out-houses as yet. The tree-trunks, the road, the out-buildings, the garden, every object, wore that aspect of mesmeric passivity which the quietude of daybreak lends to such scenes.

(chapter 24)

Here again Hardy finds a marvellously precise phrase ('mesmeric passivity') that exactly catches the dazed but immediate silence of early morning.

These two examples, it will be noticed, have to do with love (Grace's emotions) and nature (Melbury's garden). *The Woodlanders* marks the highest point of Hardy's handling of these two subjects. His interest in love is founded on his conviction that 'the way things are' for man can be most thoroughly explored by a treatment of the matter in which man is most involved and most vulnerable – love. Hardy's stories of love, because this is their foundation, naturally interact with the environment in which they are set, and the country which he knew so well is thus pressed into service to help reveal the true nature of what is going on among the humans.

There is, however, another aspect to Hardy's fiction, the 'cosmic' allegorical level which looms so large in *The Return of the Native* and *The Mayor of Casterbridge*. In his two final major novels Hardy integrates this ambitious tendency towards the universal with the love-and-nature theme of *The Woodlanders*. *Tess* and *Jude* attempt to go further, and our question must be whether, having achieved near-perfection in his less ambitious style, Hardy went on to achieve the same result on the broader canvas.

6

Tess of the d'Urbervilles (1891)

In Hardy's two last major novels, *Tess of the d'Urbervilles* and *Jude the Obscure*, his manner of integrating a love story into its natural environment is expanded to its widest dimensions. A third level, as it were, is added, and this is the symbolic, allegorical and cosmic element found in *The Return of the Native* and *The Mayor of Casterbridge*. A vivid general picture of man's relationship to the cosmos emerges in *Tess* and *Jude*, and the success of these novels depends on Hardy's ability to unify this general picture with his love story and its natural background. In *Tess*, particularly, this unification works almost perfectly. In this novel Hardy succeeds in integrating the personal emotions of an obscure girl with an intense study of nature and an overall view of the cosmos and the meaning of man's existence. All this is set within a realistic historical framework, so that while *Tess* is about love, nature and the cosmos, it is also, without any disruption of its unity, about nineteenth-century beliefs concerning religion and morality. It is the novel in which Hardy integrates all these elements most thoroughly; as a result it is not easy to separate the different strands of the novel's symbolism. However, it is possible to go some way towards this by telling the story of *Tess* from various points of view: it can be seen as a love story, a pastoral romance, an allegory of man's progress through the world, and a study of late-nineteenth-century agnosticism in its impact on a Christian or supposedly Christian society.

'TESS' AS A LOVE STORY

Tess Durbeyfield, a partly educated village girl, meets a handsome young gentleman, Angel Clare, at a village dance and is attracted by him. Her impecunious family, having discovered that they are descended from a line of local landowners supposed extinct, send Tess, with her pretty face, to 'claim kin' with some rich gentry living nearby who have assumed the ancient name of d'Urberville, rightfully hers. Much as Tess's mother expects, these 'cousins' include a young man, Alec d'Urberville, who becomes interested in Tess. He gives her employment on his estate and eventually seduces her. She spends a few weeks as his mistress but soon leaves him and returns home, against his wishes, pregnant. She has a baby which dies.

To conceal her shame and earn her bread Tess moves south and takes work at Talbothays dairy where she discovers Angel Clare to be living. During the ensuing months they fall in love. Tess constantly refuses Angel's offers of marriage because of her 'past'; he takes her refusals as proof of her virgin modesty. At last she yields and marries him. On their wedding night Angel confesses that he has previously had an affair with a woman; encouraged by this Tess confesses her affair with d'Urberville. Angel feels he has been duped, tricked by an apparently 'pure' woman. He leaves Tess and soon goes to Brazil. Tess, her wedding ring on a string round her neck, goes back to farm work. Angel, partly because he is very ill in South America, does not write to her and she starts to despair of his return. Meanwhile, Alec d'Urberville meets her again and his passion for her is rekindled to the extent that he abandons his new whim of being an evangelical preacher and starts to pursue her again. He is abhorrent to her, but when her weak-minded family fall upon hard times on the death of her father, d'Urberville supports them, and the price of his support is Tess's body. She goes to live with him.

Angel Clare then returns, chastened and clearer-eyed. Not knowing Tess's situation he tracks her to Sandbourne, to the elegant lodgings she now shares with d'Urberville, and, more than a year after their abortive wedding, comes once more face to face with his wife. Hysterical with grief and frustration, Tess murders d'Urberville and rushes out in pursuit of the now despairing Clare. They are united in a belated, bizarre but successful honeymoon as they hide for a week or so in an empty house. Moving from their shelter, they are caught on Salisbury Plain. Tess is tried for murder and executed. As something of an afterthought, Angel is left hand in hand with Tess's sister, 'Liza-'Lu.

'TESS' AS A PASTORAL ROMANCE

Tess Durbeyfield, a pretty girl from the North Dorset village of Marlott in the Blackmoor Vale, having attracted Angel Clare momentarily at the village 'club-walking', finds herself, one winter's night, the unwitting destroyer of her father's livelihood. She falls asleep at the reins of his cart and, in an ensuing accident, his horse is killed. His trade of 'haggler' must now be pursued on foot.

The local parson, an antiquarian, has discovered that the Durbeyfields are descendants of an important family of landowners now supposed extinct, the d'Urbervilles. In their impoverishment they send Tess to 'claim kin' with some local gentry of that name who turn out to have appropriated it for reasons of snobbery only. Tess makes an impression on the scion of this family of parvenus, Alec. He loads the village girl with roses from his hothouses and feeds her with strawberries. Subsequently he creates employment for her by putting her in charge of his mother's poultry-yard. This is the first of a number of associations between Tess and birds – later we see her regretfully wringing the necks of pheasants who have been winged during a shoot, and later still we find her several times compared to a bird caught in a trap. She is also frequently associated with other animals and insects.

One night, during their return from a rustic revel, Alec and Tess make love. She does not find him attractive, but there is a fatal passivity about her which, combined with the situation in which the seduction occurs, apparently leads her to offer no resistance. The episode occurs on a warm, foggy September night when Tess is extremely tired, and it occurs in the open air. Nature, unheeding of social proprieties or even of the exact tastes of the individuals involved, brings man and woman together thus in response to her need for procreation.

It appears that Tess and Alec have an affair of some weeks' duration, and in October Tess trudges home, pregnant. She has the baby in the early summer, and we next see her suckling it during the harvest of that August. Of it we learn that 'her corporeal blight has been her mental harvest'. Soon, however, it dies and is buried in a corner of the churchyard. Several years now pass until, one spring, Tess begins to feel her hopes rising a little with the rising sap. She leaves Blackmoor, the Valley of the Little Dairies, and journeys to the Froom Vale, the Valley of the Great Dairies, where there is work for her. In the advancing summer she becomes a competent milkmaid and a natural denizen of the rich landscape. As her life thus blossoms and brightens she falls in love with the same Angel Clare whom she met at the beginning of the novel. He is studying agriculture at Talbothays, the dairy where Tess works, and he in his turn falls in love with her. He justifies his interest in her by observing how she will make the sort of wife who will be able to assist him in the management of the farm he plans to take once he has finished his studies.

For a long time she refuses him. None the less there is an under-current of emotion that is drawing them together with the inexor-able force of natural law. They are likened to two streams converging in a valley. Tess is the bashful milkmaid, Angel her ardent swain; their courtship is set against a background of dairy activity and in an entirely traditional rustic setting. In the lush, sappy heat of a Wessex summer Tess and the other milkmaids sigh on sleepless beds in paroxysms of passionate devotion, while the milk oozes from the cows' udders and everything in nature is in abundance. Only the journey of Angel and Tess to the railway station imports a breath of the modern world; otherwise everything at Talbothays is subservient to the pastoral. Even Angel's learned and facetious comparisons of Tess to various goddesses sound appropriately Arcadian.

When Tess at last agrees to marry Angel, the wedding takes place at the dead of winter, on New Year's Day. The pastoral looks as if it has been disrupted here: the highest point of their love comes at the lowest point of the year. But nature is not mistaken. As the lovers sit in their gloomy rented farmhouse on their wedding day, and the weather changes for the worse, Tess confesses her affair with Alec and Angel's love is instantly frozen. They separate and spend more than a year apart, Angel learning wisdom through his hope-less struggle to make a success of farming in the unfavourable environment of Brazil and Tess suffering in the lonely pursuit of the roughest sort of farm work in Wessex. During the summer subse-quent to her marriage she obtains dairy work, but under less congenial circumstances than at Talbothays. By winter time, the milking season at an end, she is driven to a 'starve-acre' upland farm where she is engaged in backbreaking work in the teeth of bitter winter winds. She endures stoically, hoping for two sorts of spring.

But with the seasonal spring Angel does not come. Tess gets news that her mother is unwell, and she returns to Marlott, where, by one of life's little ironies, her mother recovers but her father dies. His death brings virtual ruin to the family.

The parvenu Alec d'Urberville appears again and offers to assist the Durbeyfields. Unlike Angel, who learns to love the land at Talbothays and learns its power to resist in Brazil, Alec is shown to be an evil, alien, uprooted, dangerous figure partly through his dissociation from nature. For him, in the early stages of the novel, a hill or a strawberry or a poultry-yard are merely means to the end of seduction; and so now, when he reappears in Tess's life and tries once more to win her, he is always seen as separate from the rural life around him. Either he is dressed as a town man in the fields or he is on horseback, above the labourers; or, when he does put on a smockfrock and start digging, it is only to be near Tess for long enough to try to gain his ends with her. When she walks away he burns the smockfrock.

But the rural economy is changing. The Durbeyfields are displaced and impoverished. Alec assists them, and the price of his help is that Tess should leave off her country work, country clothes and country ways, and become his mistress at Sandbourne, an elegant seaside town beside, but not attached to, Egdon Heath. Angel returns to seek his estranged wife and eventually tracks her to Sandbourne. His first thoughts on entering the town, as he does not know of her new position relative to Alec, are about how few cows there are for her to milk there. Indeed, there are none: at Talbothays there was natural fulfilment, a pastoral idyll, love: at Sandbourne there are smart clothes and a travesty of love.

Tess murders Alec and escapes inland with Angel. They cross Egdon, hide in deep country, are eventually caught on Salisbury Plain. Tess is taken to the town of Wintoncester and hanged. Angel is left with a country girl, 'Liza-'Lu, Tess's sister, to love.

'TESS' AS AN ALLEGORY

Tess Durbeyfield, a maiden, sees but fails to dance with Angel Clare, a personification of grace, at a traditional village occasion into which he has descended. She is dressed in white and carries a white wand and white flowers. Alone among the maidens, she is marked by a red ribbon in her hair. A little later, when she is driving at night, her father's horse is killed in a collision and the maiden is ominously stained with its blood. The collision is no fault of hers but she feels guilt at having thus damaged her family's livelihood.

To make amends for her supposed fault, Tess agrees to save the family fortunes by, in effect, begging from rich relatives. These 'relatives', assumed to be such because their name (d'Urberville) is the uncorrupted version of Tess's own, are in fact spurious. One of them, Alec d'Urberville, represents the snares into which human innocence can walk. His real surname, Stoke, and his aura of cigar smoke mark him with faintly devilish qualities. He tempts

Tess by offering her strawberries, much as Satan offers Eve an apple, and by loading her with roses, on the thorns of which she significantly pricks her chin. Eventually she succumbs to him and they make love. The maiden is a maiden no more: she has learnt the lesson that 'the serpent hisses where the sweet birds sing'. She is pregnant: she sees her future life as 'a long and stony highway' along which she must tread. In spite of all this, and in spite of everything we discover about her she is, perhaps surprisingly, described as 'an almost standard woman'. Is this, then, the story of Everywoman's pilgrimage?

Tess christens her child Sorrow. Sorrow is the result of man's involvement with the world, the natural child, at any rate, of woman's involvement with man, perhaps the fruit of original sin. Sorrow, the baby, dies. Tess's sorrow seems likely to die with it, but, unlike the baby, the mother's trials are capable of resurrection. However, she rallies after the baby's death and moves away to a place where she is unknown. Nature appears to heal her at the dairy she goes to, but the seed of new sorrow is sown, because there at Talbothays, complete with harp, is Angel Clare again, ready to sing and talk his way into her heart and soul. Angel and Tess, twice specifically linked to Adam and Eve, fall in love and find themselves, indeed, in the same position that Adam and Eve occupy once they have been banished from Eden: it is a mishap to be alive, they agree, but at least there is their love for each other. The garden at Talbothays dairy comes to represent the lost Eden to them.

Just as Bunyan's Christian is a pilgrim, so Tess several times sees herself as being on a pilgrimage through life. She feels that her life is in some way a penance, an expiation for the sin of being born. But, unlike Christian, Tess is no mere symbol, no abstraction. She is Everywoman in flesh and blood, passionate, physical, luxuriant.

Tess and Angel marry on New Year's Day. On their wedding night, Angel, as Adam or Everyman, confesses a past sin. Tess confesses her sin in return. We are clearly told that in nature she has committed no sin at all, that her behaviour – seen objectively – has been quite natural; but man exists under a different dispensation from the animals: man is cursed with consciousness, guilt, self-accusations and social flagellations. As Tess tells the story of her affair with the tempter Alec, the coal in the fireplace glows red and puts Hardy in mind of a 'Last Judgement luridness'.

Angel judges. His judgement is that Tess is guilty, as she agrees; and he punishes her as God is said to punish the damned by removing his divine presence from her. He wants to love her, as we see when he sleepwalks with her in his arms before they separate, but he is blind at that time and cannot rise above the self-destructive urges of mankind, since, like Christ, he is God *and* man. Tess walks penitentially barefoot beside him as she leads him back to his solitary bed, still asleep.

Left without angelic grace or protection, Tess stoically suffers hardship and loneliness, hoping against hope that she will be forgiven or that she will die. She attempts to call upon Angel's father, theologically a stern patriarch, in fact kind to sinners, but her cry never reaches him. Numberless social and personal inhibitions keep her from intruding upon this God-the-father figure: indeed, when she arrives at his village she cannot see him at first because he is in church. Her long, hard journey to visit this source of help and comfort is in vain.

While Angel, by experiencing and witnessing suffering in a distant land, is learning that it is at times better to be human than to be divine, the tempter returns to Tess. Everywoman, Eve, is beset by the same difficulties, offered the same choice, lured into the same sin as she always is. The snake is always there. Alec d'Urberville is momentarily possessed by a spirit of evangelical Christianity, but nature prevails and his powerful desire for Tess blows away his new religious resolutions like mist. But if natural forces prevail over ideology, so do the social and psychological forces that man has himself chosen. On the one hand Mrs Durbeyfield can say of Tess's pregnancy that ' 'Tis nater, after all, and what do please God!' and on the other hand, society's view of Tess's relationship with Alec and, above all, the traumatic psychological effect it has on Tess herself, indicate that mankind is at variance with 'nater'.

The angel returns having learnt the lesson of humanity, but too late. Tess has already yielded again to the tempter. In despair she destroys her destroyer in a way that will inevitably destroy herself. After a brief experience of fulfilled human love (the only paradise available: Angel explains at this point that there is no life after death) Tess is offered as a sacrifice, on Stonehenge, to the twin gods of nature (the sacrifices at Stonehenge were to honour the sun) and man's blighted social and psychological arrangements (the policemen who take her to her death). Angel, now to be presumed quite free of all commitment to religious or social dogmas, leaves the scene with 'Liza-'Lu, Tess's sister, like Adam with another Eve leaving Eden, hand in hand, bowed but stoical.

'TESS' AS A STUDY OF NINETEENTH-CENTURY BELIEF

It is not necessary to recapitulate the entire plot again to illustrate how much of it turns on questions of religious beliefs. What follows is not really a fair summary of the novel, but makes the point the more clearly for omitting irrelevant sections.

A parson who perhaps has not quite enough to do informs John Durbeyfield of his illustrious ancestry. Angel Clare meets Tess Durbeyfield when on a walking tour with his ardently Christian brothers. Angel dances, though not with her, when he should be hastening on to the village where the three are to read another chapter of *The Counterblast to Agnosticism* before going to bed. Tess goes to 'claim kin' with a supposed d'Urberville cousin who proves to be a libertine and a cynic. He seduces her. She is a Wessex heathen with some vivid scraps of Old Testament theology stuck on to her paganism. As a heathen daughter of nature she yields to d'Urberville: as a nominal Christian she develops an oppressive sense of guilt and a strong conviction that she deserves punishment.

Tess is in agonies lest the baby she has by d'Urberville, Sorrow, should be denied heaven because it has not been properly baptized. The parson whom she consults on this point is a man who has undergone 'ten years of endeavour to graft technical belief on actual scepticism'. He is inclined to tell her that Sorrow, having only been baptized by Tess herself, cannot join the blessed, but he wants to be kind to her: 'The man and the ecclesiastic fought within him, and the victory fell to the man.' He tells her (truthfully, some will say) that all baptisms will be 'just the same' in their results.

Meanwhile Angel Clare realizes that he is unable to accept the Christian doctrines of his father (a vicar) and his now ordained brothers. Similarly he is unable to show any interest in Mercy Chant, a young lady of intense Christianity marked out for him by his parents. Mercy Chant is described as an 'emanation' of the walls of his father's church.

Angel becomes something of a pagan at Talbothays while Tess, under his influence, becomes something of an agnostic. He has already abandoned thoughts of Cambridge and the Church and is studying to become a farmer.[1] The revelation of Tess's 'past' does

---

[1] All this reflects Hardy's own experiences quite faithfully. His friend and mentor, Horace Moule, one of several ordained sons of a vicar and a Cambridge don, had severe problems with his faith and ultimately committed suicide. Hardy at one point found himself asked to witness Leslie Stephen's renunciation of Holy

not shock Angel in a religious sense so much as in a personal and conventional one, although, of course, his personal feelings and his social conventions are partly grounded in centuries of Christianity.

And Angel's father, who is responsible for Alec d'Urberville's temporary conversion, gives us a brief insight into one of the less attractive sides of Christian belief. His personal charity does not altogether compensate for the rigour of his sectarian opinions. Tess's sense of guilt clearly stems from her childhood conception of an avenging deity whose lesson for man is that his 'damnation slumbereth not.' D'Urberville turns out to be Tess's 'damnation', although not in quite the sense intended in that text. His evangelical enthusiasm is short-lived, and the man in him overcomes the ecclesiastic. This scheme – nature asserting her rights against religion and morality – is one of the motifs of the novel: Tess, for all her scruples, twice becomes d'Urberville's lover, impelled at least in part by nature's reckless urges; Angel chooses farming instead of the Church and, eventually, chooses Tess in preference to the letter of the law; Izz Huett knows that it will be sinful to live with Clare in Brazil, but she agrees to go; Angel's mother is un-affectedly delighted when he returns from Brazil – and Hardy specifically comments on the natural strength of her maternal feelings and their capacity to outweigh any scruples she may have as to the state of Angel's beliefs; as we have seen, 'the man' over-comes 'the ecclesiastic' in the case of the parson consulted about Sorrow's baptism and in the case of Alec himself. There are stronger forces in man than those created by faith, especially waning faith.

All this is a picture of some of the currents of belief and dis-belief that coexisted in Britain towards the end of the nineteenth century. By implication Hardy introduces into the story the volume *Essays and Reviews* of 1860 in which many of the Church's more traditional and dogmatic teachings were questioned;[2] further, he refers to Malthus, whom we may take as an instance of objective

---

Orders. In the *Life* it is recorded that Hardy contemplated trying for Cambridge as late as 1865. Cambridge automatically meant acceptance of Anglican ortho-doxy (in that undergraduates had to sign a document professing belief in the Thirty-Nine Articles of the Church of England's doctrine) and often led to Holy Orders. There are clear parallels, too, between Hardy's reading and Angel Clare's.

[2] *The Counterblast to Agnosticism* which the Clare brothers are reading represents the *Replies to 'Essays and Reviews'* which appeared in 1862. Cf. the first note on p. 44 of the New Wessex paperback edition of the novel.

investigation, and to Voltaire and Huxley, whose clear-minded objectivity, in two different centuries, brought them into conflict with orthodox religious teaching. At one level, then, Tess's story comes to us as the struggle of Hardy's contemporaries to reconcile reality as they saw it (including natural forces and social conventions) with their belief in an approximately Christian supernatural scheme. At moments we can almost feel Hardy breaking through the surface of his story and attempting to address us directly on this subject of belief. For example, we are carried along with Tess in her assumption that Alec d'Urberville's brief bout of Christianity is wrong-headed, and Hardy seems to be challenging us when he reveals that her simple scepticism destroys Alec's faith: she doesn't 'believe in anything supernatural' and her 'drops of logic' fall into 'the sea of his enthusiasm' with devastating effect. It is Hardy, we notice, who chooses the words 'logic' and 'enthusiasm'. And at times Hardy's presence as commentator is even more apparent. Early in the novel, for instance, a paragraph describing the shiftless muddle of the Durbeyfield household concludes with the sentence

Some people would like to know whence the poet whose philosophy is in these days deemed as profound and trustworthy as his song is breezy and pure, gets his authority for speaking of 'Nature's holy plan'.

(chapter 3)

The voice here can only be Hardy's own, talking directly to his Wordsworthian contemporaries.

INTEGRATION

I have looked at *Tess of the d'Urbervilles* in four different ways, and I think they are the four most important ways, but they do not, of course, exhaust the novel. For one thing, its greatness stems from the integration of these four levels with one another and with the further levels to be discerned in its dense texture. I should like to examine two simple examples of this integration, although I believe it to be a spirit that permeates the novel so thoroughly that any page will yield similar instances.

First there is the famous subtitle of the novel: 'A Pure Woman'. Once we have read Tess's story we react to this on at least four levels. Yes! we say, Tess is pure because she is a child of nature, compounded of the milk, butter and honey on which she lives. Then she is pure in her loves: Alec takes advantage first of her innocence and later of her desire to protect her family from utter ruin; Angel she loves with an absolute fidelity. But we are also aware of the challenge in Hardy's choice of adjective: by Victorian, Old Testament and extreme Christian standards Tess is by definition impure as soon as Alec has made love to her. The tension between these opposing conceptions of purity gives rise to a fourth level on which Tess exists as an exemplar, a test-case as it were, Purity itself as it might appear in a modern morality play: on this level Tess is a figure of allegory, a focus of significance of cosmic scale. All these things arise together from Hardy's subtitle.

Second, there is the example of Stonehenge. As a place of sacrifice it determines a special sort of attitude that we must take towards Tess: she is the allegorical victim, the doomed tragic figure, the innocent lamb that must bleed for the supposed good of mankind, the useless sacrifice. But then it is also the place at which Tess is most completely exposed to nature; it is to her what the heath is to Lear: it is a centre for sun-worship, a 'Temple of the Winds'; in the palm of the great hand of Salisbury Plain it offers Tess to the sky. Within it her love story comes to an end. Her great happiness with Angel, like the happiness of all human love, is evanescent, and here it ends. Furthermore, it is here that society – in the shape of sixteen policemen – society, in the eyes of which Tess is hopelessly impure, an adulteress and a murderess, steps in and claims its revenge. All these things come together at Stonehenge, and with them other levels that I have not yet mentioned in connexion with *Tess*, notably the historical perspective, the view into the past that loomed so large in our discussion of *The Mayor of Casterbridge*. For Stonehenge is old, part of those historical depths that Tess so fears when she is in her darkest moods. Like every story, Tess's is only one of the many strands that constitute history.

These are examples that show the many facets that Hardy's best writing reveals. It is in this richness of resonance, rather than in psychological insight, that his greatness lies.

'TESS' AS TRAGEDY

I have mentioned tragedy several times in my discussion of Hardy, notably in connexion with *The Return of the Native* and *The Mayor of Casterbridge*. *Tess* is obviously tragic, too, as can be inferred from an allegorical reading of the novel. Tess is a tragic protagonist, flawed by a 'fatal passivity', a 'reckless acquiescence in chance', tainted perhaps by spent blood, bitterly ready to assume guilt where the blame is not really hers, capable of wishing that she had not been born. Behind these qualities we feel in Hardy's mind the presence of Sophocles and Shakespeare. The tragic resignation of Desdemona to her death, for instance, and her great devotion to her husband, find parallels in Tess's story. Similarly we feel that the grotesque incongruity between Tess's 'crime' and its punishment is like the incongruity between the supposed 'sin' of Oedipus and his punishment.

Hardy's handling of tragic motifs is not merely a literary exercise, yet he appears to be conscious of his reading when he considers the structure of Tess's fate. The last paragraph of the novel opens with a sentence that makes this clear enough. Tess is hanged:

'Justice' was done, and the President of the Immortals, in Aeschylean phrase, had ended his sport with Tess.

Just as Sophocles appears as a sort of clue at the beginning of *The Woodlanders*, Aeschylus appears here at the end of *Tess*. So does Shakespeare, if we take up the hint offered by this word 'sport' and associate it with Gloucester's statement in *King Lear*:

As flies to wanton boys are we to the gods;
They kill us for their sport.

Less ambiguously, Angel quotes *Lear* when he admits that Tess, in being seduced, was 'more sinned against than sinning'.[3]

But this is only one level at which Hardy wants to stimulate a tragic consciousness. He also drops hints sufficient to make us aware of the inherently fatalistic temperament of his Wessex country people. For them, as perhaps for the Greeks and Elizabethans, there is a sense of doom, of the uselessness of kicking against the pricks, that is reinforced by the extremer forms of their Christianity: the Calvinist doctrine of Predestination, for instance, as espoused by Alec d'Urberville's temporary brethren and by Mr Clare, is a Christian version of Fatalism or Determinism. Below this rather superficial layer of Christian belief is a layer of primitive country fatalism indicated by the existence of the 'conjurors' mentioned in chapter 21 of *Tess*. A conjuror predicts what the future will hold; man's own actions cannot alter the course of events: he can merely conform to the dictates of fate as forecast by magic. This superstitious view of the universe gives rise to other forms of fortune-telling, and, sure enough, we find Mrs Durbeyfield possessed of a copy of *The Compleat Fortune-Teller*. In fact these Wessex minds are deeply impregnated with superstition: 'Like all the cottagers in Blackmoor Vale, Tess was steeped in fancies and

---

[3] There are several other references to Shakespeare in the novel, notably to stern moments in *Macbeth* and *Hamlet*.

prefigurative superstitions' – thus Hardy comments on Tess's pricking her chin on d'Urberville's gift of roses. Tess herself expresses the hope that Angel's failure to dance with her when they first met will prove 'no ill omen' for them now. Similarly she is upset by the ominous 'afternoon crow' of the cock on her wedding day.

When things are going well for Tess, in the last days of her courtship at Talbothays, she puts together her sense of the ominous and her Old Testament conception of retributive justice in a way that adds up to a perfect tragic picture of the world:

'I don't feel quite easy,' she said to herself. 'All this good fortune may be scourged out of me afterwards by a lot of ill. That's how Heaven mostly does . . .'

(chapter 32)

This view of the future arises from a view of the past that is also purely tragic: Tess has 'an almost physical sense of an implacable past which still engirdled her' (chapter 45). Caught in the web of fate, she again and again states or implies that she wishes she had not been born or at least that she could now die. Continuing to live is, however, her fate for the moment, and in this she 'acquiesces' even to the point of feeling that her punishment is deserved. Her stoicism almost reaches the point of masochism as she confronts cruel destiny in the shape of Alec, whom she has just struck on the mouth:

'Now punish me!' she said, turning up her eyes to him with the hopeless defiance of the sparrow's gaze before its captor twists its neck. 'Whip me, crush me . . . I shall not cry out. Once victim, always victim, – that's the law!'

(chapter 47)

And yet what is this 'law' she refers to? Here again, Hardy's unifying vision is at work: with that one word 'law' he indicates a tragic dimension (the protagonist's sufferings must go on remorselessly until his death), a consciousness of the scapegoat that appears in primitive religions, an Old Testament view of the fate of such as Job, and a vaguely conceived reference to Christ who came to 'fulfil' the law and gave his life to do it. But all these are only images, myths and metaphors. The reality to which they correspond is simply the way things are, and the way things are is that the actual never comes close to the possible, the achievement never matches the aspiration, the Intention is never Fulfilled. Commenting on Angel's harshness to Tess, Hardy sums this up:

Men are too often harsh with women they love or have loved; women with men. And yet these harshnesses are tenderness itself when compared with the universal harshness out of which they grow; the harshness of the position towards the temperament, of the means towards the aims, of today towards yesterday, of hereafter towards today.

(chapter 49)

Here it is quite clear that what Tess sums up as a 'law' is not intended by Hardy to be the subject of personal blame. Jehovah punishing Israel, the gods punishing Lear, God tormenting sinners – these are only images of harshness: Hardy does not really blame God; the harshness arises out of the nature of things, out of today towards yesterday, out of the way things are.

Not surprisingly, Hardy integrates nature into his picture of man's tragic fate. He makes a certain play with the stars, for instance. Tess's little brother Abraham quizzes her about stars during their fateful night ride when the horse Prince is killed (chapter 4), and later, at Talbothays, Tess attracts Clare's attention by explaining to Dairyman Crick that if she lies on the grass at night and looks at a star she soon feels herself to be on the star and no longer in her body (chapter 18). As the dairyman's reply indicates, it is because she is both sensitive and a country girl, used to being out of doors, that Tess considers the stars at all: it is perfectly natural that they should appear in her story just as they do in Bathsheba Everdene's story (see FFMC, 1 and 2). But our stars are more than this: they are also symbolic of the fate that governs us; where they lead we must follow. 'Then I defy you, stars!' shouts Romeo, but within hours he and Juliet are dead. With this in mind Hardy's treatment of the 'twinklers' turns out to be an image of his philosophy of fate's indifference to man; Tess and Abraham are on the cart:

[Abraham] leant back . . . and with upturned face made observations on the stars, whose cold pulses were beating amid the black hollows above, in serene dissociation from those two wisps of human life.

(chapter 4)

Abraham wonders if God is in some way 'on the other side' of the stars, and the naïveté of this leads us to question God's very existence, especially when we consider that the stars, which are 'serenely dissociated' from man, are, in Abraham's picture, closer to Earth than God is.

In this way we can see Hardy as having written a modern

version of a tragedy. We know that behind the struggles of man with the gods or with God that make up most tragic literature there is a deeper layer of meaning in which man is struggling with Fate or Destiny. Hardy cuts away the gods and God, although he uses them as symbols; makes Fate impersonal, so that the capital letter becomes inappropriate; and leaves us with an ultimate tragedy in which the struggle is simply between man and the way things are.

NATURE IN 'TESS'

I have already considered *Tess* as a pastoral romance and indicated that the natural background to this novel is an important part of its powerful, integrated picture of the world. Besides this, *Tess* contains some of Hardy's richest and best writing about nature, which is worth considering in its own right. Only in *The Woodlanders* does Hardy come close to the intensity of realization achieved in *Tess*.

Some of the natural description in *Tess* can stand independently as a record of rustic life. The harvesting that takes place during Sorrow's brief experience of the world, for instance, is vividly portrayed; so are the milking operations at Talbothays and the field work at Flintcomb-Ash. Even in these examples, however, the descriptions are not gratuitous embellishments to the story. The harvest in the fields parallels the 'harvest' that Tess has reaped in the shape of Sorrow, the rich milk-yield at the dairy parallels the quality of Tess's and Angel's love, Flintcomb-Ash is a penitential purgatory and so on. This general ability of Hardy's to integrate the action of his novels with its natural background rises to new heights in *Tess*.

We can see this more clearly if we examine in some detail this harvesting episode. It constitutes the opening paragraphs of chapter 14. Hardy describes the sunrise that opens this August day and pays particular attention to the sun, whose present appearance seems enough to explain sun-worship immediately:

The luminary was a golden-haired, beaming, mild-eyed, God-like creature, gazing down in the vigour and intentness of youth upon an earth that was brimming with interest for him.

Among the things illuminated by the first rays of the sun is a reaping machine, painted bright red by man and a brighter red by the sunrise.[4] With this machine in action the harvesting begins. So far

---

[4] There is always something a little sinister about bright colours in Hardy. We may remember Farmer Shiner's name (UGT), Sergeant Troy's flashing sword

so good. But food for one species, man, means death for other species: rabbits, hares, snakes, rats and mice retreat into the centre of the field as the reaping machine works round it in decreasing circles, and are 'every one put to death by the sticks and stones of the harvesters'.

Against this ambiguous natural background Tess appears; before she does so Hardy describes the other harvesters, first the men and then, with this commentary, the women:

Those of the other sex were the most interesting of this company of binders, by reason of the charm which is acquired by woman when she becomes part and parcel of outdoor nature, and is not merely an object set down therein as at ordinary times. A field-man is a personality afield; a field-woman is a portion of the field; she has somehow lost her own margin, imbibed the essence of her surrounding, and assimilated herself with it.

Man and nature can be integrated in Hardy, but not as intimately as woman and nature.

This proves to be even more clearly the case when we come into the love-laden summer air at Talbothays. Even in the harvesting sections we have just examined there is an association of sexuality with Hardy's woman/nature equation: Tess holds her sheaves of corn to bind them 'in an embrace like that of a lover'; the stubble scratches at the 'feminine smoothness' of her arm, and it bleeds. At Talbothays even the educated Angel Clare has 'made close acquaintance' with 'the seasons in their moods, morning and evening, night and noon . . . and the voices of inanimate things' (chapter 18). Here the urge towards 'sweet pleasure', which has risen as the sap has risen in the trees, draws Tess and Angel together; it also arouses the desires of three other milkmaids.

As the season 'develops and matures' nature achieves an astonishing florescence:

---

and red uniform (FFMC) and Diggory Venn's red clothes and face (RN). In *Tess* we find Alec d'Urberville's gig 'highly-varnished', the railway train seen by Angel and Tess as an alien being has 'gleaming cranks', the turnip-slicing machine at Flintcomb-Ash (an instrument of torture for Tess) has 'a bright blue hue of new paint', and the threshing machine there is described as 'a red tyrant'. Shininess and bright colours, it seems, represent wealth and modernity. For poor men who aspire to social prestige and the hands of ladies there is something threatening about the casual flashiness of the rich and well-bred. For a Wessex rustic, used presumably to a world of earthy colours, there is something genuinely ominous about the gleaming machinery of modern civilization.

Rays from the sunrise drew forth the buds and stretched them into long stalks, lifted up sap in noiseless streams, opened petals, and sucked out scents in invisible jets and breathings.

(chapter 20)

The sexual imagery in a passage such as this is not belied: in the room where the milkmaids sleep the hot summer air seems to be hot for another reason:

The air of the sleeping-chamber seemed to palpitate with the hopeless passion of the girls. They writhed feverishly under the oppressiveness of an emotion thrust upon them by cruel Nature's law.

(chapter 23)

As the Talbothays episode moves to a climax Hardy makes this connexion between natural forces and sexual forces explicit:

Amid the oozing fatness and warm ferments of the Froom Vale, at a season when the rush of juices could almost be heard below the hiss of fertilization, it was impossible that the most fanciful love should not grow passionate. The ready bosoms existing there were impregnated by their surroundings.

July passed over their heads, and the Thermidorean weather which came in its wake seemed an effort on the part of Nature to match the state of hearts at Talbothays Dairy . . . And as Clare was oppressed by the outward heats, so he was burdened inwardly by waxing fervour of passion for the soft and silent Tess.

(chapter 24)

This direct association of man and nature is almost pure Pathetic Fallacy, as is the description of Tess and Angel making their sad return-visit to Talbothays after the fiasco of their marriage:

The gold of the summer picture was now gray, the colours mean, the rich soil mud, and the river cold.

(chapter 37)

Nature echoes man just as man echoes nature.

This process is obviously at work on Flintcomb-Ash as well. Marian and Tess crawl over the 'desolate' fields like flies, their only companions 'gaunt spectral' birds blown thither by frozen winds from 'behind the North pole' (chapter 43). We need nothing more to tell us that this is the nadir of Tess's existence.

Following an old tradition in literature, Hardy continues the marriage between man and nature into the grave. In several of his poems this is clearly expressed; in, for instance, 'Transformations' (CP p. 472) or 'Voices from Things Growing in a Churchyard' which opens with the lines

> These flowers are I, poor Fanny Hurd,
>> Sir or Madam,
> A little girl here sepultured.

(CP p. 623)

In *Tess* this fantasy (the conceit that the flowers *are* Fanny, a proposition that is only true on a purely physical level) is even less optimistically expressed. Considering her past, Tess at one point realizes that

Whatever its consequences, time would close over them; they would all in a few years be as if they had never been, *and she herself grassed down and forgotten.*

(chapter 14; my italics)

The agricultural image that Tess conjures up for her own burial indicates the absolute intimacy Hardy wants to establish between man and nature – in this case between a woman's body and the Wessex earth.

CHRISTIANITY AND 'TESS'

In discussing *Tess*, and in previous chapters, I have mentioned allegory, Darwinism, the Old Testament and nineteenth-century belief. Most of these topics are directly related to Christianity, but my discussion has tended to eschew Christian aspects and to edge off into considerations about the cosmos, about tragedy and about nature. I think that this is just, since Hardy was always more inclined to use Christianity as an emotional matrix for the growth of symbols than as a central element in his thinking. However, a special tone starts to enter his handling of Christianity in *Tess*, and the importance of this becomes clear when we consider *Jude* and ponder the astonishing number of Christian references and themes in that novel.

I think that there are probably two reasons for the emergence of Christianity as a theme towards the end of Hardy's career as a novelist. It seems reasonable to suggest that at the age of fifty, when *Tess* was written, Hardy had a less respectful view of Christian doctrine, though not necessarily of Christ or of the

Church itself, than he had at the age of twenty-five when he was still able to contemplate a career as a clergyman. That may be one reason why he felt more able to discuss religion in his later novels. My other suggestion is equally simple: as an established novelist in the 1890s Hardy could afford to be a good deal less careful about the opinions of his audience than he had to be as a struggling unknown in the 1870s.

Whatever the reasons, it is certainly the case that Christianity looms larger in *Tess* than in any previous Hardy novel, and that it looms larger again in *Jude*. There is a rather laboured treatment of the question of baptism in *A Laodicean* (the very title of that novel is a reference to the New Testament) and there are plenty of references to parsons and churches throughout the Wessex novels; but Christianity does not appear as a central concern of any of the main characters before *Tess*. There is a possible exception in Clym Yeobright, in *The Return of the Native*, whose personal development culminates in his becoming a lay-preacher of sorts in a way that reminds us of Alec in *Tess*. I would stress this concept of personal development: Clym moves from being a Paris jeweller to being a teacher, a furze-cutter and at last a preacher. Angel Clare moves from conventional Christianity to a sceptical agnosticism; so does Tess herself, and so will Jude. The move *towards* Christianity is left to the villain, Alec. Hardy is mainly interested in examining the loss of faith and its effect on the development of the person concerned. One of the more original results of this loss of faith is that Hardy's main characters, in the absence of God, start themselves to take on some of the attributes of God and of Christ.

The Clare family first brings Christianity into *Tess*; from one point of view it is a novel about Angel's progressive loss of faith. But most of the comments on Christianity come to us directly from Hardy himself. It is his idea to paint 'THY, DAMNATION, SLUM-BERETH, NOT' on the stile in front of Tess (it comes as a slight shock to us to discover that this text is taken not from the Old Testament but from the New); then it is Hardy, in pursuit of his thorough association of Tess with nature, who writes this of her evening walks during her pregnancy:

Her flexuous and stealthy figure became an integral part of the scene. At times her whimsical fancy would intensify natural processes around her till they seemed a part of her own story . . . A wet day was the expression of irremediable grief at her weakness in the mind of some vague ethical being whom she could not class definitely as the God of her childhood, and could not comprehend as any other.

But this encompassment of her own characterization, based on shreds of convention, peopled by phantoms and voices antipathetic to her, was a sorry and mistaken creation of Tess's fancy – a cloud of moral hobgoblins by which she was terrified without reason. It was they that were out of harmony with the actual world, not she.

(chapter 13)

Here Christianity is not directly referred to, but the sorry muddle of Tess's mind is certainly intended to reflect the 'Christian' and social teaching that she has had. She is 'terrified' by 'moral hob-goblins' because she has committed fornication, and this is a sin about which a Christian should feel guilty: under the guise of talking about Tess's unnatural conscience Hardy is presenting the unnatural conscience prescribed by Christianity.

This is made obvious when we read the description of what Tess imagines will happen to Sorrow if he is not baptized:

She thought of the child consigned to the nethermost corner of hell . . . saw the arch-fiend tossing it with his three-pronged fork . . . to which picture she added many other quaint and curious details of torment sometimes taught the young in this Christian country.

(chapter 14)

Here Hardy is quite definitely intruding on us: the irony of 'this Christian country' is all his own. When, a few paragraphs later, we find Tess baptizing the child 'SORROW . . . in the name of the Father, and of the Son, and of the Holy Ghost' we can hardly avoid misreading the ritual words so that they mean that Father, Son and Holy Ghost are the origins of Sorrow's sorrow.

Hardy's own intrusions continue through the novel; but after a time Tess herself reaches a point where her natural paganism and her experience of suffering combine with Angel Clare's sceptical teaching to bring her to an intellectual point of view almost identi-cal to Hardy's own. Even before going to Talbothays she interrupts her own chanting of the *Benedicite* ('Bless ye the Lord') with the comment 'But perhaps I don't quite know the Lord as yet' (chapter 16). This tendency of Tess's to adopt Hardy's own views, as expressed in his intrusion and asides, culminates in her destruction of Alec d'Urberville's temporary religious enthusiasm (chapter 46) where, interestingly, Tess claims to have a religion and to believe in 'the *spirit* of the Sermon on the Mount' although she doesn't believe in 'anything supernatural'.

Angel Clare, meanwhile, the part-author of these views of

Tess's, also expresses Hardy's views as we know them from the *Life* and as we know them from his other novels and his poems. Angel explains to his father that he cannot conscientiously take Holy Orders:

I love my church as one loves a parent . . . but I cannot honestly be ordained her minister . . . while she refuses to liberate her mind from an untenable redemptive theolatry.

(chapter 18)

At first reading, this may sound as if Angel is a fully believing Christian who has a scruple about some small technical detail called 'redemptive theolatry'. An analysis of what this term actually means, however, and a consideration of the conversation with his father that follows, in which Angel gives a few more of his opinions, show that he does not believe in the Resurrection, the divine nature of Christ, or even that Christ's mission on earth had supernatural significance. By most definitions Angel is not a Christian at all, and the position that he shares with Tess represents at least a stage in the development of Hardy's own thinking. We will find this same trio of hero–heroine–author ranged critically against normal Christian doctrine in *Jude*. In *Tess* the three are brought together in at least one place: when Angel returns home to Emminster Vicarage after his first sojourn at Talbothays he is full of Tess's heathen spirit; he finds his family's Christianity to be 'like the dreams of people on another planet', and, in what are unmistakably the tones of Thomas Hardy, he is described thus:

Latterly [i.e. at Talbothays] he had seen only Life, felt only the great passionate pulse of existence, unwarped, uncontorted, untrammelled by those creeds which futilely attempt to check what wisdom would be content to regulate.

(chapter 25)

In this striking summary of Angel's state of mind, hero, heroine and author are united. Tess's pagan involvement in nature at Talbothays is the 'great passionate pulse of existence' that Clare has come up against: he has been altered by it and has accepted its wisdom, and Hardy clearly approves of this development in his hero's views, as the second part of the sentence makes clear. It is interesting to see Hardy here entering the lists behind the figure of his own character: at first it seems as if the sentiments conveyed are only Angel's, but their breadth, their switch into the present tense and their self-assured quality derive from some other mind, a mind that is not involved in a taxing emotional situation such as that of Angel when visiting his father's house. From Hardy's mind, in fact.

To sum up this matter of the personal intellectual development of Hardy's heroes and heroines, we can say that they move, through the hard school of life, towards something like Hardy's own position. If it is objected that Hardy has no fixed philosophy, and therefore no 'position', I think the objection can be met. It may be true that Hardy did not have a consistent philosophy, but it is equally true that in novel after novel and poem after poem he passes opinions on a number of topics which are forthright and usually echo one another accurately. Towards these opinions Angel, Tess, Jude and Sue painfully move.

Besides this matter of personal development away from Christian views, there is the curious question of Hardy's tendency to replace God and the divine Christ by man. This appears quite markedly in *Jude*, but there are traces of it in *Tess* which I shall try to follow.

Tess herself briefly acquires divine status in the eyes of her young brothers and sisters when she baptizes Sorrow:

> The children gazed up at her with more and more reverence . . . She did not look like Sissy to them now, but as a being large, towering, and awful – a divine personage with whom they had nothing in common.
>
> (chapter 14)

In the eyes of Angel, in the early mornings at the dairy, Tess seems a very 'divinity', Artemis or Demeter, and he thinks, in the 'luminous gloom' of the dawn, of the 'Resurrection hour', little knowing that 'the Magdalen might be at his side' (chapter 20). This addition of an ironic Christian touch to the basic identification of Tess with the divine is several times developed in the novel. Tess's feeling of being unworthy of Angel is described as a 'thorny crown'; her patience under Angel's neglect of her leads Hardy to quote St Paul's famous description of charity and to conclude that 'she might just now have been Apostolic Charity herself'; Angel's mother is influenced by his enthusiasm for Tess to the point that 'she had almost fancied that a good thing could come out of Nazareth – a charming woman out of Talbothays dairy'; when Tess walks to Emminster, Mercy Chant finds her boots in a hedge and attributes them to 'some imposter who wished to come into the town barefoot, and so excite our sympathies', a vague reference that just associates Tess with Christ and Mercy with the Pharisees; when Tess overhears Alec d'Urberville's sermon at Evershead, his text concerns the doctrine that Christ is 'set forth, crucified' among

Christians: the Christ set forth in Wessex is Tess herself; finally, at a more mundane level, when the care of her brothers and sisters falls on Tess's shoulders, she muses:

If only she could believe [in Providence] . . . how confidently she would leave them to Providence and their future kingdom! But, in default of that, it behoved her to do something; to be their Providence.

(chapter 51)

Thus Hardy keeps on jarring us, opening new vistas of possible metaphor, making us think about the supernatural and about Christianity as he likens his heroine to God, to goddesses, to the Magdalen and to Christ. Just as frequent, however, is the association of Angel with God, especially in Tess's eyes. His name, of course, points to the divine, and Hardy is at some pains to show us what a perfect being he becomes for Tess. Even before their marriage he can do no wrong, and afterwards she feels that she has 'delivered her whole being up to him' (chapter 37). At times her worship of him seems ominous to Tess herself:

She tried to pray to God, but it was her husband who really had her supplication. Her idolatry of this man was such that she herself almost feared it to be ill-omened.

(chapter 33)

And, indeed, her idolatry wrecks her judgement, so that when the divine Angel metes out to her suffering and punishment she welcomes it, with the masochism of the martyr, as just: 'I agree to the conditions, Angel; because you know best what my punishment ought to be' (chapter 37). Her long letter to Angel that concludes chapter 48 reads very like a human address to divine ears, a *De profundis*: 'The punishment you have measured out to me is deserved . . . only [be] a little kind to me . . . I live entirely for you . . . it has been so much my religion ever since we were married to be faithful to you . . .' and the letter ends with an appeal to Angel to come to her and to save her from what threatens her – the onslaughts of the devil, Alec. Tess's 'reckless acquiescence' in all that Angel has commanded also accords him divine status:

she had adhered with literal exactness to orders which he had given and forgotten . . . [she] admitted his judgement to be in every respect the true one, and bent her head dumbly thereto.

Angel, struck with remorse, remembers her in his turn: 'How her eyes had lingered upon him; how she had hung upon his words as if they were a god's!' (chapter 49). When he returns from his Brazilian ordeal, Angel looks like 'Crivelli's dead *Christus*'.

At Stonehenge, Angel, asked by Tess whether there is a life after death, remains silent 'like a greater than himself'. The silence implies that Angel feels there to be no life after death, the 'greater' is Christ, tempted by Pilate to make rash claims. Here we have an example of the breadth of reference Hardy gains by using Christian parallels, an example that perhaps sums up Hardy's purposes in this connexion. Christ was the supremely suffering man, the archetype of all suffering men and women. Christ was pure and faithful; his reward at the hands of the world, and at the hands of his Father, was ignominy and death. Such are the rewards of men and women at the hands of the world and at the hands of an indifferent fate. For all his greatness, Christ's suffering is in the end irrelevant if there is no life after death. Like Christ, Tess suffers here for no reward hereafter.

7

Jude the Obscure (1895)

FLESH AND SPIRIT

One of the many causes of Tess Durbeyfield's tragedy is Angel Clare's lack of sensuality. Had sexual desire been stronger in him, we are told, he might have made love to Tess on their wedding night in spite of his profound shock at discovering her not to be a virgin; but 'his affection itself was less fire than radiance' and he is not like those 'who remain sensuously infatuated with what they intellectually despise' (TD, 36). This surprises and alarms Tess, who has not been aware of this hard edge to his character:

> She was appalled by the determination revealed in the depths of this gentle being she had married – the will to subdue the grosser to the subtler emotion, the substance to the conception, the flesh to the spirit.
>
> (chapter 36)

Perhaps Angel Clare is not so much short of libido as exceptionally capable of putting mental and spiritual values before physical satisfaction. Here Hardy is touching on a delicate theme that lies beneath some of his other novels – for instance beneath his handling of Clym Yeobright and Eustacia Vye in *The Return of the Native*; it is the theme of the 'deadly war waged between flesh and spirit' that he describes in the Preface to *Jude the Obscure*.

This theme, taken up at length in *Jude*, is not altogether easy for modern readers to adjust themselves to. We are inclined, being influenced by writers such as D. H. Lawrence, to see no separation between the carnal and the spiritual: Lawrence recommends a sort of modern materialism in which, for example, making love can be the supreme *spiritual* experience. I think we have been less inclined since Lawrence's day to see the spiritual as a nebulous region cut off from the physical; we are more inclined to locate it in the here and now, in our experience of other people, of nature and of specific works of art. Hardy, at the end of the nineteenth century, stands uncomfortably between the old, Christian view of the unavoidable opposition between flesh and spirit and the modern, Lawrentian view. In *Jude the Obscure* this is only one of many ambiguities (ambiguities which, rather than proving Hardy inconsistent, prove him instead highly sensitive to the currents of change at work in his lifetime). This 'flesh versus spirit' ambiguity can be stated simply: physical desire for Arabella leads Jude away from the things of the spirit (learning, Latin, the New Testament); conversely, the spiritual side of Jude's relationship with Sue is threatened by her lack of sexual drive.

I have started my discussion of *Jude the Obscure* with this point about flesh and spirit because it is a good example of what is most important about that novel. *Jude* is an allegory, a sociological novel and a psychological study, but its importance is that it is an allegory about the fate of man as he is caught between two worlds, a sociological novel about a man caught between classes (and stages of social development), and a psychological novel about the traumatic personal lives of two people caught between desire and duty. The common denominator here is the concept of being 'caught between' things, and the example of 'flesh versus spirit' illustrates it perfectly: the trap is ambiguous and therefore doubly inescapable. What is more, the one example is also a summary of these three aspects of the novel.

Allegorically we can see Arabella as flesh and Sue as spirit, with Jude caught in between. *Sociologically* we can derive the whole plot from the flesh–spirit dichotomy: given the social conditions under which Jude lives, he cannot fulfil himself spiritually by going to Oxford but is forced to fulfil himself physically with Arabella by marrying her – for conventional reasons yet also against his will. Similarly, Sue's struggles are generated by her rebellion against 'spiritual' values as embodied in the ecclesiastical nature of her life at Oxford *and* by her rebellion against the physical expectations of sexually conventional men. When she breaks and collapses at the end of the novel she falls back into an extreme pietistic spiritual self-abasement before God *and* an extreme physical self-abasement before her husband. *Psychologically*, of course, the novel springs from the interaction between Jude's temperament and his environmental influences, and from the interaction between Sue's temperament and her situation. In Jude's temperament the call of the flesh is strong, but so is the call of idealistic scholarship; his environment casually encourages both aspects: Phillotson's early influence is strong, and so is the physical appeal of Arabella. In Sue's temperament there is little of the carnal, but her mind quickly catches at notions of personal liberty that immediately put her in a position where she should logically feel sexually free: her freethinking derives from her early environment and from a reaction against the excessive piety of Christminster, but her agnosticism, like Tess's, conceals primitive fears of divine wrath: her neurasthenic inability to enjoy sexual freedom is made worse by her cosmic terrors. For both Jude and Sue the flesh and the spirit are still at war.

In my first chapter I suggested that Hardy's novels and poems are about love in the sense that Hardy finds it to be the most important human experience. I added to this, however, the corollary that love is also the area of experience which most perfectly illustrates the moral, social, religious and psychological problems of mankind; it is the catalyst that sets action going and it naturally involves the very things that a novelist is most concerned with: personal spiritual development, rivalry and jealousy, marriage and divorce, public opinion and private feeling, family life and position, the significance of money, looks, luck and talent, the moral worth of the individual and other major topics. Love is a big hook that brings everything else up with it.

Now all this applies to *Jude* clearly enough: on the simple hooks of Jude's two different passions Hardy is able to hang a novel of universal significance. Perhaps, however, in concentration on the cosmic, universal importance of his work he has begun to lose touch with the other essential component of his greatness, his ability to integrate a love story with its natural background. In *Tess of the d'Urbervilles* he achieves a perfect balance: the novel is about Tess's love; the story of her love is woven into an intensely realized natural background; and the result quickly turns into a novel that takes on wide allegorical meanings of the sort that are termed universal. In *Jude* the middle item of these three is less prominent. In place of, say, the rich summer at Talbothays and its importance as a setting for love, we are given the stone of Christminster, the red brick of Leddenton and even the back streets of Aldbrickham (Reading). The setting is appropriate, of course, and Hardy certainly knows what he is doing, but we too should be aware of what he is about. He chooses to leave Wessex altogether in several parts of the novel, and a good deal of the borderland area of Wessex that he does describe is wide, bare and chalky, as far as possible in tone from the Froom Vale. *Jude* is set in a harsher, more modern world than any of the novels we have discussed so far.

Interposed between the love story and its cosmic significance in a novel like *Tess* is a level of natural integration. (It is slightly absurd to talk of 'levels' when the whole point is that Hardy *integrates* the different elements in his work, but criticism always involves analysis, and analysis is the breaking down of wholes into parts.) In *Jude* this natural level starts to give way to an urban social setting in which Hardy was less at home, although this development seems to have been a necessary move on his part. It appears that he was increasingly concerned to present his views on a range of social and moral issues which necessitated an emergence from Wessex. If we look back to *Far from the Madding Crowd* we at once feel the difference between that novel and these later works, especially *Tess* and *Jude*. In *Far from the Madding Crowd* Hardy does not really present any definite picture of the world: I mean, for all his comments and asides, the structure of his plot does not bend us strongly towards any particular opinion or any particular picture of reality. Increasingly, however, as we read through the later novels, we find that Hardy's plotting does bend us towards a definite world view. In *Tess*, this is still fully supported by a brilliant integration of the plot into its natural background. In *Jude*, Hardy's didactic purposes begin to overwhelm him, and, although he produces a powerful and disturbing novel, there is a sense of thinness and even of slight caricature about it that makes it less successful than *Tess*.[1] Had Hardy continued to write novels, it is possible that they would have degenerated into polemics, which may be one reason why he stopped doing so. Interestingly, his very first attempt at fiction, the destroyed novel *The Poor Man and the Lady*, was rejected as being too violent a social satire.

THE STRUCTURE OF 'JUDE'

I have claimed that Hardy has a didactic purpose that starts to emerge in his later novels, and that it is the structure of his plots that particularly pushes us towards the point of view that he wants us to consider. In the case of *Jude* this is very clear. Hardy himself pointed out that the plot of the novel is 'almost geometrically constructed' (*Life* p. 271). An examination of this geometrical structure is rewarding.

Jude Fawley, living in the village of Marygreen, is helped as a boy by the local schoolmaster, Richard Phillotson, who shortly

---

[1] Hardy himself commented on this in the *Life*. He felt he had given the bones of the story but had not done it justice and called it 'a miserable accomplishment . . . when I compare it with what I meant to make it' (p. 272). Of course we would hardly agree with the adjective 'miserable', but we can see that the density of developments and themes in the novel might have required a *longer* book, if nothing else. This point emerges in the summary of *Jude* that I offer immediately below: I use far more pages to tell the story than I have needed for the other novels.

moves away to the university town of Christminster (Oxford). Jude aspires to follow him and, keeping his faith alive by distant glimpses of the lights of Christminster, he learns, in spite of all vicissitudes, a good deal of Latin and Greek. To keep himself alive, he adopts the trade of stonemason, but pursues his studies relentlessly. His dreams of scholarship are shattered, however, by a love affair with a vulgar, cheerful and sensual village girl, Arabella, who tricks Jude into marrying her by pretending to be pregnant. The couple are not well suited and Arabella soon departs for Australia with her parents. After their final altercation, Jude drowns his sorrows in drink.

Left alone, he resumes his studies and his dreams of Christminster, although he now begins to think of becoming a clergyman rather than a scholar.[2] Motivated by the old desire at least to see Christminster, and by a new desire to meet a cousin of his who lives there, Sue Bridehead, Jude walks to Christminster and takes a job as a stonemason. He soon finds that this has brought him no nearer to his academic and religious goals, but it has brought him Sue. In spite of many misgivings (he is, after all, legally married to Arabella) Jude and Sue fall in love, he unambiguously, she with many doubts, withdrawals and teasings.

Together they go to visit Phillotson, who, far from having become a star in the academic world, is still a village schoolmaster with the difference only that the village in question is a little closer to Christminster than Jude's old village was. The conventional Phillotson is attracted by Sue and sees that she would make a useful assistant in his school, a post she soon fills. Jude, scornfully rejected by the colleges of Christminster and in despair about Sue, gets drunk, disgraces himself in front of Sue, loses his job and returns to Marygreen. Thus he has twice been brought back to his starting-point. These phases of his life are marked by Hardy's division of the novel into parts, of which there are six: Part First, 'At Marygreen', ends with the breakdown of Jude's marriage to Arabella and with a bout of drunkenness; Part Second, 'At Christminster', ends with the dashing of his academic hopes, his premature despair about Sue, and again with a bout of drunkenness.

In Part Third Jude goes to the cathedral city of Melchester, again to be nearer Sue, who has gone there to attend a teacher-training college, and again to be near something that may satisfy his intellectual ambitions – in this case the cathedral, whence he

---

[2] A marginal distinction. Oxford (and Cambridge) dons were all in Holy Orders until the late nineteenth century.

expects some sort of theological training to come to him in the same way as he expected learning somehow to seep out to him through the walls of the Christminster colleges. Again he loses Sue, who goes through with her perverse plan of marrying Phillotson (Jude even has to 'give her away'). So again his ambitions are thwarted; the nearest he gets to theology is his work on the cathedral masonry. This last thwarting is partly the result of Jude's conversations with the freethinking Sue: he cannot become a preacher in even the humblest capacity when he is no longer a believing Christian. Part Third ends not with a reversion to drink but with a disappointment connected with drink: Jude goes to visit the composer of a hymn he admires, only to discover that the man has given up writing sacred music for the more lucrative business of selling wine.

In Part Fourth Sue is married and living with Phillotson at Shaston. Jude burns his religious books and yearns for Sue. Sue finds her husband's sexual demands repugnant, and, when she shows this in an unmistakable manner by jumping out of her bedroom window, Phillotson, in a moment of enlightened generosity, lets Sue go and join Jude.

Part Fifth sees Sue and Jude living together, although they have not consummated their union sexually. Both their marriages have gone through the divorce courts and the divorces are now granted: ironically, Phillotson's case against Sue is based on her supposed adultery. Ominously, Jude now finds himself forced to adopt his child by Arabella, sent to him from Australia. This gloomy and tragic child, nicknamed 'Little Father Time', is soon followed by Arabella herself. She has fallen on hard times, visits the house in Aldbrickham where Jude and Sue are living, and asks for help. Her visit provokes Sue's jealousy and that same night Sue and Jude become lovers. This initiates a period of happiness together which reaches a climax when they visit the Great Wessex Agricultural Show; immediately after this, things start to go wrong for them. Because they cannot face the marriage ceremony, they live together unmarried and their neighbours make them uncomfortable; Jude becomes ill and cannot work; they drift away from Aldbrickham and eventually settle again in Christminster. By this time they have two children of their own, as well as Little Father Time, and in the nightmare of trying to get lodgings in Christminster Little Father Time becomes possessed of the idea that he and the other children are somehow in the way, obstructing their parents' chance of happiness. As a result he murders the two younger children and hangs himself. This carnage almost unhinges Sue's mind, and from this moment on, increasingly convinced that a malignant fate has heaped this horror upon her with a purpose, she turns away from her freethinking and back to the arms of the Church. For Jude, however, the deaths of the children are only a bitter confirmation that all is not well with the world and that therefore God is not in his heaven. Sue's self-abasement before the altar of St Silas' church inevitably leads her to attempt some sort of reparation that will appease the wrathful divinity there worshipped. This takes the shape of a rejection of her relationship with Jude and a conviction that she is really the wife of Phillotson. Eventually she goes back to Phillotson and they are again married. Jude, meanwhile, has been more or less taken over, in his bitterness and illness, by Arabella, whose second husband, one Cartlett, is now dead. She gets Jude drunk and in that condition makes him marry her again. Their brief second life together is not happy and Jude in effect kills himself by walking in bad weather, when already ill, out to Marygreen, where Phillotson is once again schoolmaster, to visit Sue. In this, their last meeting, Sue's passion for Jude is revealed, almost for the first time. Jude returns to Christminster where he dies with the noisy festivities of the 'Remembrance games' ringing through his death-chamber.

The structure of this plot, even as it appears in a brief summary, is obviously the result of careful and deliberate planning. What is revealed by it is precisely that mixture of love and thwarting that I spoke of in chapter 1. The main thrust of the novel is the love of Jude and Sue for one another: the structure of the plot is designed to show how that love is neatly thwarted at every turn. Here we see the Immanent Will weaving its 'artistries in circumstance'.

Jude's early thwarting (of his scholarly ambition) is a preliminary to his great thwarting: it is brought about by an involvement in the carnal side of love (Arabella). His second thwarting (of scholarly and ecclesiastical hopes) is brought about by his involvement with Sue and is at least partly the result of his intellectual involvement with her. For a while Jude and Sue have a reasonably satisfactory relationship together, both physical and intellectual, but both aspects break down under the impact of the children's death; Jude's great thwarting occurs when Sue finally withdraws from him both physically and intellectually.

Phillotson's thwartings parallel Jude's to some extent. His early ambitions of scholarship come to nothing. His second ambition, represented by his headmastership at Shaston, is thwarted by his involvement with Sue. His relationship with her is in part destroyed by her freethinking, which influences him. At the end of the novel what he gets back is a travesty of the former Sue: this woman he remarries has contorted her mind into unnatural beliefs which parallel her masochistic will to force herself to share his hated bed.

Arabella's life is not exactly happy, but she is protected from the worst sufferings by a cheerful and vulgar insensitivity. She is rarely thwarted because her ambitions are not sufficiently high to attract the anger of the gods: if Jude is an unsatisfactory husband, as he twice is, she can and does get another; if she is taken with a religious fervour, she can abandon it when it is no longer convenient. In this way she plays a sort of Alec d'Urberville to Sue's Tess and Jude's Angel Clare.

The main 'geometrical' structure, then, is based on these thwartings that keep bringing the four main characters 'back to square one'. Jude's profession never rises above that of stonemason – he is always thrust back to that. His last wife is his first wife, his deathbed is in the city of his earliest dreams, he dies childless as he was at the beginning of the novel, he is neglected at the end as he was at the beginning. Sue ends the novel involved in the same high-church Anglicanism that we found her engaged in when we first met her; her last husband is her first; she, too, is again childless. Phillotson ends the novel exactly as he began it, as schoolmaster at Marygreen; his wife is again Sue. This theme is pursued even in the details of the plot: the 'physician' Vilbert wrongs the young Jude over the matter of the classical textbooks early in the novel and at the end wrongs him again when he shows an interest in Arabella while Jude is dying upstairs. Such parallels can be multiplied.

This structuring of *Jude the Obscure* forces us to ask the questions that Hardy wants us to ask. These questions can be summed up with the generalization offered in my discussion of flesh and spirit, that the novel is about people caught between two worlds. As we watch the antics of Jude, Hardy's 'poor puppet', we have to consider him as a being trapped between the physical and the intellectual, between social propriety and the unconventional, between one class and another, between religious belief and freethinking, between the old world and the new. Each of these traps cries out for an escape-route. We *must* ask whether a man should put spirit before flesh, whether society is right to demand that Jude put flesh before spirit after he has made love with Arabella, whether there is a divine order behind the self-negating plan of Jude's life. The rigid and ironic destiny that decrees that Jude's last state shall be as his first even raises the cosmic question about free will and determinism: is man only an impotent insect crawling beneath an indifferent sky or can he, in spite of that sky's indifference, be the master of his fate and the captain of his soul? Might he not be able to be this *because of* the sky's indifference?

All these questions are thrown up by the structure of *Jude*. For reinforcement they are also discussed overtly in the novel. Jude and Sue talk a great deal about religion, marriage and love; Phillotson is even provided with a friend, Gillingham, for the express purpose of airing the questions of marriage, divorce and personal freedom; everybody who appears in the novel has an opinion to add, even down to Widow Edlin with her 'Weddings be funerals 'a b'lieve nowadays.' Hardy himself joins in the discussion in places, and usually his opinion is pretty apparent behind the characters' talk. We feel that he is being less than frank when he opens the chapter that follows the scene in the Registry Office, where Sue and Jude fail to get married, with the words

> The purpose of a chronicler of moods and deeds does not require him to express his personal views upon the grave controversy above given.

(Part Fifth, chapter 5)

Hardy's views are clearly present in every move his characters make and in every twist of the plot.

In spite of this, or because of it, the greatness of *Jude* lies in its plotting. Hardy fits a complex story together brilliantly and effortlessly. Every detail serves his overall purpose and the work is absolutely homogeneous. The homogeneity is generated by a didacticism that readers and critics often find too strong, especially in comparison with the homogeneity of *Tess*, which is, literally, perfectly natural. Certainly there are moments in the novel when Hardy presses his points home with embarrassing insistence; but I think he is always completely consistent: he knew what he was doing in writing this novel and we should give him the credit of sticking to well-designed if dangerous guns. Written at the end of a century of prudery and damaging concealment, *Jude* is like a door open on to the modern world in which, for all its horrors, improvements have been made, along lines advocated in *Jude*, in the vexed business of the regulation of sexual relationships.

MARRIAGE AND SEX IN 'JUDE'

It should by now be clear that *Jude the Obscure* is about love and that, although this is central, Hardy uses love as a means of involving the reader in large social psychological and religious questions. These three are all linked in the question of marriage. What exactly does this novel say about marriage?

The tone of Hardy's attitude is set by his description of Jude's marriage to Arabella. He devotes a separate paragraph to summarizing this event; it reads:

And so, standing before the aforesaid officiator, the two swore that at every other time of their lives till death took them, they would assuredly believe, feel, and desire precisely as they had believed, felt, and desired during the few preceding weeks. What was as remarkable as the undertaking itself was the fact that nobody seemed at all surprised at what they swore.

(Part First, chapter 9)

The chapter in which this paragraph appears concludes with another paragraph that again questions the good sense of Jude's marriage (and, by implication, of any marriage under similar circumstances); Jude is described as being 'caught in a gin which would cripple him'.

It begins to look as if Hardy may be turning entirely against marriage; but a few pages later Jude comes to this moment of enlightenment:

Their lives were ruined, he thought; ruined by the fundamental error of their matrimonial union: that of having based a permanent contract on a temporary feeling which had no necessary connexion with affinities that alone render a life-long comradeship tolerable.

(Part First, chapter 11)

This harks back to the claim, made at the end of *Far from the Madding Crowd*, that Gabriel and Bathsheba may be happy because their love has grown up as they worked together side by side. Hardy is again saying that this sort of love is the only rational basis for a marriage. Sexual passion (the 'temporary feeling') is irrelevant, it seems; at least, its presence or absence is as nothing compared with this 'comradeship' that alone ensures happiness. Yet if we look at Hardy's words again, we see that he is not even claiming the possibility of happiness: comradeship based on 'affinities' can render married life 'tolerable'. So we are almost, but not quite, being urged to reject marriage out of hand.

The marriage question next appears in relation to Sue. Her letter asking Jude to 'give her away' is highly sarcastic about this 'giving': Sue feels it puts her in the category of 'a she-ass or a she-goat', and Jude, for all his emotional torment, is still able objectively to think, 'She does not realize what marriage means!' (Part Third, chapter 7). After Sue has become 'Mrs Phillotson' Jude naturally rejects that name and comments,

You are dear, free Sue Bridehead, only you don't know it! Wifedom has not yet squashed up and digested you in its vast maw as an atom which has no further individuality.

(Part Third, chapter 9)

Once Sue has settled at Shaston and has come to discover 'what marriage means', her highly sensitive and intelligent mind starts to play around the questions of what is wrong with her situation, and what is wrong with the institution of marriage. She finds that she does not want to give her physical love 'continuously to the chamber-officer appointed by the bishop's licence to receive it' (Part Fourth, chapter 1). Then she begins to see a difference between a marriage that is 'a religious ceremony' and a purely secular marriage; with her new views on religion, of course, she can only see it as a secular institution, and *that* she sums up as

A sordid contract, based on material convenience in householding, rating, and taxing, and the inheritance of land and money by children, making it necessary that the male parent should be known.

(Part Fourth, chapter 2)

Later in the same chapter, feeling increasingly trapped by her marriage (like Tess, Sue is often likened to a bird), she exclaims,

It is none of the natural tragedies of love that's love's usual tragedy in civilized life, but a tragedy artificially manufactured for people who in a natural state would find relief in parting!

(Part Fourth, chapter 2)

Here Hardy is moving towards his consideration of divorce. This exclamation of Sue's is part of her conversation with Jude; discussing the same matter with her husband she says,

Why can't we agree to free each other? We made the compact, and surely we can cancel it.

(Part Fourth, chapter 3)

I am directly attributing this view of divorce to Hardy, although the opinions I am quoting come from the mouths of his characters. I think there is every justification for the attribution. We can *see* that Sue is right: her marriage *is* a tragedy. No good arguments are presented on the other side; indeed, Sue persuades Phillotson to let her go, and he, in discussion with Gillingham, shows himself to be enlightened in his turn:

> I had not the remotest idea . . . that merely taking a woman to church and putting a ring upon her finger could by any possibility involve one in such a daily, continuous tragedy as that now shared by her and me!
>
> (Part Fourth, chapter 4)

Gillingham presents the conventional view of Phillotson's situation ('Do go back and make up your mind to put up with a few whims'); but as he walks home Phillotson says to himself, 'So Gillingham, my friend, you had no stronger arguments against it than those!' (Part Fourth, chapter 4). 'It' here is Phillotson's decision to allow Sue to go away. We are clearly intended to sympathize with this conversion to a liberal view.

There is another, and deeper, discussion of marriage when Sue has left Phillotson and is living with Jude. Both Jude and Sue are understandably afraid of marrying, once their divorces have come through, and a good deal of Part Fifth is devoted to their qualms and uncertainties. The trouble is that the only sure thing that their experiences have taught them is that marriage is a dangerous and potentially sordid business:

> I think I should begin to be afraid of you, Jude, the moment you had contracted to cherish me under a government stamp, and I was licenced to be loved on the premises by you. Ugh, how horrible . . .
>
> (Part Fifth, chapter 1)

Here Hardy seems again to be entirely antagonistic towards marriage, and it must be admitted that, from this point of brief *unmarried* happiness onwards, marriage takes some hard knocks in the novel. Hardy moves beyond mere advocacy of divorce to the more extreme position adumbrated in his presentation of the first marriage, that between Jude and Arabella. Not only do the appalling mockeries of the remarriages (Sue's to Phillotson, Jude's to Arabella) cast doubt on the institution by representing it as a sort of inescapable, legalized torture-chamber; Hardy also makes some rather pointed asides whose gratuitousness shows that they are the deliberate self-expression of a committed author. Arabella and Cartlett leave the bar-tent at the Great Wessex Agricultural Show 'in the antipathetic, recriminatory mood of the average husband and wife of Christendom' (Part Sixth, chapter 5). Here, incidentally, Arabella's bad temper arises partly because she has seen the simple and spontaneous happiness of Jude and Sue as they hold hands at the show: unmarried, they can be happy. When Arabella has managed to catch Jude for the second time, she shows her wedding ring to her friends with the comment, 'There's the padlock, see' (Part Sixth, chapter 7). Once they are remarried they live together again, but their landlord suspects them of being unmarried:

He was about to give them notice to quit, till by chance overhearing her one night haranguing Jude in rattling terms, and ultimately flinging a shoe at his head, he recognized the note of genuine wedlock; and concluding that they must be respectable, said no more.

(Part Sixth, chapter 8)

I think that the Bishop of Wakefield was probably right, holding the Christian view of marriage, to fling his copy of *Jude* into the fire. He saw, presumably, that the novel not only advocates divorce but leaves very little room for the possibility of rational marriage at all.[3]

Although 'marriage' is not simply a euphemism for 'sex' (it is a social, psychological and religious matter as well as a sexual one), Hardy is always interested in passionate love, and he juggles increasingly openly with the trio love–sex–marriage. Much of what I have said about Hardy has concerned two parts of this trio, love and marriage, and I would like here, while discussing the novel in which he treats it most openly, to try to consider the third part, sex, rather in isolation.

It is interesting that in *Jude* Hardy attempts the portrayal of a passionate man and a 'fastidious' woman. His earlier men have been surprisingly sexless, while his earlier women have tended to be passionate. This is partly because he is writing according to a convention and partly because he really chooses to deal with people of this sort. In his earlier novels, where he is still relatively conventional, this is quite marked, but there is a development towards the *Jude* situation: the men liven up somewhat or, at least, are discussed as sexual beings rather more openly, and the women

---

[3] It is tempting to speculate about Hardy's own marriage. His first wife, Emma, with whom he was on decreasingly good terms, had become a sadly unattractive person by the 1890s. How much of *Jude* is autobiography? Hardy mentions his own cousin, Tryphena Sparks, in the Preface. Is she the model for Sue? Such questions may interest the curious, who are referred to Robert Gittings' excellent two-volume biography (see Reading List).

subside. In every Hardy novel, however, there is some evidence of female passion. Thus Bathsheba (and Fanny Robin) in *Far from the Madding Crowd* seem to be sexually aroused by Troy, while Troy's feelings, like Boldwood's and Oak's, have a detached, cerebral quality about them. This is only a faint impression, one that is hard to substantiate, but if we think of the abandon with which Bathsheba falls in love against her better judgement and the abandon with which Fanny follows Troy from barrack to barrack we surely find a sexual flavour in it that is quite absent from Boldwood's self-obsessed obsession or Oak's steady devotion.

Similarly Eustacia Vye in *The Return of the Native* is presented as sexually passionate, while even her lover, Damon Wildeve, is presented as colder and more 'civilized'. We get the impression that Lucetta in *The Mayor of Casterbridge* actually desires Donald Farfrae, while he seems more concerned with her status and glamour. Then Hardy starts to change: Grace Melbury in *The Woodlanders* is not presented sexually at all, while Fitzpiers certainly is; Giles's devotion to Grace, on the other hand, is like Oak's devotion to Bathsheba, not overtly sexual, and he contrasts interestingly with Fitzpiers, who, in the course of the novel, makes love to Suke Damson and perhaps to Mrs Charmond as well as to Grace. What is interesting here is the alien status of Fitzpiers (and of Mrs Charmond): they are from the great wide world of gentry and education that lies beyond the borders of Wessex; Hardy feels free to mention their sexuality in a way he does not feel free to discuss the libidos of the 'natives'. In *Tess* we find passionate women in the Talbothays milkmaids, although Tess herself has to remain something of an enigma, and we find two upper-class male 'outsiders', Alec and Angel. Alec is distinctly lecherous; Angel, though undersexed, at least has his temperament explained to us. This motif of the sexual 'outsider' disappears in *Jude*, and the underlying development of Hardy's fiction in this connexion is made apparent. The passionate woman is present in Arabella and the cold woman in Sue, while Jude represents both the strong libido that Hardy has previously only been able to attribute to 'outsiders' and the undersexed idealism of Angel Clare.

What is so striking about *Jude* is the frankness that Hardy suddenly brings into his writing. I have tried to sketch out a plan of the sexuality of some of the characters in his earlier major novels, but in all honesty we have to say that before *Jude* Hardy's novels contain no analytical treatment of sex at all; they belong to an idiom in which we can see the sexual forces at work under the surface but have to translate what we see into something clearer and more comprehensible. We have to *assume* almost everything. We have to infer Troy's sexual attractiveness, for instance, from his clothes, his profession, his amorous talk and the symbolism of the sword exercise; a veil of darkness is thrown over Bathsheba's real responses to Troy as a male body. Even Eustacia's sexuality is something that we gather from the metaphors used for her, from her disquieted yearnings and from physical descriptions that concentrate largely on her head: she becomes ecstatic if her long hair is brushed, she has full lips, and so on. Tess and her fellow milkmaids move a little beyond this and we are left in no doubt that Marian and Izz desire Angel physically, but we still have to assume a great deal about the three main characters. Angel is probably rather idealized in his sexlessness, although we do learn that in his bitterness he considers taking Izz to Brazil and there living with her unmarried; Alec, however, for all his swagger, is a stock lecher and libertine, and Hardy leaves us to assume all the details of his sexuality without comment. Tess herself is left completely to our powers of assumption and inference, and Hardy carefully avoids attributing any sexual desires to her at all.

When we come to *Jude* it is as if we have emerged from a Victorian world of allusion and innuendo into a recognizably modern world. First, Hardy's pointers or clues to the characters' sexuality are far more obvious (Arabella throws a pig's pizzle at Jude to attract his attention; she has large breasts while Sue has small breasts; and so on) and, second, Hardy actually starts to *discuss* sexual problems. His discussion is not always direct and, in Sue's talk for instance, is often hesitant and embarrassed, but it is a genuine discussion.

Early in the novel Jude is impelled towards Arabella by a force that is unmistakable in origin:

> As if materially, a compelling arm of extraordinary muscular power seized hold of him – something which had nothing in common with the spirits and influence that had moved him hitherto. This seemed to care little for his reason and his will . . . and moved him along, as a violent schoolmaster a boy he has seized by the collar, in a direction which tended towards the embrace of a woman . . .
>
> (Part First, chapter 7)

This powerful sexual drive is present in Arabella, too. She tells her friend Anny, in 'a curiously low, hungry tone of latent sensuousness', that although she has got Jude to care for her, she wants more than care:

> I want him to have me – to marry me! I must have him. I can't do without him. He's the sort of man I long for. I shall go mad if I can't give myself to him altogether.
>
> (Part First, chapter 7)

Arabella's first attempt at seduction is on a hilltop where she and Jude rest after they have chased an escaped pig. The running has 'blown' them and they lie down side by side:

> 'We've run all this way for nothing,' she went on, her form heaving and falling in quick pants, her face flushed, her full red lips parted, and a fine dew of perspiration on her skin.
>
> (Part First, chapter 8)

This is a pointer towards Arabella's sexuality, of course, rather than a discussion of it, but its import is blatant: Arabella is described as she would be if she were making love. The connexion is so obvious that Hardy does not need to comment.

The most explicit discussions of sex appear in Sue's conversations with Jude, as for example during their talk at Marygreen after Aunt Drusilla's funeral. Sue admits that she finds herself unable to respond sexually to Phillotson; her stammerings represent not only her own difficulty in expressing this but also the birth-pains of the free discussion of sexual topics in literature and, perhaps, between educated people in life. The anti-sexual conventions of nineteenth-century society can be seen cracking as she speaks to Jude:

> I – I think I must be equally honest with you as you have been with me. Perhaps you have seen what it is I want to say? – that though I like Mr Phillotson as a friend, I don't like him – it is a torture to me to – live with him as a husband! – There, now I have let it out . . .
>
> (Part Fourth, chapter 2)

For all her embarrassment, Sue elaborates on this point, and the discussion continues; further, it is taken up later in the novel in several places. The result is that when Sue finally 'gives in' to Jude and asks, 'I am not a cold-natured, sexless creature, am I, for keeping you at such a distance?' (Part Fifth, chapter 2), we automatically read the word 'sexless' in its modern colloquial meaning (= not passionate) rather than in its basic meaning of 'hermaphroditic', I think this may be the earliest such usage.

Towards the end of the last section I mentioned the pig's pizzle that Arabella throws at Jude. In saying that it was a 'pointer' to a sexual significance (obvious enough) I was in effect saying that the pizzle was a symbol. As in his other novels, Hardy employs symbolism frequently and effortlessly in *Jude*. As in his other novels, the symbolism tends to be taken from nature and from religion in a way that integrates these two levels and points outward to the cosmic significance behind his story. I have said that *Jude*, set only on the fringes of Wessex, does not depend on its natural setting for its strength in the way that *The Woodlanders* or *Tess* does. In spite of this there are a number of natural symbols in the novel that are worth considering. The slaughtering of the pig (Part First, chapter 10) is the most outstanding of these, the pig standing as the representative of all victims and scapegoats and sacrifices. Jude's pity for the animal and his bewilderment about the morality of its fate perfectly illustrate man's reaction to the casual in- difference of nature. 'Pigs must be killed', says Arabella. 'Poor folks must live'; and so it is, but Jude is disgusted and upset by the killing all the same. The blood that stains the snow symbolizes all the suffering generated by existence: it is hideous and meaning- less, but it is necessary. Besides this, the intense physicality of the scene of the killing makes it a symbol of Jude's degradation with Arabella: he has responded to the call of his flesh and the pulse of his blood, and it has brought him to this grotesque wallowing in gore. Arabella, with Jude's own assistance, is slaughtering his hopes and aspirations, leaving only a limited physical satisfaction.

Similarly the rabbit caught in the gin (Part Fourth, chapter 2) symbolizes Jude himself, caught up in the powerful machinery of his obscure fate, and it symbolizes Sue, caught in the psychological and social trap of her marriage. Jude puts the rabbit out of its agony rather as Little Father Time puts the younger children out of the world, and rather as casual destiny will put Jude himself away.

If Arabella comes to symbolize the physical and the gross in her association with pigs, Sue comes to symbolize the spiritual and delicate in her association with birds. The first animals Jude is kind to in the novel are birds and, later, he offers Sue not the trap which she so fears (marriage) but a 'nest'.

Moving 'up' from the natural to the cultural level, the sym- bolism includes, for instance, almost every aspect of the buildings and places mentioned. Sometimes this is completely obvious, as when Christminster symbolizes Jude's aspirations when he sees it as a glow on the horizon, or when it symbolizes dead and useless learning ('Sarcophagus' College); or Melchester cathedral, which not only *is* a great Christian institution but also symbolizes the Christian Church as such. At other times these symbols need a little explanation. Thus, Hardy provides the conventional Gillingham with a town called 'Leddenton' to live in: lead does not sound intellectually promising. Or, on occasion, Hardy gives us a full explanation of the symbol: when Phillotson and Sue marry they move to Shaston and take a house there called 'Old-Grove Place' which seems to symbolize the old-fashioned and conventional values that so oppress Sue, and so it is:

It is so antique and dismal that it depresses me dreadfully. Such houses are very well to visit, but not to live in – I feel crushed into the earth by the weight of so many previous lives there spent.

(Part Fourth, chapter 1)

Moving 'up' again, we find ourselves involved in the immense web of Christian and religious symbolism that is one of the most extraordinary and striking elements in the novel. In discussing *Tess*, I pointed out how in his last novels Hardy does not say *less* about Christianity than before (as we might expect from the development of his own views), but more; in the case of *Jude*, much more. I also pointed out that his characters, as they lose their religious faith, start to take on themselves some of the characteristics of God and of Christ. The degree to which this is done in *Jude* creates a pattern of religious symbolism which is both extraordinary and striking, both unusual to the point of blasphemy and puzzling to the point of obscurity.

First, there are over one hundred direct references in the novel to Christianity, Christ and the Church. More references, in other words, than there are to all the things we would normally consider the novel to be about; more than to education in all its aspects, more even than to sex, love and marriage. This does not make Christianity more important in the novel; after all, when marriage *is* mentioned it is discussed at length; quantity, anyway, is an unreliable measure. But the number of references is a fact that should make us want to know what all this Christianity is doing in *Jude*. We can start by looking at its more significant appearances.

Christminster is not only interestingly named, from our point of view, but is also associated with Jerusalem. When Jude first hears what the town looks like from a distance at sunset, he immediately thinks of 'the heavenly Jerusalem'; when he sees its distant lights this impression is confirmed. Hardy even suggests what version of 'the heavenly Jerusalem' is in Jude's mind ('more of the painter's imagination and less of the diamond merchant's'). This theme is developed by the vocabulary of Jude's distant views of the city: its smoke is 'incense' and its lights at night give it a 'halo' (Part First, chapter 3). Later, of course, there is the exhibition in Christminster of the actual model of Jerusalem.

The chapter in which Jude has his visions of the distant seat of learning concludes with five staccato propositions that represent his thinking about it; the two first are:

'It is a city of light,' he said to himself. 'The tree of knowledge grows there.'

(Part First, chapter 3)

Later he announces:

Christminster shall be my Alma Mater; and I'll be her beloved son, in whom she shall be well pleased.

(Part First, chapter 6)

This quotation from St Matthew implies that Christminster is God and that Jude is Christ. During the Arabella episode, however, Jude goes twice into a room where there is a picture of Samson and Delilah. He is obviously Samson to Arabella's Delilah (at the end of the novel, when Arabella lures the broken Jude back to her, she sees him as her 'shorn Samson') but we should not forget that Samson has what are called typological affinities with Christ: both sacrificed themselves, at any rate.

When Jude first goes to Christminster he chooses to walk, entering the city on foot. His first experiences there involve the intense Christian atmosphere of the shop where Sue works and, of course, the many churches of the town. When Sue sees him at the exhibition of the model of Jerusalem he is peering so intently into 'the Valley of Jehoshaphat that his face [is] almost hidden from view by the mount of olives' (Part Second, chapter 5). The associations hint that Jude is Christ-like in his sufferings.

During his drunken night in Christminster Jude recites the Nicene Creed in Latin, and Hardy quotes a substantial part of the Latin in his text. The next day, having walked to Alfredston, he sits down wearily by a well 'thinking as he did so what a poor Christ he made' (Part Second, chapter 7). When he has decided to abandon his Christminster plans and to train for some humble level of the priesthood we read this:

He considered that he might so mark out his coming years as to begin his ministry at the age of thirty – an age which much attracted him as being that of his exemplar when he first began to teach in Galilee.

(Part Third, chapter 1)

Like Christ, Jude has been rejected by Jerusalem and will now try in humbler places. But from even the humblest he is to be driven out, until he dies despised and rejected of men. Meanwhile the associations between him and Christ are reinforced. When Sue has left Phillotson and joined him, he exclaims at one point, 'Crucify me, if you will!' (Part Fourth, chapter 5). When Jude and Sue return to Christminster with the children, Jude 'preaches' to the crowd as the 'solemn stately figures in blood-red robes' collect for the Judgement Day. The crowd stares at Jude 'like the Lycaonians at Paul'. When he cannot get lodgings, he says, 'Leaving Kennetbridge for this place is like coming from Caiaphas to Pilate!' When Sue tells him that she has seen Phillotson in the crowd she answers, 'He is evidently come up to Jerusalem to see the festival like the rest of us' (Part Sixth, chapter 1). When Jude and Sue finally separate, Jude declares, 'Then let the veil of our temple be rent in two from this hour!' (Part Sixth, chapter 3). After this he becomes the pale and corpse-like figure of the Christ met on the road to Emmaus.

In other words Jude's life is hung on a sketchy outline of Christ's; the blueprint is faintly visible under the many levels of Hardy's story, and we are the more receptive to it in that there are so many other Christian and biblical themes in the novel, mostly with symbolic rôles. There are biblical epigraphs to some of the parts, as well as a Christian epigraph to the whole novel. Jude frequently quotes scripture, and his deathbed oration to empty air is an extensive quotation from the Book of Job. We naturally think of that other Job figure, Mayor Henchard and perhaps wonder about the equation Job = Jesus = Jude. Jude's name is that of an apostle at least. Sue, too, has biblical and Christian associations that cannot be accidental. She is 'the Ishmaelite'; she first appears in an aura of high-church ritual (the same aura in which she ends, of course); after the death of the children her 'cup of sorrow' is 'full'; when she deals Jude the final cruel blow of leaving him, the text in her mouth is 'charity seeketh not her own'; remarried to Phillotson she chooses to wear a coarse calico nightgown of which

Widow Edlin says that it is 'no better than very sackcloth o' Scripture!'; when she steels herself to re-enter Phillotson's bed at the end of the novel she says, 'I will drink my cup to the dregs!' and again, 'I must drink to the dregs!' Like Christ in the garden she herself chooses to drink the cup of suffering, and in both cases the motivation is the same: God's will is to be done.

So Sue, like Jude and like Tess, is a suffering Christ figure, and Hardy has erected an extensive scaffolding of Christian reference to make these parallels inescapable. It is almost as if Hardy has accepted, for his poetic purposes, the claim that Christ stood for all humanity when he suffered, and now turns that equation about to claim that any suffering human *is* Christ.

THE OLD WORLD AND THE NEW

Jude the Obscure is the first modern novel. Balanced as it is between the nineteenth century and the twentieth, it is inevitable that it should select elements from the old world that point towards the new. Sue is not the first confused and distressed heroine in fiction, but she must be one of the earliest whose confusion and distress are explicitly sexual; she must also be the first fictional heroine to appear in male clothes for the reasons Hardy seems to have had. Her brief adoption of Jude's clothes simultaneously emphasizes the closeness of the cousins and the potential independence of women. Sue the tormenting tease and Sue the religious extremist are not forerunners of female emancipation; but Sue in Jude's best suit, talking about her earlier boy-friend with whom she lived on equal, though 'sexless', terms certainly belongs to the modern world. 'How modern you are', Jude says to her. Not that modern women always wear men's suits or lack sexual drive, but Sue's unhappy type was one of several stages in the development of women from undereducated sex-objects trussed up in inconvenient clothing to betrousered equals with educational opportunities.

On a different topic, that of Natural Selection, we find Hardy again bringing a nineteenth-century problem into a twentieth-century focus. Little Father Time is of a type (as are Jude and Sue) that is quite unfitted to survive; so much is direct from Darwin. But his suicide note ('Done because we are to menny') is Darwinism as it appears in the overcrowded modern world.

Or again, consider Sue's view of the value of personal liberty. As it centres on the question of marriage it is largely nineteenth-century, and she cites Mill, one of that century's proponents of divorce. But the passage of Mill that she actually quotes on this occasion, although entirely apt, is pure existentialism. Heidegger's warning against 'inauthentic existence' is perfectly summed up in the lines:

[He] who lets the world . . . choose his plan of life for him, has no need of any other faculty than the ape-like one of imitation.

(Quoted in Part Fourth, chapter 3)

I think that the novel's direction can be encapsulated in the phrase Hardy uses when the enlightened Sue is watching Jude's struggle with Christianity and other conventions. She is interested in him 'as one might be interested in a man puzzling out his way along a labyrinth from which one had one's self escaped' (Part Third, chapter 2). The 'labyrinth' is Christian belief (represented by the dense tissue of Christian references surrounding Jude) but it is also all the other conventional and social beliefs that follow this basic belief. In fact, it is the whole fabric of nineteenth-century thought that Jude is puzzling his way out of. His tragedy, and Sue's, is to be situated between this old world and the new. The new world does not seem like a promised land, but at least it is an escape from the labyrinth of the old world. What is wrong with that labyrinth is that it lives by the letter that killeth and not by the spirit that giveth life; in fact the 'letters of the law' *are* the labyrinth. Direct from the Christian religion come the letters of the commandments that 'kill' Sue when she tries to obey them. Hence the poignancy of the scene in the church where Sue is literally trying to restore the letters of the law. Direct from the social structure in which Jude lives come the other 'thou shalt nots' listed by Sue:

There is something external to us which says, 'You shan't!' First it said, 'You shan't learn!' Then it said, 'You shan't labour!' Now it says, 'You shan't love!'

(Part Sixth, chapter 2)

These prohibitions seem to be directed towards him from an old world which he is trying to break out of, just as the ten commandments rise up against Sue and prevent her from breaking out of that same world. Sue sinks back into the old world, but she has helped Jude push open the doors to the new. Jude's body is one more obscure corpse among the many scattered about that doorway: Hardy mourns over it, but the doors are not shut again.

8

A Pair of Blue Eyes (1873), The Trumpet-Major (1880) and the Minor Fiction

HARDY'S MINOR FICTION

A glance at the table of Hardy's published work given at the end of the Introduction shows that the six novels I have discussed are the smaller part of Hardy's output. Together with *Under the Greenwood Tree*, they constitute the seven Novels of Character and Environment – by any standards Hardy's major work.[1] Apart from these there are the Romances and Fantasies (four novels and one volume of short stories), the three Novels of Ingenuity and a volume of stories entitled *A Changed Man*. I intend in this chapter to say something about the two most significant of the Romances separately, then something about the remaining novels and then something about the short stories.

It is best to be frank about this minor work. My view is that it *is* minor and that its principal use is as an aid to the greater understanding of the major work. I think that the educated reader can enjoy *A Pair of Blue Eyes* and *The Trumpet-Major* in isolation, and perhaps some of the stories, but I think that the greatest value of the other novels is for the Hardy student or enthusiast for whom they will amplify aspects of the major work. A study of 'Hardy's heroines' or 'Hardy and religion' will profit from a consideration of the minor novels; considered in their own right they have an undoubted fascination but cannot honestly be seen as great literature.

'A PAIR OF BLUE EYES' (1873)

This novel is autobiographical and almost completely conventional. It is dangerous and probably pointless to speculate about the first of these qualities, but the opening scenes parallel quite closely the description of Hardy's first meeting with his first wife in Cornwall in 1870, given in the *Life*.[2] Elfride Swancourt has

---

[1] The two other titles listed as Novels of Character and Environment are volumes of short stories.
[2] Cf. pp. 65–74.

much in common with the young Emma Gifford with whom Hardy fell in love; and the young architect who visits her, Stephen Smith, can be seen as a partial version of the young Hardy. Smith is the son of relatively humble villagers, a fact he is at some pains to conceal: and this uncomfortable position between two worlds was certainly Hardy's own.[3] More important, Smith represents all people who, in a class-conscious society, have had to practise concealment as their talents have raised them from their original sphere.

The relationship between Elfride Swancourt and Stephen Smith is not strikingly conventional in itself, but most of the further developments of the plot are handled in conformity with the conventions of minor Victorian fiction. Hardy's own voice is not entirely absent but the main thrust of the novel develops in a manner that is not comfortably Hardy's own. He is, for one thing, a little out of place in the grand Cornish scenery of the book, and for another he deals with passion rather too delicately and conventionally, so that we find it hard to feel *with* any of the main characters. Thus, Stephen Smith has an older friend, a Londoner and an intellectual, Henry Knight, who visits Cornwall and falls in love with Elfride once Stephen has gone to India to make his fortune. Knight, who is a study of the relationship between passion and propriety, cannot bear the thought that Elfride may have been kissed by anyone before himself. In this he resembles Angel Clare in *Tess*; but where Angel integrates this conventional obsession into a larger whole that involves us in a conflict between the social and the natural, Knight strikes us as little more than a prig, a man whose maturity is called into question by his psychological quirk.

Elfride is caught between two loves, Smith and Knight, and to some extent she embodies the true love of the maiden for the honest young lad struggling with the false love she feels for an older man who is her intellectual and perhaps social superior. This trap is in Hardy's own territory, but we are not taken deeply enough into Elfride's reactions for Hardy's strength to show itself.

Propriety has been offended because Elfride and Stephen, before his departure for India, have spent the night together in two trains, first up to and then down from London, in an abortive elopement. This indiscretion was witnessed by the melodramatic character old Mrs Jethaway, an avenging figure who hates Elfride because her disdain brought Mrs Jethaway's son, Felix, to an

---

[3] In fact Stephen's father is exactly what Hardy's was, a 'master-mason'.

early grave. At one point Elfride and Stephen discover themselves to be sitting on this very grave, and this is one of several places in the novel where Hardy introduces a burial motif. Young Smith, for instance, has come to Elfride's father's parish to organize the restoration of the church there, a job which inevitably involves scenes in the graveyard. Then Elfride acts as a sort of second mother to the children of a local widower, Lord Luxellian, whose family vault we twice visit for extended periods. Finally, the train that brings Smith and Knight, separately, back to Cornwall from London has an ominous black coach attached to it which turns out to contain the coffined body of Elfride.

From this the novel's structure can be inferred. 'The poor man', Stephen Smith, courts 'the lady' and departs for India. In his absence an older, richer gentleman, Henry Knight, courts her. Neither is successful. Elfride escapes from their rivalry into the shadowy arms of a local peer and shortly dies. There is much coincidence and contrivance in this. Knight does not realize that the young woman whom Smith has praised to him is the Elfride with whom he falls in love. Old Mr Swancourt does not realize that Smith is the son of a local mason. Smith and Knight several times talk at cross-purposes about Elfride. Mr Swancourt marries a woman who turns out to be a distant relative of Henry Knight's, which is how Knight is invited to spend time in Cornwall. Knight turns out to be the reviewer of a light romance written by Elfride. Stephen sends Elfride £200 which he has saved in Bombay, and she receives the present on the morning after Knight has left a valuable pair of earrings on her dressing-table, also as a present. When Stephen returns from Bombay he goes to Liverpool and thence by boat to Bristol; as he sails up the Bristol Channel he looks towards the Cornish coast through a telescope and sees Knight and Elfride looking at *him*, also through a telescope. Thus the contrivances develop through the novel to the final great coincidence whereby Stephen, Knight and the body of Elfride all travel down to Cornwall together on the same train, each unaware of the others. It is interesting that Hardy comments on coincidence early in the novel:

Strange conjunctions of phenomena, particularly those of a trivial, everyday kind, are so frequent in an ordinary life that we grow used to their unaccountableness, and forget the question whether the very long odds against such juxtaposition is not almost a disproof of it being a matter of chance at all.

(chapter 8)

Here Hardy makes the assumption that coincidence is the work of chance, but draws our attention to the *prima facie* improbability of such an assumption. In the world of his fiction the novelist creates the 'juxtaposition', but who creates it in the 'real' world?

A Pair of Blue Eyes, then, is marred by conventionality and contrivance, and its value as autobiography is necessarily concealed from us. It is also marred by Hardy's efforts at social satire. These involve aristocrats and London, as they do in all his lesser novels, and they are not happy. The scene in Hyde Park in this novel, for instance, is in transparent imitation of a rather uninteresting literary convention that was already showing signs of weariness in the hands of Thackeray in 1847. Hardy is simply not very good at aristocrats or at brittle urban satire.

This is not to say, however, that the novel is altogether a failure. I have singled it out as the best among Hardy's minor novels because it does have several moments of insight, comedy and narrative power that rank with the best of their kind.

Stephen Smith travels to the Swancourts' house for the first time in a 'dog-cart' driven by a Cornish local who is none the less amusing for the fact that his accent and manner of speech are not Cornish at all. His tales to Stephen of how the first Lord Luxellian came by his title and other matters are most attractive.

King Charles came up to him like a common man, and said off-hand, 'Man in the smockfrock, my name is Charles the Second; will you lend me your clothes?' 'I don't mind if I do,' said Hedger Luxellian . . .

(chapter 2)

Another rustic, William Worm, almost rises to the Joseph Poorgrass[4] level, being particularly remarkable for the permanent noise in his ears of fish frying.

At a different level there are some well-articulated moments of confusion and embarrassment such as Henry Knight's purchase of the earrings. He is quite unable to decide which pair to buy, and loses sleep, money and time in his 'tergiversation', which reduces him to 'a perfect heat of vexation'. The lengthy paragraph that describes this (chapter 20) is realistic and witty and quite without the strain into which Hardy's prose so often slips when his characters are beyond the boundaries of Wessex.

One of the most remarkable episodes in the novel is that in which Knight and Elfride nearly fall off the Cliff Without a Name to their deaths. Elfride climbs quickly to safety, but Knight is left for several minutes suspended above the abyss by his hands alone.

[4] Cf. *Far from the Madding Crowd.*

Hardy embarks at this point on a *tour de force* in which he achieves briefly that quality of integration which I have stressed in previous chapters. The episode (chapters 21–2) is far too long to quote here, but it stands out, among all Hardy's writings, as the point at which he most successfully brings together the past and the present, the eternal, malevolent cliff and the individual beings thrown up by time, from fossils to Mr Henry Knight. It is also an exciting and dramatic description of that staple situation of adventure stories, the narrow escape from death.

I think it is only in episodes such as this that *A Pair of Blue Eyes* rises to a level of success at which it can claim an independent existence. It may say something about changing critical criteria that this novel received lavish praise from Coventry Patmore, and was the novel of Hardy's that Tennyson most admired and that Proust would most have liked to write.

'THE TRUMPET-MAJOR' (1880)

There is a lightness about *The Trumpet-Major* that we do not find elsewhere in Hardy except in *Under the Greenwood Tree*. Like that earlier novel, it is a love story in which there are tangles and disappointments and a sour note at the end. But in neither novel does the gloom set in too darkly. Certainly we are sympathetic to John Loveday in his wooing of Anne Garland and, certainly, he does not win her. When he walks out at the end of the novel it is without Anne and in the direction of a battlefield in Spain where he will meet his death, but his hopes are kept alive through most of the story, and Anne does promise her hand at the end to John's brother Bob, with whom we also have some sympathy. Moreover all Anne's suitors – John, Bob and Festus Derriman – are capable of bearing up under the weight of their varying infatuations. This is very different from the situation, for example, of Giles Winterborne in *The Woodlanders*, who is almost literally killed by Grace Melbury because he loves her. Giles's death is generated by the tragic forces within the novel, as is Mayor Henchard's death, and Tess's and Jude's. John Loveday, on the other hand, is killed long after the action of the novel is over, on an irrelevant battlefield in Spain. So although *The Trumpet-Major* ends with a death, it is not a tragic death. The novel is not even formally a tragedy; often enough it is a comedy, and in general it is a romance if not a fantasy.

Like *The Dynasts* it is the product of Hardy's lifelong interest in the Napoleonic War. A good deal of the novel is given over to the public events of that period, particularly as they affected dwellers on the South Coast of England where Napoleon was planning his invasion. Thus it is a historical novel, with all that that implies, as well as another variation on the theme of love's tangles. As a historical novel it suffers from some of the weaknesses of Scott's much earlier experiments, notably from an indulgence in historical detail and incident for its own sake. What we learn about the bustle of the South Coast as Englishmen prepare to meet the invader is interesting and even at times amusing, but it does not always have much to do with the story of the loves of Anne Garland. George III, for example, appears on occasion, more to impress the reader with Hardy's insight into George's interesting character than to advance the plot. The scene of the amateur drilling of the impromptu volunteers (chapter 23), although high comedy in Hardy's best tradition, is really only excellent background.

The Trumpet-Major can be said to succeed in what it sets out to do rather better than *A Pair of Blue Eyes*; but it does not set out to do so much. It is as if Hardy wanted to make some use of the Napoleonic War material he had collected so extensively, and chose, very naturally, to graft it on to the plot that came most readily from his pen, the ephemeral quadrangle of three men in pursuit of one woman that had been successful in *Far from the Madding Crowd* and other novels. This ambition is largely achieved in *The Trumpet-Major*, but not the ambition to write a great novel. A second-order success of this sort is naturally not as uneven as a novel, such as *A Pair of Blue Eyes*, that tries to be more and fails; none the less it has moments of insight and integration that are remarkably impressive in this rather bland context.

As an example, Festus Derriman's old uncle, Benjamin, lives in a decayed mansion called Oxwell Hall, and in describing it Hardy uses his most wryly observant and idiosyncratic style of description (chapter 6). One of the themes of the description is, precisely, that integration between nature and man which we have so often seen at work in the major novels. The Hall is built round a courtyard within which the miserly old Derriman keeps livestock; so it is built round a 'bed' of mud, manure and animals; the walls of the rooms are as damp as the walls of a cave, and mushrooms are growing up between the chinks of the larder floor.

As for the outside, Nature, in the ample time that had been given her, had so mingled her filings and effacements with the marks of human wear and tear upon the house, that it was often hard to say in which of the two or if in both, any particular obliteration had its origin.

(chapter 6)

Everything about the house bespeaks its owner's neglect, miserliness and slovenliness, but ominous signs from the human point of view (the Hall belongs to an 'extinct' aristocratic family; it is in ruins and filthy) are neutral or even hopeful from the point of view of nature: the pigs and geese thrive, as do the mushrooms. Nothing could more appropriately set off the person of the house's owner, old Derriman. Beneath the skin of his face, we are told, his skull can be seen; like the house he is on the way down fortune's slide, and his decay, too, is the direct action of nature in the shape of time; but if the house's decline also paradoxically means nature's advance, what are we to say of a man's decline? It is enough for nature that she can turn Oxwell Hall into a mushroom bed, but is it enough for nature to turn the wondrous piece of work that is man into worm's meat? Apparently.

In a more cheerful vein Hardy gives us a splendid description of the preparations for the wedding feast of Bob Loveday and his love, Matilda (chapter 16). The rustic mixture of lavishness (a pig is killed, and four chickens, and there is stuffed veal, pigeon pie and much else besides) with parsimony (the chickens are only 'supernumerary') is topped off with rural nervousness at the approach of a fine town lady (they kill the smaller and tenderer pig). Nor is this all, for behind their bustle is Hardy's ironic consciousness, in which we share, that Matilda is no fine lady at all and is quite used to rougher fare than the best pork. There is a gusto in Hardy's prose that entirely wins our sympathies and sustains his description at a level above the merely conventional. Of the Casterbridge 'strong beer' laid in for the occasion, for example, we are told much:

It was of the most beautiful colour that the eye of an artist in beer could desire; full in body, yet brisk as a volcano; piquant, yet without a twang; luminous as an autumn sunset: free from streakiness of taste; but, finally, rather heady . . . Anybody being brought up for drunk and disorderly in the streets of its natal borough, had only to prove that he was a stranger to the place and its liquor to be honourably dismissed by the magistrates, as one overtaken in a fault that no man could guard against who entered the town unawares.

(chapter 16)

Amusing as it is, even this passage rouses the suspicion (as does the whole novel) that in it Hardy is indulging himself, as a historian and a folklorist, in irrelevancies and that in stepping aside from his main purpose in the novel he steps aside from his main concerns as a novelist.

THE MINOR NOVELS

Hardy's first published novel was *Desperate Remedies* (1871). It lives up to its title in its slightly desperate construction, its principal fault being that it is constructed too much. It may be obvious to suggest that this difficulty arose because of Hardy's architectural training, but *Desperate Remedies*, as a glance at its contents page will show, is written according to a blueprint. Hardy said of his last novel, *Jude the Obscure*, that it was constructed 'almost geometrically'; so this quality of being carefully planned persists throughout his novels. To be carefully planned is not in itself a fault, but it can become one if it is carried to excess. In *Desperate Remedies* it verges on the absurd. Hardy was consciously trying to write a novel with a complex plot, as he had been advised to do, and his success is painful. For a complex plot to satisfy, it has to be satisfyingly ingenious. Hardy, it seems, did not have the ingenious mind of Wilkie Collins or Dickens: we never reach the point in any novel of Hardy's where we are overcome by the delicious sensation of total bafflement that Dickens arouses in us, the sensation of helplessness in the hands of an author who, alone and by magic, will somehow bring all things to a satisfactory conclusion. The dissatisfaction is in large part because we are not able fully to believe in or sympathize with the characters in the Novels of Ingenuity (*Desperate Remedies*, *The Hand of Ethelberta* and *A Laodicean*), and our failure is attributable to certain manners and mannerisms of Hardy's prose. We have arrived, inevitably I think, at the question whether Hardy 'writes badly'.[5]

Of course, Hardy writes brilliantly. The opening chapter of *The Return of the Native* should be in any anthology of English prose and reaches a height that Hardy often reached. But he never writes neutrally; he never settles for the merely adequate or conventional; there is always something more. I would challenge readers to open any Hardy novel at any place and to read at random imagining that he had to guess the author. Within two

---

[5] A critical chestnut. Cf. e.g. Lord David Cecil, *Hardy the Novelist* (see Reading List), and, for a profounder treatment, the Hardy chapter of David Lodge's *Language of Fiction* (London: Routledge and Kegan Paul, 1966), pp. 164–88.

sentences, or at most three, he will find that the tone and the cadence of the English are quite unmistakable, apart from the other pieces of evidence such as Hardy's curious nomenclature, his use of dialect or his characteristic use of quotations. This tone and this cadence usually work very well, but sometimes they betray him into strange quirks and oddities. By always avoiding a neutral style Hardy takes an enormous risk: when inspiration fails him he has no safety-net into which he can fall.

It is impossible to separate things like tone and cadence from the other elements in a piece of prose; they are interdependent with what is being said in that particular tone. Form and content are finally inseparable. Consequently it comes about that where a writer's inspiration fails in terms of content, the failure will be signalled in the form.

As an example we can consider Hardy's insistence on Cytherea Graye's walk and posture in *Desperate Remedies*. It does not strike us as a very happy idea that the girl's attractiveness should depend on her capacity to move gracefully; it is something that we can imagine but are inclined to dismiss as weak and improbable. When she is interviewed by Miss Aldclyffe, who wants a lady's maid, Cytherea is at first informed that she will not do:

Cytherea turned away to the door. The movement chanced to be one of her masterpieces. It was precise: it had as much beauty as was compatible with precision, and as little coquettishness as was compatible with beauty.

And she had in turning looked over her shoulder at the other lady with a faint accent of reproach in her face. Those who remember Greuze's 'Head of a Girl', have an idea of Cytherea's look askance at the turning. It is not for a man to tell fishers of men how to set out their fascinations so as to bring about the highest possible average of takes within the year: but the action that tugs the hardest of all at an emotional beholder is this sweet method of turning which steals the bosom away and leaves the eyes behind.

Now Miss Aldclyffe herself was no tyro at wheeling . . .

(chapter 4)

Here is the sort of trap into which Hardy falls when his idiosyncrasies lead him astray. Having decided on an unhappy idea, his inability to write neutrally means that the idea becomes less and less happy. Cytherea turns away from the older woman, and her movement is a 'masterpiece', which is hardly the word for so momentary a thing as a movement, and, what is worse, it 'chances' to be a masterpiece: the slightly archaic 'chance' has sonorous overtones which, although employed successfully elsewhere by Hardy, are unnecessary here. The elaboration of the idea that follows ('It was precise . . .') is contained in an aphoristic sentence of the most perfect shape: beauty–compatible–precision, coquett-ishness–compatible–beauty. But for all its balance, the sentence is meaningless at first and even second reading, and this is because it refers to a vaguely defined physical gesture to which it is not particularly appropriate.

Next comes the comparison with a painting, a favourite device of Hardy's. Instead of trying to describe Cytherea he lapses into pedantic parallels. No doubt the Greuze painting does capture on canvas the evanescent moment of the backward glance of the girl, but unless we are familiar with the picture we have to take this on trust. It is as if Hardy were trying to describe an unknown quantity x by likening it to an almost-unknown quantity y; the comparison hardly helps, and looks like showing off. As in the previous sentences, Hardy is trying too hard. His 'masterpiece', his 'precision' of 'beauty' and his Greuze are all too strong, too much for the context.

Next he uses two more favourite devices, the biblical quotation and the generalization from a particular incident. The quotation in this case is grotesque, even blasphemous, and pointlessly so. The 'fishers of men' were the first apostles; here they are women who wish to attract men. The tastelessness is apparent even to a non-Christian; there is no inner connexion between Christ's metaphor and Hardy's. The extension of the metaphor does not improve it: even in Hardy's sense Cytherea is not a 'fisher' – quite the reverse – and the only other candidate for the title is the female reader of the novel, who may well reject it. When we come to the generalization, to the effect that the over-the-shoulder parting glance is the most effective action a woman can take to interest a beholder, we are not convinced.

In the concluding sentence, Hardy seems to have thrown his hand in altogether. To escape from the sexual irrelevancies of the preceding paragraph he has to turn back to Miss Aldclyffe to reassure us that her interest in Cytherea is aesthetic and not erotic. In doing so, he almost destroys her. The apparently frank logical step implied by the 'now' lends the sentence unpromising weight (obviously this matter of turning is going to be discussed for another paragraph) and the words 'tyro' and 'wheeling' have the wrong meaning and the wrong tone. A 'tyro' is a beginner, an apprentice, and the word implies that the graceful turn, as executed so spontaneously by Cytherea, is a matter of training. 'Wheeling' is military or ornithological, anything but delicately sexual.

Desperate Remedies is not nearly so bad a novel as this analysis implies. There are moments of insight and examples of well-chosen words and phrases in the book, just as there are moments of oddity and quirkiness even in *The Woodlanders* and *Tess*; but I think that here, in the Novels of Ingenuity, Hardy's faults can most clearly be seen. They amount to a sort of alienation of the reader à la Brecht. After reading the description of Cytherea turning we simply cannot take her or Miss Aldclyffe seriously any more. When this method of Hardy's is successful (as it largely is in the major novels) we delight in the ironic distance imposed between author and character. When we read, for instance, that Eustacia Vye would have done well on Olympus 'with a little preparation' (RN, Book First, chapter 7) we are being held at just the right arm's length from an uncritical immersion in her rich and sensual personality. But when we are expected to become involved in the destinies of a rather conventional girl and the unstable woman who employs her, and to identify with them through imagery and language such as I have quoted, we find it cannot be done: instead of coming closer to them we draw off in alienated consciousness of their contrivance and absurdity.

We can learn much from *Desperate Remedies* about Hardy's views and concerns. As in all the novels, there are asides and interjections that certainly contribute to our overall picture of Hardy's work. For example:

With all, the beautiful things of the earth become more dear as they elude pursuit; but with some natures utter elusion is the one special event which will make a passing love permanent for ever.
(chapter 1)

This is a commonplace elsewhere in Hardy, but its presence here helps to confirm it as his constant view, and his way of expressing it, although confident, opens the door to the possibility that 'some natures' are perhaps not altogether in the right; certainly it is not everyone, according to this dictum, who is doomed to perpetual dissatisfaction. Here is a less commonplace observation:

If anything on earth ruins a man for useful occupation . . . it is the habit of writing verses on emotional subjects which had much better be left to die for want of nourishment.
(chapter 3)

Something of the same sentiment is expressed in his poem 'I Look into My Glass', of which the first stanza runs

I look into my glass,
And view my wasting skin,
And say, 'Would God it came to pass
My heart had shrunk as thin!'

(CP p. 81)

Here the poet laments his sensitivity: emotional subjects are dangerous. The relevance to Hardy of the other part of the quotation from *Desperate Remedies* (that emotions are kept alive by writing poetry) is apparent from his whole poetic career.

In at least two places in *Desperate Remedies* Hardy finds his own voice, and we are given moments of insight of the sort we experience with Henry Knight as he clings to the cliff face in *A Pair of Blue Eyes*. As Aeneas Manston tries to kill time by wandering about in the Strand he sees, without taking much notice of it, the great procession of humanity as it flows past him:

Each and all were alike in this one respect, that they followed a solitary trail like the inwoven threads which form a banner, and all were equally unconscious of the significant whole they collectively showed forth.

(chapter 16)

Earlier in the novel Manston peers into a rainwater butt and learns the converse lesson, this time in microcosm:

Staves of sunlight slanted down through the still pool, lighting it up with wonderful distinctness. Hundreds of thousands of minute living creatures sported and tumbled in its depth with every contortion that gaiety could suggest; perfectly happy, though consisting only of a head, or a tail, or at most a head and a tail, and all doomed to die within twenty-four hours.

(chapter 12)

Evidence that, even in his lesser works, Hardy's broad-ranging imagination is never altogether dormant is met again in *The Hand of Ethelberta* (1876) and *A Laodicean* (1881). In the first of these, one of Hardy's love stories is unsuccessfully grafted on to a social satire; the novel, subtitled 'A Comedy in Chapters', is a light and attractive tale of some charm. Perhaps because of the satirical concern of the novel Hardy offers us everything at a superficial level, even Ethelberta's heart and hand. Although we miss the insight and scope of the major work, we have here a fast-moving and intriguing, if unconvincing, story. Its greatest interest may be in the ambiguous attitude towards class adopted by Ethelberta. She is the daughter of a butler, and is therefore from approximately the same point on the social scale as Hardy himself. Like Hardy, but much earlier in life, she rises, and to the very highest levels of society. The most interesting and convincing emotion displayed in the novel arises from this position of Ethelberta's. She wants to help her parents and her numerous brothers and sisters: this is the spur with which she drives herself upwards; also, she wants to succeed and to be admired. But she is on dangerous ground once she moves above her own level, and she frequently suffers real and imagined insults. She is not altogether happy in high life. Like Jude Fawley (and Tess Durbeyfield and Grace Melbury and Thomas Hardy) she is in what Raymond Williams has called the 'border country' between classes.[6]

Paula Power, George Somerset and Captain de Stancy, the main characters of *A Laodicean*, are also in border country. George Somerset, a young architect, is obviously so, and in Hardy's own way. Paula is the heiress to millions but is obsessed by not being of an 'old' family; de Stancy, on the other hand, is all old family but has no money. Paula has not established her claim to a place in the county aristocracy in spite of her money. De Stancy cannot lose his place as an aristocrat, but he cannot maintain it either. These contrapuntal ironies occupy Hardy at length in this weak novel, largely dictated from a sickbed. Nearly all of his commoner themes and motifs appear here in various forms, and this interests the Hardy student, but none of them is developed organically 'inside' the plot; the novel, far from showing an integrated and worked-out unity shows bits and pieces of Hardy's mind scattered about in a thin story.

In the year following *A Laodicean* Hardy wrote *Two on a Tower* (1882), which is a clear bid to return to the seriousness and scope of *The Return of the Native* (1878): it is not successful in this, and, interestingly, there was a four-year gap between *Two on a Tower* and *The Mayor of Casterbridge* (1886), the novel which ushers in the greatest phase of Hardy's career as a novelist (1886–96). It is almost as if the mainstream of Hardy's inspiration deserted him after *The Return of the Native* for seven years during which he produced only two novels, and those weak. *Two on a Tower* has a setting which reduces Egdon Heath to insignificance just as Egdon reduces men to insignificance; it is set against the heavens. The hero is Swithin St Cleeve, an aspiring astronomer whose involvement with the heroine, Lady Constantine, is brought about by her possession of a tower which he uses

6 See Reading List.

as an observatory. For most of the novel he looks on her as a benefactress who is kind enough to purchase him a good telescope and to help finance his studies; she is, after all, ten years his senior. But she falls in love with him and, ultimately, he with her. Their union is hampered by the uncertain status of Lady Constantine's husband, supposed dead in the heart of Africa. After Swithin and Lady Constantine have secretly married, the husband is found to be, indeed, dead, but his death occurred after the secret marriage, which is therefore invalid.[7]

There are several features of this story to interest the student of Hardy. First there is the matter of the astronomical background. Swithin is lyrical about the immensities of space and we can feel Hardy's own awed sense of the universe gaining on him as he talks:

The actual sky is a horror . . . You would hardly think, at first, that horrid monsters lie up there waiting to be discovered by any moderately penetrating mind . . . Impersonal monsters, namely, Immensities . . . monsters of magnitude without known shape . . . Those are deep wells for the human mind to let itself down into . . . And to add a new weirdness to what the sky possesses in its size and formlessness, there is involved the quality of decay. For all the wonder of these everlasting stars, eternal spheres, and whatnot, they are not everlasting, they are not eternal; they burn out like candles . . .

(chapter 4)

In the sentence that follows, Hardy even has Swithin *pitying* the stars for their evanescence, a conceit that gives a good image of Hardy's calm realism. It is true that space is a horror, and it is also true that the stars are pitiable, just as it is true that for all man's grandeur and suffering he is in the end a useless passion. The one point reflects the other: it takes a human mind to see the horror and the pathos of the stars and, conversely, it is because of the indifference to him of the universe that man's plight is so hopeless; as Swithin puts it, 'It is just the same in everything; nothing is made for man.'

Nature takes second place to this quasi-supernatural background, although, of course, there are several descriptions of

---

[7] It is worth noticing how constantly Hardy worries at this question; what is a legal marriage? The details of matrimonial law play a substantial part in the plots of DR (where the marriage is invalid because Manston's wife is still living), FFMC (where Bathsheba hides behind the legal point that she may not remarry for seven years after Troy's disappearance, his body not having been found), RN (where Wildeve fails initially to procure the right licence), TT (as described here), WL (where Melbury tangles with the new divorce law), TD (where, in the original version, Alec stages a mock marriage in order to seduce Tess) and, of course, JO *passim.*

natural scenes. The first sentences of the first and seventh chapters, for instance, have a curious, grotesque and almost surrealist effect.

On an early winter afternoon, clear but not cold, when the vegetable world was a weird multitude of skeletons through whose ribs the sun shone freely . . .

(chapter 1)

A fog defaced all the trees of the park that morning; the white atmosphere adhered to the ground like a fungoid growth from it, and made the turfed undulations look slimy and raw.

(chapter 7)

Hardy is unromantic about nature: he describes it honestly in its beauty and honestly in its less pleasant aspects.

A third feature of the novel is the equation it makes between love and deception. Swithin is an artless young man, but once the scales fall from his eyes and he sees that Lady Constantine is in love with him, Hardy comments:

St. Cleeve's sudden sense of new relations with that sweet patroness had taken away in one half-hour his natural ingenuousness. Henceforth he could act a part.

(chapter 13)

When they decide to get married they feel that they have to keep the matter secret; various complex arrangements are discussed, and Lady Constantine exclaims, 'See what deceits love sows in honest minds!' (chapter 15). Love is a great but dangerous power, spreading deceit and suffering, and levelling men down. When Swithin, in turn, falls in love with his patroness, we read:

The alchemy which thus transmuted an abstracted astronomer into an eager lover – and, must it be said? spoilt a promising young physicist to produce a common-place inamorato – may be almost described as working its change in one short night.

(chapter 14)

It is as well to bear this view of love in mind, as a counterbalance to the natural assumption that love represents the highest human value in Hardy. Love, after all, frequently kills in his novels. Usually the deed is carried out through a third agency (Egdon Heath, the law) but in *Two on a Tower* the effect is immediate, and the novel ends with Lady Constantine dead in Swithin's arms, killed directly by the vicissitudes of her affair with him.

The Well-Beloved (1897), Hardy's last published novel, takes up a theme that was obviously one of Hardy's minor but abiding concerns. It tells the story of a man, Jocelyn Pierston, whose fate it is to fall in love with a certain face, whoever possesses it. Thus the simple plot concerns his amatory interest in three generations of girls from the same family: mother, daughter and granddaughter. These three, all of whom are called Avice Caro, develop the well-beloved face when they are about twenty, so Pierston falls in love with them respectively when he is twenty, forty and sixty. This theme works well enough in Hardy's poetry, for instance in 'Heredity' (CP p. 434) and in a poem itself called 'The Well-Beloved' (CP p. 133), but is a very slight structure on which to build a novel. None the less there is a haunting quality about this bizarre plot, and by the time we meet Avice number two the novel has developed something of the tone of *Lolita*. Even Pierston wonders whether there may not be something 'abnormal' about a love in which adolescent yearning for the unattainable and voyeurist masochism predominate. Like *Jude the Obscure* this slight novel casts up for our consideration the nice question of the balance we strike between unconfined sexuality and social sexual conventions, and between these and the ideal of romantic love. These are cast up but they are not really explored and explained as they are in *Jude*. Hardy subtitled *The Well-Beloved* 'A Sketch of a Temperament' and that is the level it is written at; we are left with a sketch which haunts us, but are puzzled to know what to do with it.

Hardy's four volumes of short stories (thirty-six stories and nine brief pieces collected as 'A Few Crusted Characters') are made up largely of oddities and curiosities, many of them taken from country gossip and tradition, and of examples of 'life's little ironies' in the shape of stories that turn on the chance intrusions of fate. Nearly all of them echo some aspect of the novels.

The debt to country gossip is freely admitted in the Preface to *Wessex Tales* (1888) in which something is said about the traditional sources of four of the seven stories in that volume. There is even a later addition to the Preface in which Hardy points out that although he had no original source for another of the stories (called, significantly, 'A Tradition of Eighteen Hundred and Four') he was surprised to be told that the incident recounted in that story corresponded to a 'real tradition'. In other words, he was at some pains to establish the truthful basis of his tales, and can be seen here as the chronicler of country events, concerned that traditional stories should be recorded. On the other hand, this antiquarian purpose was certainly not Hardy's only motive. It is noticeable that he selects certain sorts of tradition to retail, and he handles them in his own characteristic manner. He says at the end of his Preface that 'the stories are but dreams, and not records'.

The second point about the stories (that they explore the ironic concatenations of fate) largely applies to the other three volumes. *Life's Little Ironies* (1894) lives up to its title: for instance, in the story 'A Tragedy of Two Ambitions' circumstances so arrange themselves that two brothers, Christians and clergymen, are able to hear their father drowning and deliberately to delay going to his rescue in time to save him. This piece of inhumanity, far from bringing them the expected release from worry, destroys their peace of mind and their self-contentment. The outstanding story in *Life's Little Ironies*, however, is 'An Imaginative Woman', a story in which a woman staying in lodgings in 'Solentsea' falls in love with the young poet who normally occupies the room she has taken. Her imagination leads her to develop a passion for him even before she has met him. He, meanwhile, in his loneliness, writes passionate verse to an imaginary woman. Eventually he commits suicide and in his suicide note explains that he has taken that step for good reasons, but that perhaps he would not have done so had there been some female 'tenderly devoted' to him. Mrs Marchmill, the imaginative woman, has never revealed herself to the poet except in letters signed with a false, masculine name. Here two lives are destroyed by that little irony; and, after Mrs Marchmill's own death, her husband even repudiates his little son, because, by some mysterious influence, the boy looks like the dead poet. Little ironies can breed big disasters.

Hardy's third volume of stories, *A Group of Noble Dames* (1891), combines narrative about the whims of fate with a pseudo-traditional background. Each of the stories is told by a different member of the South Wessex Field and Antiquarian Club, and this, together with the historical material incorporated into the tales, gives the impression that we are listening to minor Dorset legends. But once again we are really listening to Hardy's view of the perversities of circumstance. To give one example: in the story of Anna, Lady Baxby, Anna is married to a cavalier nobleman during the Civil War and finds herself besieged with him in his castle by her Parliamentarian brother. This is a typically ironic Hardyan trap: Anna has not chosen the war, nor has she chosen which side to support, but here she is, painfully caught. First she tells her brother that he must change sides; then, annoyed with her husband, she steals out of his bedroom intending to join her brother; she puts on her husband's hat and cloak and is accosted by a girl who has been waiting to keep an assignation with Baxby; in her jealousy, she becomes a Royalist once more and returns to keep an eye on her husband. That is all. The interest of the story for Hardy must lie in its only marked characteristic, which is the part played by tiny chances and unforeseeable turns of events in deciding major issues of principle.

A Changed Man (1913) is a collection of various sorts of story written over a period of twenty years or more. One of them, 'The Waiting Supper', shows Hardy at his most grotesquely mannered in his pursuit of the ironic twist. Christine loves Nicholas, but circumstances dictate that she should marry one Bellston, who turns out to be a bad lot. Bellston disappears and, after the legal period has expired, Christine and Nicholas decide to marry. On the evening before the wedding a messenger arrives with Bellston's luggage and says that Bellston himself will shortly arrive. He never does, but since his existence seems to be confirmed by the luggage, Nicholas and Christine have to postpone their wedding until the legally required seven years are again up. By that time they have rather lost heart. One day, when they have started to grow old, Bellston's skeleton is found in the nearby river; it appears that he was accidentally drowned there on the night when he should have followed his luggage to the house. So Nicholas could have married Christine on the day that he planned to, and Hardy adds the twist that Bellston's skeleton has lain under the water only a few yards from the place to which the lovers used frequently to walk and where they so often lamented their fate.

I have given a brief sketch of this and of some other stories to show the relationship they bear to the novels. The macabre, heavily structured and ironic plot of *Jude the Obscure*, for instance, has something in common with that of 'The Waiting Supper'. Jude's interest in Sue Bridehead is aroused, before he has met her, by her photograph and by 'the idea' of her, in a way similar to Mrs Marchmill's interest in the young poet. Tess's defeat when she tries to visit old Mr Clare's parsonage is caused by a chance encounter rather in the way that Lady Baxby's loyalties are altered. These parallels do not constitute the only interest of the stories, of course, but they are instructive and important.

I think it is interesting, finally, to consider Hardy's style in his stories. He is brisker, shallower, more direct, less allusive, less metaphorical, more concrete and less sensitive. If we consider the opening passages of some of the stories this is at once apparent:

The widely-discussed possibility of an invasion of England through a Channel tunnel has more than once recalled old Solomon Selby's story to my mind . . .

('A Tradition of Eighteen Hundred and Four')

Here stretch the downs, high and breezy and green, absolutely unchanged since those eventful days . . .

('The Melancholy Hussar of the German Legion')

It was an eighty-cow dairy, and the troop of milkers, regular and super-numerary, were all at work . . .

('The Withered Arm')

Something delayed the arrival of the Wesleyan minister, and a young man came temporarily in his stead . . .

('The Distracted Preacher')

When William Marchmill had finished his enquiries for lodgings at the well-known watering-place of Solentsea in Upper Wessex, he returned to the hotel to find his wife . . .

('An Imaginative Woman')

The man who played the disturbing part in the two quiet feminine lives hereunder depicted – no great man, in any sense, by the way – first had knowledge of them on an October evening, in the city of Melchester . . .

('On the Western Circuit')

In these examples we are presented with the personality of the storyteller (of two storytellers in the first case) or with a specific piece of information, or a lot of information all at once, or a story-teller *and* information, as in the last example. We are not in much doubt, here or when the stories are in mid career, that these *are* stories. Hardy finds the right 'gear' in which to tell his tales; he presses on to the point with few digressions. Here, if anywhere, is the 'country' Hardy, the fireside tale-teller; but this is a very different Hardy from the author of the major novels.

9

The Poems

Hardy is unique in being a major novelist and a major poet. All his verse was published after he had stopped writing novels, but it appears that he actually wrote verse throughout the seventy years of his adult life. His earliest extant poem, 'Domicilium', may have been written as early as 1857, and his last poems were apparently dictated from his deathbed. This extraordinarily long period of productivity accounts for the great number of poems that constitute the *Complete Poems*,[1] nearly a thousand lyrics, ballads, odes, satires and epitaphs. Some of them can be clearly dated; most cannot. Hardy revised many of them after they were written, sometimes years after. Some of the most famous of them were generated by emotions connected with events of half a century earlier. In other words, his poems are held together by a web of cross-reference that we may at first find disconcerting. We are used to the idea that a poet develops chronologically; we expect to see that development from volume to volume as the writer matures, and we are cheated of this in the case of Hardy. Once we have accepted that we cannot watch him develop, however, we can turn it into an advantage: as it is not often possible to make excuses for Hardy such as 'This is an early work', we are forced to take each poem independently and on its merits. Hardy had every opportunity of altering or suppressing poems, and we can be sure that the poems we do have are largely as he intended us to have them.

Hardy's poetry, however, comes to us as a coherent and consistent whole not merely because he was able to lay it all on the Procrustean bed of his later taste. It really seems that in many ways he himself did not develop from his early views, and that he never radically changed his mind either about life or about the sort of poetry he wanted to write. This sort of semi-biographical speculation is, of course, dangerous, but I think we must try to

[1] By this I mean James Gibson's definitive edition so-called. See Introduction, p. 4 above, for details.

account for the fact that the same ideas, world view and poetic techniques appear in poems written in the 1860s and in the 1920s. Hardy's poetry is extraordinarily homogeneous and highly characteristic: it can usefully be seen as a whole, and each individual part of that whole is unmistakably Hardy's own.

Neither Hardy's reputation as a novelist nor the reputations of his poetic contemporaries (Yeats, Pound, Eliot) should be allowed to obscure his achievement as a poet. His voice has come to be as important an influence on modern poetry as the method and style of Yeats or Eliot. Hardy is direct where they are obscure, and perceptive where they would perhaps not be concerned to look. It is futile to attempt a ranking of such writers, but it is significant that Philip Larkin and Helen Gardner have included so many poems by Hardy in their new Oxford books of verse.[2]

I have said that Hardy's work is about love and that he achieves an integration of love with the natural world and, beyond that, with a view of the cosmos. These three concerns are certainly present in his poems.

HARDY'S LOVE POETRY

Nearly half of Hardy's poems are concerned with love. This average is not maintained in his last three volumes, but even there love is an important topic: in *Late Lyrics and Earlier*, *Human Shows* and *Winter Words*, a quarter of the poems concern love. The love poetry characteristically comes in groups, at the beginning of *Wessex Poems*, for instance, or towards the end of *Poems of the Past and the Present*. A number of Hardy's poems are partly or entirely about love even when they appear to be about something quite different; thus, 'Panthera' (CP p. 280) contains a moving description of Panthera's love for Mary, although the poem is principally about Christ's paternity. Conversely, in 'The Bride-Night Fire' (CP p. 71) Hardy uses a love story for purposes other than those concerned with love; the poem's strength lies in its marvellous dialect, its narrative force, its bizarre detail and the strange tale it relates, not in what it says about love. On the whole, however, Hardy's poetry is as often about love as about all other topics put together.

The first thing that strikes us about this love poetry is that it tends to be impersonal. Hardy several times claimed that his verse

---

[2] Cf. Introduction, p. 3 above, for details.

was often 'dramatic and personative in conception',[3] and so it is.
He frequently speaks in the voices of others, and this imposes a
distance on the emotions he deals with: adopting other personalities keeps him impersonal. Thus, for instance, he has four Shakespearean sonnets of high quality which are collectively entitled
'She, to Him' (CP pp. 14–16). These appear to be early work
(they are dated 1866), and it is remarkable that as a young man
Hardy could choose to adopt the *persona* of a woman resignedly
asking for a little warmth and companionship from her lover and
proudly proclaiming fidelity although she has been scorned. 'She'
begins

> When you shall see me in the toils of Time,
> My lauded beauties carried off from me,
> My eyes no longer stars as in their prime,
> My name forgot of Maiden Fair and Free . . .

This opening quatrain from the first of the four sonnets is spoken
in the voice of a woman whose 'beauties' include eyes like stars;
it is, moreover, the soliloquy of a woman imagining herself as she
will be when she is old. Yet it is a love poem written by a twenty-six-
year-old man. This curious phenomenon is not unique to this
sequence of sonnets: Hardy speaks through a female *persona* time
and again. Consider the following titles: 'She at His Funeral',
'The Seasons of Her Year', 'Her Late Husband', 'Tess's Lament',
'She Hears the Storm'; these are only a few of the love poems in
which he impersonates a woman. Although most of his love poetry
is written from a masculine point of view, we need to account for
the large proportion of poems written as though by women, and
the even larger number written from a neutral point.

I suggest that Hardy did not differentiate between male and
female love. He seems to have seen love as an indifferent but
overwhelming force striking blindly among humanity like a sort
of divine disease. Certainly there is a parity in the novels between
the loves of the men (Boldwood's sudden infatuation, Giles Winterborne's patient devotion, Jude's ambiguous passion) and the loves
of the women (Eustacia Vye's obsessive need for love, Tess's
patient martyrdom, Sue Bridehead's ambiguous anti-passion).
What differentiates these loves is not sex but personality; Boldwood's love is more different in kind from Gabriel's than it is from
Bathsheba's brief infatuation with Troy. Once one has noticed this,

---

[3] Preface to *Wessex Poems*. Cf. also the Prefaces to *Poems of the Past and the Present*
and *Time's Laughingstocks*.

the impersonality of Hardy's love poems becomes more comprehensible. It also explains why it does not matter that we are really unable to decide whether a poem such as 'I Worked No Wile to Meet You' (CP p. 606) is spoken by a man or a woman. (The impersonality here is heightened by the subtitle 'Song'.) The first stanza sounds like a man speaking:

> I worked no wile to meet you,
>   My sight was set elsewhere,
> I sheered about to shun you,
>   And lent your life no care.

This feels as though it must come from a man who is remarking that he did not pursue a certain woman. But the second stanza opens 'You did not seek to see me', which seems to indicate the opposite, for if 'you' is a woman, then, in an Edwardian context, it is not surprising that she did not actively pursue the poet; but the poet *is* surprised, so perhaps the speaker is a woman and 'you' a man. This sort of ambiguity is unimportant, since Hardy is patently concerned with the intolerable chanciness of love rather than with, say, the praise of a particular woman.

A similarly neutral quality is present in other poems, such as 'Long Plighted' (CP p.140) in which one aged lover inquires whether it is now worth while to marry the other. Nowhere in the poem are we given any indication as to the sex of the speaker, who always refers to the other as 'dear', a favourite word in the poetry, and equally applicable to men or women. Another such word is 'friend', which takes impersonality a stage further in that it is not sex-specific and equally vague as to the relationship between the two parties. Thus we are left puzzling over 'An Experience' (CP p. 615), which, although it is not one of Hardy's major poems, is an excellent example of his impersonal method:

> Wit, weight, or wealth there was not
>   In anything that was said,
>   In anything that was done;
> All was of scope to cause not
>   A triumph, dazzle, or dread
>   To even the subtlest one,
>   My friend,
>   To even the subtlest one.
>
> But there was a new afflation –
>   An aura zephyring round
>   That care infected not:

It came as a salutation,
    And, in my sweet astound,
    I scarcely witted what
        Might pend,
    I scarcely witted what.

The hills in samewise to me
    Spoke, as they grayly gazed,
    – First hills to speak so yet!
The thin-edged breezes blew me
    What I, though cobwebbed, crazed
    Was never to forget,
        My friend,
    Was never to forget!

What is this poem about? 'An Experience' is the most general of titles. It is an experience of some sort of friendship, perhaps love if we interpret the second stanza imaginatively: a friendship that seemed commonplace either in general ('*All* was of scope to cause not/A triumph') or in one particular instance (the opening lines?). But we get no idea of the exact nature of the experience, or of how it gained 'a new afflation' or of how or why this 'aura' could be echoed by grey hills and cold breezes. All we know is that Hardy himself, assuming that he is not being 'personative', has not forgotten the experience. In this way we are thrust from the extremely impersonal level, at which this sort of poem is so generalized as to verge on the meaningless, straight on to the extremely personal level at which we have to say that the poem must have had some particular significance to Hardy that is unavailable to us.

This is the next remarkable point about Hardy's love poetry: though it is strangely impersonal it is also intensely personal.[4] In the famous 'Neutral Tones' (CP p. 12), for instance, we find both qualities. Two characters, lovers, are present in the poem, and though we naturally assume the speaker to be the man, Hardy himself perhaps, it is nowhere made clear that this is so. The poem associates the neutral tones of a winter's day with the 'loss' both lovers have sustained by loving; but the winter's day is not merely symbolic: it is a real, bitter memory. There we have the ambiguity: the poem is applicable to any lovers at the frozen end of love, and we can relate to it on a very wide general level, but it is also a vividly realized poignant moment from the poet's personal experience, a memory that rises up in him fully detailed:

[4] Of the 947 poems in CP, 155 begin with the word 'I'.

We stood by a pond that winter day,
And the sun was white, as though chidden of God,
And a few leaves lay on the starving sod;
   – They had fallen from an ash, and were gray.

In this first stanza only the first two words refer to the lovers; the rest is description. The description is symbolic, but it is also the exact observation of a countryman automatically noticing details at a traumatic moment.

This personal aspect of Hardy's love poetry is at its strongest in the sequence of poems written after his first wife's death and collected as 'Poems of 1912–13'. Coming to these, as we nearly all must, armed with the knowledge that they are *not* 'dramatic or personative' we can leave out of account Hardy's distancing of himself from emotion, and credit every memory and every movement of his mind with a complete personal involvement. I think that sometimes, as in 'An Experience', Hardy's impersonal technique can alienate us from him, but when he moves on to this personal ground he always takes us with him. Here he is direct, passionate and, above all, perceptive. He creates poetry from the welter of commonplace pangs and ponderings that make up our reaction to the destructive magnitude of death. So we recognize the reaction, are struck by Hardy's unerring observation of it, and are strongly inclined to believe in the true emotion behind each poem. 'The Walk' (CP p. 340) is an excellent example:

You did not walk with me
Of late to the hill-top tree
   By the gated ways,
   As in earlier days;
   You were weak and lame,
   So you never came,
And I went alone, and I did not mind,
Not thinking of you as left behind.

I walked up there today
Just in the former way;
   Surveyed around
   The familiar ground
   By myself again:
   What difference, then?
Only that underlying sense
Of the look of a room on returning thence.

The beautiful simplicity of this arises from the calm matter-of-fact tone Hardy adopts and from his avoidance of all metaphor, all intricacy of rhyme and rhythm and all inversion and complication of speech. Very few poets can succeed in the absence of these elements. What we *are* offered is one curious moment of sad wonder, one insight into the nature of loss clearly and poignantly presented; but for all this simplicity the emotion in the poem is too complicated for invention, too odd not to be Hardy's own. The general sense of loss is known to everybody and is apparent in the opening lines; the personal emotion is guaranteed by the personal details; the two merge in the last line where the 'room' is certainly the poet's own room – he means what he says – but is also all rooms that have changed aspect after a death or after any sort of loss.

This combination of the simple and the personal runs all through the 'Poems of 1912–13' and gives them a haunting intensity. It is really extraordinary how this works: Hardy must be the first major poet to have had the courage to seem naïve; I can imagine few poets before his day prepared to open a poem with the lines

> How she would have loved
> A party today! –

That this opening of 'Lament' (CP p. 344) now sounds relatively normal to a modern reader is an indication of Hardy's importance as an influence on modern poetry. Not all of the 'Poems of 1912–13' are at this level of directness, however, and at least one, 'Beeny Cliff' (CP p. 350), employs the long, bounding, alliterative lines of Swinburne which give it an air of complexity that is not entirely belied by its straightforward grammar.

Certain love poems of Hardy's combine the impersonal with the personal in an unusual way. These are the poems that he wrote about women and girls whom he *might* have loved. Sometimes these women are real and sometimes they are imaginary; but always the distance in time or the long odds against success contrive to distance the beloved both from Hardy and from the reader. The result is a number of poems that are personal to Hardy's memory and imagination but impersonal too in that they are principally exercises in nostalgia, the products of a distant emotion recollected in a regretful near-tranquillity. This is not intended as an adverse criticism. It is the very stuff of a ballad-writer to construct dramas and to re-enact the emotions that they generate; thus 'My Cicely' (CP p. 51) is a love story which although it is

distanced at once by its subtitle, which is the unspecified date
'17—', works as a poem about an imaginary love. This method is
greatly enhanced when the woman involved is one whom the poet
himself has known and admired, or one whom he might have
loved had things been otherwise. A major poem that falls into this
category is 'Thoughts of Phena' (CP p. 62), of which this is the
first stanza:

> Not a line of her writing have I,
>   Not a thread of her hair,
> No mark of her late time as dame in her dwelling, whereby
>   I may picture here there;
> And in vain do I urge my unsight
>   To conceive my lost prize
> At her close, whom I knew when her dreams were upbrimming
>   with light,
>   And with laughter her eyes.

This is magnificent in its bold rhythm and self-confident air of
elegy; and these formal aspects tend to impersonalize the poem.
At the same time it is intensely personal: the loss is detailed and
specific; the poet has no tangible trace of the dead woman: he
cannot even imagine what she looked like. But this is because he is
writing about a woman whom he has not seen for twenty years,
and we find that we have to take the phrase 'lost prize' as referring
both to the loss of death and to the loss that came about when
'Phena' and Hardy separated as lovers. There is controversy about
this aspect of his life. It is even possible that Hardy and his cousin
Tryphena were not lovers at all or that the episode existed only in his
mind, but in this poem there is a nostalgia both for what was, even if
it was not very much, and for what might have been, which is much.

This 'what might have been' is a constant theme. In 'At an Inn'
(CP p. 68) Hardy laments an occasion where the inn servants saw
him with another and assumed that they were lovers (if he means
himself and if the speaker is not a woman, which is unclear). The
poem asks why they were not lovers, since they seemed to be such,
and ends with a plaintive demand to circumstance to let them
again be as they then were. As we have seen so often in the novels,
it is one of the satires of man's circumstance that what might have
been has an endless power of attraction while what is can never
satisfy. Thus the poem 'To Lizbie Browne' (CP p. 130) is full of a
light, loving tenderness made the more poignant by the fact that
Lizbie was a girl Hardy had known only very slightly many years
before. He asks,

Dear Lizbie Browne,
Where are you now?
In sun, in rain? –
Or is your brow
Past joy, past pain,
Dear Lizbie Browne?

But the burden of this poem appears in stanzas VII, VIII and IX where the poet associates himself with the long-forgotten girl:

Dear Lizbie Browne,
I should have thought,
'Girls ripen fast,'
And coaxed and caught
You ere you passed,
Dear Lizbie Browne!

But, Lizbie Browne,
I let you slip;
Shaped not a sign;
Touched never your lip
With lip of mine,
Lost Lizbie Browne!

So, Lizbie Browne,
When on a day
Men speak of me
As not, you'll say,
'And who was he?' –
Yes, Lizbie Browne!

Time is to blame for this, we see: 'Girls ripen fast.' Regret is the mood of a man's memories, regret for kisses untaken, lovers uncaught. The poet's brief 'immortality' in the memories of others will not be 'immortality' in the mind of Lizbie Browne.

On survival after death through the memories of others, Hardy has several poems, notably 'Her Immortality' (CP p. 55) and 'His Immortality' (CP p. 143). Hardy never adopted Shakespeare's expedient of turning the tables and boldly claiming that the beloved is assured of immortality by the verses in which he or she is celebrated; although, without Hardy, who would have remembered Lizbie Browne a century later? But Hardy was a modest man, and his verse, in particular, has a reticent quality that is one of its great strengths: it is not the verse of a giant among pygmies but of a man among men.

I must qualify this by admitting that Hardy was not just 'a man' but a highly sensitive man. If he is the glorious exception to the rule that lyric poets do not substantially add to their reputations after the age of thirty-five, he must be credited with having retained his sensitivity to experiences such as love into the later part of his life. And so it proves. The poem that closes *Wessex Poems*, 'I Look into My Glass' (CP p. 81), makes it clear that in a universe where the susceptible suffer most this extra sensitivity is not altogether a boon:

> I look into my glass,
> And view my wasting skin,
> And say, 'Would God it came to pass
> My heart had shrunk as thin!'
>
> For then I, undistrest
> By hearts grown cold to me,
> Could lonely wait my endless rest
> With equanimity.
>
> But Time, to make me grieve,
> Part steals, lets part abide;
> And shakes this fragile frame at eve
> With throbbings of noontide.

NATURE IN HARDY'S POETRY

In his novels Hardy integrates his love stories into the natural background against which they are set. This integration is even more thoroughly carried out in his poetry, where moments of love and other experiences are framed by or commented on through their natural settings. I have quoted the first stanza of 'Neutral Tones', where the bitterness of the episode is echoed in the grey winter landscape. Other poems employ the same technique; for instance, 'At Middle-Field Gate in February' (CP p. 480). The first two stanzas describe the drops of water formed on the gate and on nearby branches by the fog, and further describe the ploughed field seen over the gate. The third and last stanza fulfils the sombre promise of this by changing tone and declaring that things were once different:

> How dry it was on a far-back day
>   When straws hung the hedge around,
> When amid the sheaves in amorous play
> In curtained bonnets and light array
>   Bloomed a bevy now underground!

This merging of an emotion with its setting, this employment of the Pathetic Fallacy, is frequent in Hardy, but it is also something that he feels he must contradict. Thus in 'On the Way' (CP p. 625) the weather is both foggy and windy, yet to the hopeful lover it is the best possible weather:

> . . . to his feet,
> Drawing nigh and nigher
> A hidden seat,
> The fog is sweet
> And the wind a lyre.

Here the movement of integration between setting and mood is complex. It does not simply operate as an irony, though that is the first thing that strikes us. The fog and the wind are described powerfully (fishes might 'fin a passage' through the mist, and drops of it gather on brambles 'with the cold listless lustre of a dead man's eye') – so powerfully that nature seems to overwhelm the footsteps of the lover or at least to reduce them to the sort of insignificance to which Egdon Heath reduces the 'wildest turmoil' of man.

Of course it is only in the passionate perception of the poet that the Pathetic Fallacy works; really there is no relationship between nature's mood and man's, and Hardy is well aware of it. In the sonnet 'A Wet August' (CP p. 578), for instance, he considers the possibility that the sunny August he remembers, 'full-rayed, fine', was just as dreary as this present wet August. Perhaps it seemed fine because of 'the golden chances seen in things' at that time, and because of the 'light' he bore within him. The ditty 'An Autumn Rain-Scene' (CP p. 612) makes this point conclusively.

I have stressed this tendency towards integration between Hardy's themes and their natural setting; it is also necessary to point out that he is one of the first poets to describe nature independently of human themes and purpose. He has a number of poems that deal with the world without any ulterior motive. There is a clutch of them in *Human Shows* which all deal with the same season of the year: 'Last Week in October' (CP p. 709), 'The Later Autumn' (CP p. 710) and 'Night-Time in Mid-Fall' (CP p. 731). The last is a good example of Hardy's direct description. Here is the complete poem:

> It is a storm-strid night, winds footing swift
> Through the blind profound;
> I know the happenings from their sound;

Leaves totter down still green, and spin and drift;
The tree-trunks rock to their roots, which wrench and lift
The loam where they run onward underground.

The streams are muddy and swollen; eels migrate
   To a new abode;
  Even cross, 'tis said, the turnpike-road;
(Men's feet have felt their crawl, home-coming late):
The westward fronts of towers are saturate,
Church-timbers crack, and witches ride abroad.

This poem is not associated with any particular mood of the poet's, nor with any experience or event beyond the stormy night itself. The poem is 'about' nature and only that. All through the first stanza we expect some sort of reference to something beyond. With the first line of the second stanza we begin to realize that we may not get it; only the final clause ('and witches ride abroad') turns our attention out away from the description and leaves us pondering these witches; are they symbols or are they a sort of serious joke?

Hardy is very good at this sort of single-minded and apparently pure description of nature. His first extant poem, the Wordsworthian 'Domicilium' (CP p. 3), has some sort of formal purpose, no doubt, connected with the original circumstances of its writing, but its immediate impact comes from its power to evoke the cottage and its surroundings. The poem has two movements: the first describes the cottage as it is now, and the second describes it as it was fifty years before the date of writing; both movements impress us with their directness. The first opens

   It faces west, and round the back and sides
   High beeches, bending, hang a veil of boughs,
   And sweep against the roof. Wild honeysucks
   Climb on the walls . . .

The second closes

   Our house stood quite alone, and those tall firs
   And beeches were not planted. Snakes and efts
   Swarmed in the summer days, and nightly bats
   Would fly about our bedrooms. Heathcroppers
   Lived on the hills, and were our only friends;
   So wild it was when first we settled here.

What is being attempted here is quite self-consciously 'poetic'. The young Hardy has learnt the power of alliteration and is experimenting with it remarkably successfully. Almost every idea introduced is supported by alliteration: the beeches bend their boughs from the back of the house, the snakes swarm in the summer, the bats fly about the bedrooms and the heathcroppers live on the hills. But this 'poetic' quality is almost irrelevant beside the direct appearance of tangible nature: the snakes seize our imaginations as they 'swarm' because of the concreteness and exaggeration of that verb, not because it begins with an 's'. Moreover the direct presentation is strengthened by Hardy's placing his key objects at the beginnings of sentences; this is clear in the passages quoted and also in such openings as

> Heath and furze
> Are everything that seems to grow . . .

and

> A stunted thorn
> Stands here and there, indeed . . .

It is appropriate that in his first extant poem Hardy pictures nature as a vivid and overshadowing setting for human existence.

In the end there is no such thing, in poetry anyway, as a pure description. Even Hardy's least-purposeful poems about nature quickly reveal an attitude towards it that implies a whole picture of the universe. 'Domicilium' is only mildly tinged with his characteristically candid *Weltanschauung*; other poems are more forceful. 'An Unkindly May', for instance (CP p. 841), shows us a shepherd counting his flock, unconscious of the weather, which is described thus:

> The sour spring wind is blurting boisterous-wise,
> And bears on it dirty clouds across the skies;
> Plantation timbers creak like rusty cranes,
> And pigeons and rooks, dishevelled by late rains,
> Are like gaunt vultures . . .

The imagery here shows the world as evil and ugly: sour, dirty, rusty, full of vultures. We are a long way from the pastoral tradition. We realize that, though the poem does not have a 'purpose' (the description is not merely the setting or background for some main action that concerns the poet), it has the deeper aim of awakening the reader to the unpleasant indifference of nature to man, or at least to the fact that nature often *is* unpleasant. Hardy frequently chooses the less-attractive times of the year as his subject: 'Shortening Days . . .', 'February', 'Last Week in October', 'At Day-Close

in November' and 'The Later Autumn', from which this stanza
is taken:

> Toadsmeat[5] is mangy, frosted, and sere;
> Apples in grass
> Crunch as we pass,
> And rot ere the men who make cyder appear.
> Couch-fires abound
> On fallows around,
> And shades far extend
> Like lives soon to end.
>
> (CP p. 710)

This 'Later Autumn' poem is, formally, going nowhere. It merely
describes characteristics of the season. But it gives a deep sense of
the evanescence and rottenness of universal nature, in which man
participates.

This leads me back to my starting point: Hardy writes poems
about nature and man together. The apparently pure or purpose-
less poem always tends to move back towards man, or at least to
establish an undertow that draws the reader towards a certain
view of the universe and therefore of man. Once again, as in the
novels, we find that the three layers (direct human interest, nature
and the cosmic) are being integrated. In some of his greatest poems
this happens quite explicitly. In 'Afterwards', for example (CP
p. 553), Hardy is considering his own death and people's reactions
to it: in between these personal (and universal) elements, and
constituting the main thrust of the poem, is a subtle movement
through a carefully chosen series of times, seasons and natural
phenomena. Will he be remembered, he asks, as someone who
'used to notice such things' as the delicate leaves of May, hawks at
dusk, hedgehogs at night, the winter sky and the irregularity of a
bell tolling on a windy night? The progression towards the grave
is faintly echoed in the move from a day in May to a winter's night.
In the last stanza the subtlest possible integration is achieved
between the poet's death, nature and the universal fact of death:

> And will any say when my bell of quittance is heard in the gloom,
> And a crossing breeze cuts a pause in its outrollings,
> Till they rise again, as they were a new bell's boom,
> 'He hears it not now, but used to notice such things'?

The poet himself is noticing this detail of the sound of a bell, and
it is *his* bell of course, his funeral knell. Beyond this is a fluctuating
breeze that cuts off the bell's sound; the phenomenon could only

---

[5] 'Toadsmeat' is a fungus.

be observed out of doors on a windy night: it is a trick of nature's. Finally there is the slightly suggested metaphor of the resurrection of the dead who may, or may not, 'rise again', renewed like the sound.

Less subtle, but also successful in its more explicit treatment of integration, is 'I Am the One' (CP p. 837). In this poem the poet observes that he is so familiar a figure – to nature, to man and to the cosmos – that he is scarcely noticed. In the first stanza he does not disturb the ringdoves in their cooing, and in the second he does not disturb the hares in their munching. In the third stanza he does not disturb a train of mourners, presumably in a grave-yard; the implication here is that the poet, too, is mourning a dead love. Nature and love (the senior human interest) come together in the final stanza in which his implied misery leads him to look askance at the stars. This is, of course, Hardy's character-istic move towards the cosmic.

> I hear above: 'We stars must lend
>   No fierce regard
>   To his gaze, so hard
>   Bent on us thus, –
> Must scathe him not. He is one with us
>   Beginning and end.'

HARDY'S NEGATIVE METAPHYSICS

Hardy's poetry is unusual in that it includes a substantial number of poems devoted to the direct exposition of his metaphysical views. Of course, we have a reasonably clear picture of Milton's view of the cosmos, and Wordsworth's and Pope's, but Hardy is almost unique in that his views are available in a series of brief lyrics. They are most fully expressed, perhaps, in *The Dynasts*, but even without that epic work we should be able to establish Hardy's metaphysics adequately from the lyrics, as we should not be able to do for Milton, Pope or Wordsworth in the absence of *Paradise Lost*, the *Essay on Man* or the *Prelude*.

Once again, the remarkable thing about this group of 'meta-physical' lyrics is their consistency. In chapter 1, I quoted the sonnet 'Hap'. This poem is dated 1866 and is thus one of Hardy's earliest, but it can be compared with a number of later poems, for example 'The Subalterns', and will be found to be consistent with them philosophically.

The 'subalterns' of this poem (CP p. 120) are not junior army officers, but the sky, the North wind, Sickness and Death. The point of the poem is that even these are subordinate to the blind laws that govern the universe. The stanza concerning the sky opens the poem, and it can be set against the opening of 'Hap'.

> 'Poor wanderer,' said the leaden sky,
> 'I fain would lighten thee,
> But there are laws in force on high
> Which say it must not be.'

'Hap' opens with the wish that 'some vengeful god' would call to the poet 'from up the sky'; the point there is that there is no god, vengeful or otherwise, to lend meaning to suffering: there are only the 'purblind Doomsters' who correspond exactly to the 'laws on high'.

Because of their own consistency these poems of Hardy's work coherently to prove that there is ultimately no coherent pattern in life. When the poet looks candidly at the universe and its blind laws he can see no sign or token of a deeper meaning, of a spiritual realm or of a god. Thus 'A Sign-Seeker' (CP p. 49) explores the idea of a sensitive soul 'pant[ing] for response' from the universe:

> But none replies;
> No warnings loom, nor whisperings
> To open out my limitings,
> And Nescience mutely muses: When a man falls he lies.

Similarly the poet in 'The Impercipient' (CP p. 67) describes himself thus:

> I am like a gazer who should mark
> An inland company
> Standing upfingered, with, 'Hark! hark!
> The glorious distant sea!'
> And feel, 'Alas, 'tis but yon dark
> And wind-swept pine to me!'

Here, incidentally, Hardy finds an image in nature, or rather in man's relationship with nature, to express his sense of cosmic emptiness. The image reinforces the opinion.

These poems are to be taken almost literally; a 'sign' in the shape of ghost or angel, a genuine 'perception' of the divine beyond, *anything* supernatural would directly affect the poet's views. However, Hardy also has another sort of poem in which he uses the apparatus of the Christian world view to make his point metaphorically. In these metaphorical poems the non-Christian abstractions (the 'Vast Imbecility', the 'Immanent Will') give place to Christian words such as 'Lord' and 'God' – for instance in 'God-Forgotten' (CP p. 123) in which Earth is described as having been created by God and then forgotten by him. Variations on this theme appear in 'God's Education' (CP p. 278) in which the poet has to tell God that death, whatever it may seem to him, is a cruelty to mankind, and 'By the Earth's Corpse' (CP p. 126) in which God claims to feel remorse for mankind's sufferings but did not alleviate them when he could have done. In a similar vein, 'The Bedridden Peasant' (CP p. 124) addresses his 'Unknowing God' in kind terms, not blaming him for the 'cleft' that separates him from man. The peasant's logic is that if God *knew* of his agonies he would prevent them but that, since he does not prevent them, he cannot know them. This condescension towards God appears even more strongly in 'A Plaint to Man' (CP p. 325) in which God asks man why man created him; God's objection is that he has been made in man's image and is vanishing beneath the onslaughts of scepticism. Not surprisingly, there is also a poem called 'God's Funeral' (CP p. 326).

I have given all these examples (and there are dozens more) to indicate the main, coherent movement of Hardy's metaphysical lyrics. The picture that emerges is unambiguous, and is exactly the picture that underlies the novels. The universe, according to Hardy, is intricately and rigidly structured; it is not possible to get 'behind' or 'beyond' the laws that control this structure; even if God existed (in other words), he too would be subject to the workings of the Immanent Will, or, to put it another way, he would *be* the Immanent Will. This is a poetic equivalent to A. J. Ayer's thesis in *Language, Truth and Logic*.[6] Ayer maintains that any propositions about what is 'beyond' the empiricially verifiable world are by definition nonsensical; similarly Hardy maintains that, in the absence of signs to the contrary, it is impossible to go beyond statements as to how things are. 'How things are' includes gravity and causality, felt good and bad, happiness and unhappiness, everything that is; anything which is added to this totality is meaningless. The totality is *metaphorically* summed up by the words

---

[6] One could say that Hardy is a logical positivist. (Ayer's book is simply the clearest and briefest exposition of positivism.) On the other hand, Hardy's language differs from Ayer's, and that makes him a very special kind of forerunner, whose links with the old world of belief very much colour his disbelief.

'Immanent Will'. This term is not to be taken supernaturally; things are not as they are 'because of' the Will: the Will is merely a word used to denote the collective dynamism of the world. Most important, the Will *is* immanent and not transcendent.

The clearest picture of Hardy's metaphysics in action is given in *The Dynasts*. As John Wain argues so cogently in his Introduction to the Macmillan edition of this 'epic-drama', Hardy was writing, although he did not realize it, for a medium then unavailable to him – the cinema. *The Dynasts*, 'an epic-drama of the war with Napoleon in three parts, nineteen acts and one hundred and thirty scenes', is constructed like the scenario of an 'epic' film. Sometimes we watch intimate action in detailed close-up, and sometimes we watch armies marching. Apart from the blank verse and some other theatrical and poetic conventions, *The Dynasts* could almost be filmed directly as a realistic historical drama. From our point of view, there is one interesting qualification that must be added to this view of the work: 'special photographic effects' would be needed to fulfil Hardy's demand for a celestial world seen at work above the action. This celestial world of 'supernatural spectators' appears frequently during the action of the drama, and its function is not so much to comment on that action as if it were a Greek tragic chorus as to use the action to illustrate the workings of the Immanent Will.

Two questions arise from this: what is the status of these supernatural spectators, and what is it that they show us? The answer to the first question is simple: in his Preface to *The Dynasts* Hardy states clearly that his spirits are only convenient devices: they have no literal significance:

They are intended to be taken by the reader for what they may be worth as contrivances of the fancy merely.

(DY, Preface)

He explains that he could not have used classical, Norse or Christian mythological figures for his purposes, as they offend against the prevalent 'Monism' of 'this twentieth century'. This word 'Monism' is our clue to an answer to our second question. The answer is that the spirits show us a monistic universe. The Immanent Will is not part of 'another' world; it is this world. Thus the ambitions of Napoleon *are* the Will; every volition and every notion *are* the Will in action. This is made explicit early in the drama. The first exchanges between the spirits establish that

the Immanent Will is unconscious, asleep, that it weaves its webs
with the automatic motion of a drowsy knitter. Then the Spirit of
the Years starts to 'lay bare the Will-webs'. We see the surface of
the earth teeming with alarmed peoples at the outbreak of the
Napoleonic War, then

> A new and penetrating light descends on the spectacle, enduing men
> and things with a seeming transparency, and exhibiting as one organism
> the anatomy of life and movement in all humanity and vitalized matter . . .
>
> (DY, Fore Scene)

This monistic 'one organism' is likened to a brain, 'evolving always
that it wots not of', a brain 'whose whole connotes the Everywhere'.
Other imagery likens the movements within the organism to
streams and to threads. Beyond the knowledge that this organism
is everything, we can know nothing; it is inconceivable that we
could learn anything of a 'Prime' entity 'that willed ere wareness
was'. Even if we assume such an entity to have existed, its existence
would explain nothing.[7]

The Dynasts is of great importance as a model of Hardy's negative
metaphysics. It also has some interest as poetry: some of the blank
verse works, although it must be admitted that a lot of it does not,
and some of the songs and choruses have the fresh quality of
Hardy's other lyrics. It is a bold experiment in a new genre, and
if it fails, it does so grandly and, in its failure, illuminates Hardy's
view of the world in a clear light.

I think it is worth pointing out two rays of hope in what may
otherwise appear to be the unrelieved gloom of Hardy's atheistic
poetry. First, there is the final chorus of *The Dynasts*, in which the
spirits feel 'a stirring' in the air, a rumour to the effect that 'the
rages/Of the ages/Shall be cancelled'; if this happens 'Consciousness' will 'inform' the Immanent Will 'till/It fashion all things
fair!' Perhaps this is only a remote possibility; but closer at hand
is the second hope, that of human society and charity. In 'A Plaint
to Man' (CP p. 325) God concludes:

> The truth should be told, and the fact be faced
> That had best been faced in earlier years:

---

[7] Hardy's universe is a closed circuit which man cannot escape from. This is the
final meaning of the idea that the Will is identical with all wills. As the Spirit of
the Years puts it at the battle of Borodino, the Will is 'A Will that wills above the
will of each. Yet but the will of all conjunctively' (DY, Pt 3, Act 1, Sc. 5).

The fact of life with dependence placed
On the human heart's resource alone,
In brotherhood bonded close and graced

With loving-kindness fully blown,
And visioned help unsought, unknown.

Reading List

In this small selection from the great mass of critical and biographical work concerned with Hardy I give details only of those works which I have found most helpful in thinking about his poetry and prose.

CRITICAL (1) *Mainly concerned with the fiction*

Cecil, Lord David. *Hardy the Novelist*. London: Constable, 1943
Gregor, Ian. *The Great Web*. London: Faber, 1974
Guerard, A. J. (ed.). *Hardy: A Collection of Critical Essays*. Englewood Cliffs, New Jersey: Prentice-Hall, 1963
Hillis Miller, J. *Thomas Hardy: Distance and Desire*. London: OUP, 1970
Lerner, Laurence. *Thomas Hardy's 'The Mayor of Casterbridge'*. London: Sussex UP, 1975
Millgate, Michael. *Thomas Hardy: His Career as a Novelist*. London: Bodley Head, 1971
Paterson, J. *The Making of 'The Return of the Native'*. Berkeley: University of California Press, 1960
Pinion, F. B. *A Hardy Companion*. London: Macmillan, 1968
Stewart, J. I. M. *Thomas Hardy*. London: Allen Lane, 1971
Williams, Raymond. *The English Novel from Dickens to Lawrence*. London: Chatto and Windus, 1970

(2) *Mainly concerned with the poetry*

Creighton, T. R. M. *Poems of Thomas Hardy*, selected with an introduction and notes by T.R.M.C. London: Macmillan, 1974
Davie, Donald. *Thomas Hardy and British Poetry*. London: Routledge and Kegan Paul, 1973
Paulin, Tom. *Thomas Hardy: The Poetry of Perception*. London: Macmillan, 1975
Pinion, F. B. *A Commentary on the Poems of Thomas Hardy*. London: Macmillan, 1976
Zietlow, Paul. *Moments of Vision: The Poetry of Thomas Hardy*. Cambridge, Mass.: Harvard UP, 1974

BIOGRAPHICAL

Gittings, Robert, *Young Thomas Hardy*. London: Heinemann, 1975
Gittings, Robert. *The Older Hardy*. London: Heinemann, in press
Hardy, F. E. *The Life of Thomas Hardy*. London: Macmillan, 1962